Contents

Part Two – Challenges and Dilemmas in Practice
Chris Beckett

Social Work Assessment and Intervention

Second Edition

Steven Walker and Chris Beckett

Russell House Publishing

First published in 2003

This Second Edition published in 2011 by:
Russell House Publishing Ltd.
4 St. George's House
Uplyme Road
Lyme Regis
Dorset DT7 3LS
Tel: 01297-443948
Fax: 01297-442722
e-mail: help@russellhouse.co.uk
www.russellhouse.co.uk

British Library Cataloguing-in-publication Data:

A catalogue record for this book is available from the British Library.

ISBN: 978-1-905541-68-3

Typeset by TW Typesetting, Plymouth, Devon

Printed by CPI Group, Eastbourne

Russell House Publishing

Russell House Publishing aims to publish innovative and valuable materials to
help managers, practitioners, trainers, educators and students.

Our full catalogue covers: social policy, working with young people, helping
children and families, care of older people, social care, combating social
exclusion, revitalising communities and working with offenders.

Full details can be found at www.russellhouse.co.uk and we are pleased
to send out information to you by post. Our contact details are on
this page.

We are always keen to receive feedback on publications and new ideas
for future projects.

Introduction

The key purpose of social work has been defined as:

A profession which promotes social change, problem solving in human relationships and the empowerment and liberation of people to enhance well being. Utilising theories of human behaviour and social systems, social work intervenes at the points where people interact with their environments. Principles of human rights and social justice are fundamental to social work.

> International Association of Schools of Social Work and the International Federation of Social Workers 2001, in: BASW, 2002

This powerful statement from a representative body of social workers from around the globe states quite clearly the twin elements that enshrine modern social work practice – the relationship between the external social world and the inner psychological experience of the individual that causes some citizens pain and suffering. In order to better understand how to help in these situations social workers need to develop the capacity to undertake assessments and interventions in a wide variety of settings with individuals, families, and groups. Such activity needs to be understood in the context of statutory duties, agency requirements, the needs and wishes of service users, and firmly underpinned by anti-racist and anti-discriminatory practice. Modern social work also needs to position itself within an increasingly Globalised world where supra-national agencies and institutions are impacting on previously unilateral policies and practices. The borders between countries are being eroded as a result of regional economic and political requirements and patterns of immigration/emigration are accelerating due to economic migration, or asylum from war and ethnic conflict. Cultural competence is now an expectation of all public services reflecting the rich, multi-cultural and ethnically diverse society, country or region that we inhabit.

The Human Rights Act (UN, 1998) symbolises the convergence in socio-political practice emanating from closer dialogue between nation states that slowly developed in the past century. It came into force in 2000 and incorporates into English law most of the provisions of the European Convention on Human Rights. The Act applies to all authorities undertaking functions of a public nature, including all care providers in the public sector. *The Human Rights Act* supports the protection and improvement of the health and welfare of children and families throughout the United Kingdom. The implications for contemporary social work practice have yet to be fully tested but practitioners need to become more familiar with the potential conflicts and dilemmas that may arise as the Act is used to challenge current practices. For example, Article 3 concerns freedom from torture and inhuman or degrading treatment. Children and young people who have been subjected to restraint, seclusion, or detention as a result of alarming behaviour could use this part of the Act to raise complaints against your practice in residential or mental health contexts.

Article 5 concerns the right to liberty, and together with Article 6 concerning the right to a fair hearing, are important to adults as well as some children and young people detained under a section of the *Mental Health Act*, the *Children Act*, or within the youth justice system. Social workers involved in such work must ensure that detention is based on sound opinion, in accordance with clearly laid out legal procedure accessible to the individual, and only lasts for as long as the mental health problem persists. In the context of youth justice work, particular attention needs to be paid to the quality and tone of pre-sentence reports that can be stigmatising. The formulaic structure of pre-sentence reports might not enable an assessing social worker working under deadline pressure, to provide an accurate picture of a young person.

Article 8 guarantees the right to privacy and family life. Refugees and asylum seeking families can become entangled in complex legal procedures relating to citizenship and entitlement. This provision can be invoked when UK authorities are considering whether a person should be deported or remain in this country. Compassionate grounds can be used for children affected by the proposed deportation of a parent in cases where a parent is not admitted. Social workers attuned to the attachment relationships of small children can use this knowledge to support Article 8 proceedings. In such circumstances the maintenance of the family unit is paramount.

Social workers involved in care proceedings or adoption work will have to consider very carefully whether such plans are in the best interests of the child but also are consistent with the child's rights under the Convention. For example, the Convention emphasises that care orders should be a temporary measure and that children should be reunited with their family as soon as possible, where appropriate. In the case of a parent with a mental health problem detained in a psychiatric hospital, the Convention could be employed by their children to facilitate regular visits if these have been denied.

Article 10 concerns basic rights to freedom of expression and in the context of adult services, is a crucial safeguard to ensuring that practitioners work actively to enable vulnerable adults to express their opinions about service provision. Social workers have an opportunity within this specific provision to articulate and put into practice their value principles of partnership and service user empowerment.

Article 14 states that all children have an equal claim to the rights set out in the Convention 'irrespective of the child's or their parent's or legal guardian's race, colour, sex, language, religion, political or other opinion, national, ethnic or social origin, property, disability, birth or other status.' This provision could be used to argue for equality of service provision and non-prejudicial assessment and intervention. Social workers need to ensure they are employing anti-racist and non-discriminatory practice and to be able to practically evidence how they are doing it.

Social work assessment and intervention are core skills for qualified social workers and fundamental learning requirements for trainee/student social workers. They have relevance to the *Human Rights Act* and featured in recent guidance on practice competencies and the latest occupational standards guidance for the Training Organisation for Personal Social Services. This book combines the two practice elements of Assessment and Intervention in an integrated way that is consistent with contemporary practice and the foundational values and skills of classic psycho-social practice.

Assessment is usually separated from intervention in the literature and practice guidance. This book aims to provide social workers with the combined intellectual and practical resources to help improve practice in these crucial areas.

Practitioners know that the two processes cannot be separated from each other. Government guidance and the professional literature have begun to accept that assessment and intervention should be seamless parts of a continuous process. It also expects there to be a therapeutic dimension to this area of social work practice:

> *The provision of appropriate services should not await the end of the assessment but be offered when they are required by the child and family. The process of engaging in an assessment should be therapeutic and perceived of as part of the range of services offered.*
>
> DoH, 2000

However, employers tend to emphasise assessment skills to the detriment of good, integrated, holistic practice. The trend towards retrenchment in social services and reduction of social work to bureaucratic care management is not meeting the needs of vulnerable service users who want more than administrative processing. Social workers who cherish their core helping skills will find this book supports and extends their practice. This book challenges the orthodoxy for compartmentalising practice processes that lead to narrow, resource-driven assessment procedures and eligibility criteria in statutory social services contexts. It also reminds staff that difficult decisions regarding rationing of human and physical resources are part and parcel of contemporary practice. We aim to offer social workers in a variety of qualified and unqualified roles and agencies a rich source of up to the minute resources to draw upon and enhance a psycho-social perspective to deliver empowering, ethical, service-user focused practice.

Recent SSI inspections have illustrated the need for social workers to rediscover their core skills of assessment and intervention, so that decision making and care planning are based on sound analysis and understanding of the client's unique personality, history and circumstances. Social workers own skills need to be seen as a resource to be used and offered in the subsequent intervention which should be based on client need rather than agency resource limitations and where services should fit around the service user rather than the reverse (DoH/SSI 2000). This book provides social work staff with an accessible, practice-oriented guide to their work in the developing modernising context of multi-disciplinary team working, joint budget arrangements, inter-agency collaboration and care management. The new graduate training environment, occupational standards, General Social Care Council, SCIE, TOPPS, and post-qualifying training requirements, all demand improvements in practice standards. This book responds to that demand and the needs of social workers to deliver high quality services in the contemporary context of practice.

National occupational standards

Six key roles for social work practitioners have been identified in the latest occupational standards guidance that together with the units and elements of practice provide detailed requirements expected of qualified professionals:

Key role 1. Prepare for and work with individuals, families, carers, groups and communities to assess their needs and circumstances:

- Prepare for social work contact and involvement.
- Work with individuals, families, carers, groups, and communities to help them make informed decisions.
- Assess needs and options to recommend a course of action.

Key role 2. Plan, carry out, review and evaluate social work practice, with individuals, families, carers, groups, communities and other professionals:

- Respond to crisis situations.
- Interact with individuals, families, carers, groups and communities to achieve change and development and to improve life opportunities.
- Prepare, produce, implement and evaluate plans with individuals, families, carers, groups, communities and professional colleagues.
- Support the development of networks to meet assessed needs and planned outcomes.
- Work with groups to promote individual growth, development and independence.

- Address behaviour which presents a risk to individuals, families, carers, groups and communities.

Key role 3. Support individuals to represent their needs, views and circumstances:

- To advocate with, and on behalf of, individuals, families, carers, groups and communities.
- To prepare for, and participate in decision making forums.

Key role 4. Manage risk to individuals, families, carers, groups, communities, self and colleagues:

- Manage risk to individuals, families, carers, groups, communities, self and colleagues.
- Address behaviour which presents a risk to individuals, families, carers, groups, communities, self and others.
- Identify and assess the nature of the risk.
- Balance the rights and responsibilities of individuals, families, carers, groups and communities with associated risk.
- Regularly monitor, re-assess, and manage risk to individuals, families, carers, groups and communities.
- Take immediate action to deal with the behaviour that presents a risk.
- Work with individuals, families, carers, groups, communities and others to identify and evaluate situations and circumstances that may trigger the behaviour.
- Work with individuals, families, carers, groups and communities on strategies and support that could positively change the behaviour.

Key role 5. Manage and be accountable, with supervision and support, for your own social work practice within your organisation:

- Manage and be accountable for your own work.
- Contribute to the management of resources and services.
- Manage, present and share records and reports.
- Work within multi-disciplinary and multi-organisational teams, networks and systems.

Key role 6. Demonstrate professional competence in social work practice:

- Research, analyse, evaluate, and use current knowledge of best social work practice.
- Work within agreed standards of social work practice and ensure your own professional development.
- Manage complex ethical issues, dilemmas and conflicts.
- Contribute to the promotion of best social work practice.

Within this broad occupational guidance framework some of the important tasks include the practical activities we aim to cover in this book. You will be expected to review case notes and other relevant literature and liaise with others to access additional information that can inform initial contact and involvement. Evaluating all the necessary information in order to identify the best form of initial involvement is crucial. The advantage of this is that it can quickly bring you up to date on what might be happening in the life of a service user. The disadvantage is that the case file may be inaccurate, or other people's perceptions are based on prejudice or misinformation.

It is important for you to be aware of your own prejudices and values when engaging with clients and to guard against making decisions based on pre-conceived assumptions about individuals and groups. Trying to evaluate what may be contradictory information or falsehood as a basis for deciding your next steps following a referral may not be as simple as it first appears. You are expected to inform people about your own and your organisation's duties and responsibilities. Identifying, gathering, analysing and understanding information is a key skill. In addition you are expected to enable people to analyse, identify, clarify and express their strengths, expectations and limitations. And you should be working with them to assess and make informed decisions about their needs, circumstances, risks, preferred options and resources.

This all sounds straightforward enough until you start to consider the complexities presented by social work clients and the multitude of personal, environmental, and relationship problems they bring to your notice. You might also wonder whether you have the time and other resources to work in the way prescribed above.

Social workers are always having to defend their organisation's lack of ability to provide what service users define as their needs. It is not uncommon to then face the fury of people who have gone through with what feels like an inquisitorial assessment process that ends up with very little in return for them. The likelihood of these tensions arising was acknowledged over 20 years ago in the first major inquiry into the role and tasks of social workers (NISW, 1982). The report described social work as comprising two strands of activity – counselling and social care planning.

The latter related to solving or ameliorating an existing social problem which an individual, family, or group experienced. All the subsequent evidence demonstrates service users value the key counselling/therapeutic skills employed in assessment and intervention activity. Social care planning relates to preventive informal or formal work to develop and strengthen communities. The problem was that social care planning can be undertaken both by practitioners and managers, resulting in tension between staff trying to juggle finite resources. The dilemmas this situation produces are considered in this book in the context of rationing and eligibility restraints that operate more strictly in statutory agencies. We examine contemporary evidence for the delivery of competent assessment, intervention and risk assessment practice. The various elements that comprise a comprehensive model of assessment and intervention practice are drawn together to articulate a synthesis of practice based on empowerment and socially inclusive practice, integrated working, and evaluating effectiveness to contribute to the building of a coherent evidence base in social work.

The occupational standards suggest that you assess and review the preferred options of people and assess their needs, risks and options taking into account legal and other requirements, and then assess and recommend an appropriate course of action for your clients. The first part of this hints at the potential for disagreement with the service user. They may have a preferred option that conflicts with your legal duties to remove their child or to detain them against their will in a psychiatric unit. The recommendation may not feel right for them, either because it is too much or too little of what they anticipated being offered. You will often be in a position of enforcing a course of action rather than recommending that it takes place. Assessment has been defined as an ongoing process, in which the client participates, the purpose of which is to understand people in relation to their environment. It is the basis for planning what needs to be done to maintain, improve or bring about change in the person, the environment or both (Coulshed and Orme, 1998). It therefore cannot be separated from intervention because of the reflexive interactive nature of the client/worker encounter.

Looking through these prescribed occupational standards is an enlightening experience in as much as they tell you very little of how to achieve them. What you are expected to achieve is deceptively simple. There are different ways in which these aims can be achieved each of which is as valid as the next. The problem is that there is no way of confidently predicting which way is the best, easiest, or most cost-effective. And that is because every service user is a unique individual. You are expected in other occupational standards to tailor your practice to the needs of that individual thereby avoiding stereotyped, institutionalised practice.

You will also bring your own individual unique self to the task of social work practice – perhaps a history of personal problems that give you some degree of insight into particular difficulties faced by some clients. Or motivation may spring from deeply held religious or political imperatives that impel you to devote yourself to helping other citizens in trouble. Whatever the motivating factor, your interpretation of these occupational standards and the practice guidance that follows may be different to other social workers in small, subtle or large ways. You will also find differences in service standards between organisations. Each local authority, health trust, or voluntary agency has discretion and flexibility in terms of how it prioritises its responsibilities under various legislative and statutory duties. All of what follows therefore needs to be placed in the context of your own local professional environment.

This is linked to central government decisions about how to apportion the local government and health budget and the variety of formulae used to rationalise political decisions. Therefore, it is very difficult in practice to undertake the task of assessment and intervention without encountering a degree of confusion, uncertainty and some dilemmas. Our aim is to bring clarity where we can, to explain where some confusion can be enlightening, but more than anything we hope this book will be a genuine resource for you to use in the complex, challenging and ultimately rewarding world of social work.

Assessment is now recognised as more than an administrative task, or as a form of gate-keeping for resources, or even as a means of determining risk. It is an intervention and thereby like many of the orthodox methods and models of intervention can be applied in a variety of ways. The distinction between assessment and intervention is unhelpful and has always restricted the vision and creativity of social work staff. We combine both aspects of social work practice in this volume in order to permit an integrated, holistic, modern psycho-social practice rooted in the principles of social justice.

Introduction to second edition

Chapters 5, 6 and 7 of Part Two have been written by Chris Beckett: all the other chapters are by Steven Walker

This second edition has been extensively revised, updated and restructured in the context of changes in social work policy and practice since the introduction to the first edition was written in 2003. This edition takes account of the practice implications embedded within, among others, the *Social Work Taskforce Report* (DCSF, 2009) *Putting People First* (DoH, 2008) *Building Brighter Futures* (CWDC, 2008) and *Raising Standards* (GSCC, 2009). In 1997 hopes were high that a government that put social justice at the centre of its policy would be able to have an impact on inequalities in modern Britain. By 2010 several authoritative reports illustrated the gap between the rhetoric and the reality of life in modern Britain (Babb, 2005; Hills et al., 2007; DoH, 2008). They showed that Britain was an increasingly divided nation where the richest 10 per cent of the population are more than 100 times as wealthy as the poorest 10 per cent of society – one of the highest levels of inequality in any modern industrialised country. They also showed that the poorest people in society die sooner and become ill younger than the richest and that social mobility was stagnant with evidence that family wealth, private education and privileged access to University remained the key determinants of career success and well-paid employment.

The ending of child poverty by 2020 was official government policy until it became apparent that this was not going to be met, and even modest reductions in child poverty were apparently hard to achieve. Social workers are among those professionals most acutely aware of how social circumstances affect a person's potential and are right to condemn the superficial efforts by all governments to tackle child poverty and other inequalities. They know that much of their work is concerned with the effects of poverty, inequality and social exclusion on individuals and families struggling to cope in a harsh and unforgiving economic system where individual greed, corporate profit, corruption and ruthless individualism are valued above mutuality, community, care for others and equality.

The latest in a long line of government reports into the future of social work produced by the Social Work Taskforce (DCSF, 2009) listed the following recommendations to guide the future development of the profession:

- Better training – with employers, educators and the profession all taking their full share.
- Responsibility for investing in the next generation and in enabling social workers already in practice to develop their skills continuously.
- Improved working conditions – with employers signing up to new standards for the support and supervision of their frontline workforce that make good practice possible.
- Stronger leadership and independence – with the profession taking more control over its own standards, how it is understood and valued by the public, and the contribution it makes to changes in policy and practice.
- A reliable supply of confident, high quality, adaptable professionals into the workforce, where they can build long-term careers on the frontline.
- Greater understanding among the general public, service users, other professionals and the media of the role and purpose of social work, the demands of the job and the contribution social workers make.
- More use of research and continuing professional development to inform frontline practice.

The problem with this list of ideas is that it came without an action plan, timescale of implementation or identified funding linked to demonstrable change. Social workers will rightly feel that this is so much more rhetoric, while they observe deep cuts in public services and welfare provision which are bound to create more need within neglected and deprived communities. At the time of writing in 2010 a new Government is embarking upon a programme of cuts and a deep-rooted ideological aversion to the public sector and the principles of the welfare state which will devastate communities and tear at the very fabric of society – testing social workers to the very limit of their endurance and resilience.

England, Scotland, Wales and Northern Ireland

Within Britain there is much diversity in the legislative and governmental guidance for social work. This text generally is based on English law for reasons of space and the avoidance of confusion. The Scottish system operates under its own legal system and system of guidance, while in Northern Ireland the Health and Social Services boards make up a very different organisational context. The devolved national assemblies in Scotland and Wales further add to this diversity. However the book contents have been adapted and designed to provide significant learning opportunities for practitioners in all the constituent countries of the United Kingdom who will find much of value here.

Using this book

The book is designed as a practical manual for use by busy practitioners, students, trainers and professional education providers requiring evidence-based knowledge and guidance to enable staff to engage with people in a supportive context. The **exposition** in the main body of the text will draw on a variety of sources, including government policy and best practice guidance, social, educational and health care theory and research findings. This will provide you with relevant information and knowledge to create the framework within which you can absorb, understand and then practically apply changes in your working context.

The **activities** you will be asked to complete are designed to help individuals, multi-disciplinary groups and teams recognise and understand aspects of practice which you might not previously have known about or considered, and will help to develop self-awareness by inviting you to relate your experience to the issues being explored. The temptation is to skip the activities – try not to because they can be valuable in ways that you might not anticipated at first sight. They are designed to give you the opportunity to bring your own experiences into the learning process, but also your responses will build up into a resource which can be drawn on in current practice contexts and future personal, professional and team development.

With this in mind, it is useful to keep a separate booklet in which to write your individual responses. Think of this as a form of **learning journal**, and record things such as experiences at work which seem to you to relate to specific activities you have completed from the workbook. This can provide useful practice material for future reference, revision, self-study on your own, in supervision, during consultation or in teambuilding and inter-agency training.

Terminology

The terminology in this book has been kept accessible as possible within the confines of the editorial guidelines and the intended audience. It is necessary however to explain how certain terms have been used in order to at least offer the reader some context to understand their use. We use the terms child protection and safeguarding children and young people synonymously throughout the text to reflect the current transitional phase of policy guidance and literature on this subject. Culture is used in places where it is specifically defined but elsewhere it is used in the sense of the organisation of experience shared by members of a community including their standards for perceiving, predicting, judging and acting.

Black is used in the contemporary accepted sense of meaning that group of people who by virtue of their non-white skin colour are treated in a discriminatory way and who experience racism at the personal and institutional level every day of their lives. 'Race' as a term is declining in use due to its origins in meaningless anthropological classifications by early imperialists seeking to legitimise their exploitation of indigenous land and wealth. It is a social construction but one which is still found in statutes, policy material and in common parlance.

Ethnicity is subject to much definitional debate in the literature but for clarity and brevity the term is used throughout this text to mean the orientation it provides to individuals by delineating norms, values, interactional modalities, rituals, meanings and collective events. Family is also a term around which there is some debate as it is both a descriptor and a socially prescribed term loaded with symbolism. In this book the term family is used to embrace the widest ethnic and cultural interpretation that includes same sex partnerships, single parent, step family, kinship groups, heterosexual partnerships and marriage, extended family groupings and friendship groups or community living arrangements.

About the authors

Steven Walker is Principal Lecturer in Social Work at the School of Community Health and Social Studies at Anglia Polytechnic University.

Chris Beckett is Senior Lecturer in Social Work at the University of East Anglia, Norwich.

Praise for the First Edition

'A thoughtful and ethically realistic book which addresses the principles and dilemmas of contemporary social work practice . . . it draws on a wide-ranging examples of practice across all the mainstream client groups . . . an engaging and stimulating book . . . reading this book has challenged my assumptions about the nature of assessment and intervention in social work practice; it has encouraged me to think critically, analytically and ethically about them and their intertwined relationships . . . it will be an important resource.' *Health and Social Care in the Community*

'An extremely informative book on which to build and develop high standards of practice and, together with the extensive further reading list, it provides the reader with a useful range of learning material.' *Practice*

'An accessible and thought-provoking guide, with succinct summaries if the main points and clear advice on common-dilemmas faced by social care professionals.' *Adoption and Fostering*

'An in-depth examination of contemporary assessment practice and contemporary models of intervention . . . an impressive resource-cum-guide.' *Care & Health*

'A vast amount of information is covered . . . The authors have also included activities and case scenarios . . . This interactive approach, coupled with a comprehensive list of further reading, makes it particularly useful.' *Community Care*

'I would recommend this book.' *Rostrum*

Part One:
Principles of Assessment and Intervention

CHAPTER 1

Modern Assessment Practice

Learning objectives

- Describe various forms of contemporary practice in assessment and how they link to intervention.
- Illustrate how effective assessment takes into account people's needs, rights, strengths, responsibilities and resources.
- Explain how an understanding of oppression and discrimination influences contemporary assessment practice.
- Evaluate tensions between policy and practice in the context of mental health, children and families and community care assessments.

Introduction

Social work assessment is often taken for granted, sometimes the subject of unwarranted attention, but always a potentially liberating and empowering experience for you and the service user. It is important to understand how effective assessment takes into account people's needs, rights, strengths, responsibilities and resources. You need to reflect on how individual practice enables you to identify clients' strengths rather than weaknesses, and work with their existing networks and communities. Organisational restrictions and resource constraints will militate against creative service user focused practice, but these need to be overcome. Understanding how oppression and discrimination influences contemporary assessment practice and service users ability to function is an important task for your practice development. The following descriptions and analyses of the policy guidance on work with clients in the context of Mental Health, Community Care, and Children and Families work are designed to illuminate areas of creative potential. The legislative context and policy guidance derived from that will be considered in terms of the changes in emphasis expected from current social work practice.

Understanding assessment

Assessment has been defined as a tool to aid in the planning of future work, the beginning of helping another person to identify areas for growth and change. Its purpose is the identification of needs – it is never an end in itself (Taylor and Devine, 1993). Assessment is the foundation of the social work process with service users. It can set the tone for further contact, it is your first opportunity to engage with new or existing clients, and it can be perceived by people as a judgement on their character or behaviour.

A good experience of assessment can make people feel positive about receiving help and their attitude to you and your agency. A bad experience of assessment can make matters worse, offend, and make problems harder to resolve in the long term. You can regard it as little more than a paper chasing exercise, involving form filling and restricting peoples' aspirations. Or you can see it as an opportunity to engage with service users in a problem-solving partnership where both of you can learn more about yourselves (Martin, 2010). A good way of measuring your progress during assessment practice is to use the concept of systematic practice (Thompson and Thompson, 2002). This requires that you ask three questions:

1. **What are you trying to achieve?** It involves considering what needs remain unmet, and acts as a focus for the assessment, helping avoid the pitfall of simply gathering a lot of information, with no clarity about what needs to be done.
2. **How are you going to achieve it?** This relates to the need to develop a strategy for achieving the identified objectives – how do you intend to get to where you want to be.
3. **How will you know when you have achieved it?** This helps to bring clarity to what can invariably be vagueness in the work process. It enables you to envisage the outcome of work and to recognise when this has been achieved – or not.

There are three types of assessment that most of you will encounter in some form or other in whatever agency you practice. They are designed to indicate the level of perceived need and seriousness and complexity of the service user's situation. These examples relate to child care practice but they are transferable to other contexts:

- **Initial assessment** – this provides a good basis for short term planning and can be used as part of eligibility criteria to determine the level of need and priority. In child care situations it is used to effect immediate child protection with a general requirement of a two week time limit.
- **Comprehensive assessment** – this takes over from where an initial assessment finishes and where more complex needs have been identified. Or it has been initiated following changes in a service user's situation where basic, but limited information already exists.
- **Core assessment** – this is used in child care cases and is a specific requirement under *Children Act 1989* guidance for a time-limited assessment in order to help inform the decision-making process in legal proceedings. The key aim is to enable all stakeholders to contribute as much information consistent with effective outcomes.

Knowing the level or depth required from the assessment is a starting point. But you need to proceed with a framework or guide to the different elements making up the assessment. If you move beyond some of your agency constraints and believe in service user focused assessment as an interactive process rather than an administrative convenience, then Milner and O'Bryne (1998) describe a helpful framework as a base for effective assessment in a variety of practice contexts:

- **Preparation** – deciding who to see, what data will be relevant, what the purpose is and what the limits of the task are.
- **Data collection** – people are met and engaged with, difference gaps are addressed, and empowerment and choice are safeguarded as we come to the task with respectful uncertainty and a research mentality.
  Weighing up the data – current social and psychological theory and research findings that are part of every social worker's learning are drawn on to answer the question: Is there a problem and is it serious?
- **Analysing the data** – the data is interpreted to seek and gain an understanding of the service user in order to develop ideas for intervention.
- **Utilising the data** – this stage is used to finalise judgements.

Milner and O'Byrne (2009) have offered a very useful way of navigating the potential complexities in assessment practice by suggesting five theoretical approaches or 'maps' to guide the modern practitioner. These are based on Psychodynamic, Behavioural, Task Centred, Solution Focused and Narrative theories, which we examine in more detail in Chapter 2. These maps, combining knowledge from Sociology and Psychology enable social workers to engage in collaborative work while maintaining a focus on the essential values necessary to lead to effective and appropriate interventions.

Practice guidance

The Social Care Institute for Excellence focused on social work assessment in a definitive document (SCIE, 2003) which reinforced the importance of three key assessment skills:

1. **Critical thinking** – this means being able to critically analyse underlying assumptions when conducting assessment and developing thinking skills to assess unfamiliar scenarios and generate plausible hypotheses from them.
2. **Research skills** – this means having advanced ability in seeking out existing reliable research evidence and developing the skills to undertake research itself. Evidence suggests that learning skills in ethnographic research or discourse analysis can enhance cultural competence.
3. **Knowledge** – the ability to conduct assessments requires not just skills but the relevant knowledge base. The demands placed upon social workers are often multi-factoral and highly complex, involving several interlocking and multiple domains. No social worker can have knowledge of every conceivable situation they may be presented with, but it is possible to acquire specialist expertise and experience or to have the ability to locate such expertise and access it.

Acts of Parliament and associated practice guidance illustrate the wealth of material that provides the framework within which your assessment practice takes place. These are the rules of engagement that permit you to take some of the most important decisions that will affect the lives of many people possibly for years and generations to follow. Some of this is prescriptive and written in administrative language that probably feels alien to your caring compassionate instincts. The power and authority offered within the law and guidance may offer comforts. Or you may feel distinctly uncomfortable in the constraints imposed on your practice and better judgement. This is however the framework in which the practice takes place and what legitimates your social work role.

Your task in managing this material is not helped by the artificial distinctions and divisions of your agency that compartmentalise families and communities into specialist areas of practice, when they are linked in all sorts of ways. The various national priorities guidance is another central government prompt to steer local authorities and other providers towards services and service user groups that it deems should receive particular attention – usually with financial incentives or penalties. The *one size fits all* guidance can also be criticised for being insensitive to particular regions or local area needs. So we can see already there are a number of layers of pressure that go towards affecting your assessment practice:

- Prescriptions for what you are meant to achieve in assessment practice occupational standards.
- Legislative injunctions setting out the legal powers and responsibilities defining your practice.
- Practice guidance documents based on research studies to offer some evidence of effectiveness and good practice examples.
- Central government budget allocations for local government that determine the scope of what your agency can provide.

We have selected the work contexts of mental health, community care and children and families to illustrate the issues, dilemmas and opportunities for your practice development in social work assessment. The government has set a variety of targets and service specifications for people with mental health problems, older people and children and families. These three broad areas cover the majority of practice situations but they are not a definitive list. Much of what follows will however, raise issues that are common to other service user groups and are therefore transferable to other areas of social work practice.

ACTIVITY 1.1

Review the above material and make a list of the legislative and practice guidances that are relevant to your work context. Now look for evidence of how these

are translated into your particular agency eligibility criteria and service specification.

Mental health assessment

The *National Service Framework for Mental Health (1999)* is now more than 10 years old. Its initial aim was to provide a focus for commissioners, providers and professionals in this complex area to improve mental health services by:

- Involving service users and their carers in planning and delivery of care.
- Delivering high quality treatment and care which is known to be effective and appropriate.
- Being suited to those who use them and non-discriminatory.
- Being accessible so that help can be obtained when and where it is needed.
- Promoting client safety and that of their carers, staff and the wider public.
- Offering choices which promote independence.
- Being well co-ordinated between all staff and agencies.
- Delivering continuity of care for as long as this is needed.
- Empowering and supporting their staff.
- Being accountable to the public, service users and carers.

The National Service Framework set national standards and defined service models for promoting mental health and treating mental illness. It put in place underpinning programmes to support local delivery and established milestones and a specific group of high-level performance indicators against which progress within agreed time-scales would be measured. It covered health promotion, assessment and diagnosis, treatment, rehabilitation and care, and encompassed primary and specialist care and the roles of partner agencies.

The 1983 *Mental Health Act* allowed for someone with a serious mental illness (or suspected of having such a condition) to be compulsorily admitted to hospital for assessment, or treatment, or for both. Changes to this legislation were introduced by the *Mental Health Act 2007* which aimed to modernise the existing *Mental Health Act 1983*. A large part of the 1983 Act remains the same. The most important changes include:

- Widening the definition of mental disorder.
- Service-users having greater say about who is their nearest relative.

- 16 and 17 year olds now being able to agree to or refuse an admission to hospital without this decision being overridden by a parent.
- A decrease in the situations where electroconvulsive therapy can be given without consent.
- A right to a special Independent Mental Health Advocate for detained patients (from April 2009).
- The introduction of Supervised Community Treatment in the form of Community Treatment Orders (CTOs).

Assessments for possible admission were set up by approved social workers (ASWs) who have completed post-qualifying training. This role has now been changed to Approved Mental Health Practitioner (AMHP) and means other non-social work staff can initiate and participate in decision-making. The three grounds for such an admission remain:

1. It is in the interests of the patient's health.
2. It is in the interests of the patient's safety.
3. It is for the protection of other people.

If one of these grounds is satisfied and the sufferer needs to be in hospital for assessment and/or treatment to be provided, then they can be admitted under the Act. However before this stage, any social worker may find themselves working in situations where they are concerned about the mental health of their client and making an assessment of the depth and severity of the client's human distress and what model of practice intervention is appropriate to their needs. This might apply in the circumstances of an adult recently discharged from hospital following a compulsory admission, a teenager who had a history of self-harming or suicide attempts, or a single young mother with severe depression.

In the case of Child and Adolescent Mental Health (CAMH) there is a tension between the requirements and expectations under the *Mental Health Act 2007 and Children Act 1989*. The social work role in CAMH has been eroded in recent years (Walker, 2003) and usually perceived as a child protection activity even though the role was historically perceived as therapeutic. As in adult mental health the social worker will find taking up the position of advocate and protecting the child or young person's rights a natural and rewarding task. National enquiries into CAMH services highlight the lack of provision and

variable quality which could be improved by more social work staff being deployed in CAMH services (DFCS, 2008).

Parents and medical staff may seek to compulsorily admit a troubled teenager to a psychiatric resource against their will under Section 2 or 3 of the 1983 Mental Health Act, or the Mental Capacity Act 2005 so issues of human rights, consent and confidentiality are paramount, requiring sophisticated assessment skills and knowledge of child development and CAMH services. As a social worker you could find yourself in a nexus involving the child, doctors, and parents all of whom could have strong and differing, feelings about the right way forward. This will test your negotiation skills to the limit. It's important to remember that a child under 16 may consent to their own admission if they are Fraser competent (previously Gillick competent) meaning they are able to understand what is being proposed.

Social workers involved in mental health assessments need to engage positively and purposively with other professionals especially psychiatrists (Golightly, 2006). This means acknowledging their medical background and training imperatives which impel them to use diagnostic manuals such as the DSM iv or ICD 10 in order to classify mental disorders. These tools are constantly evolving to enlarge the range of disorders based on observable common characteristics in clients. They are not faultless and rely on interpretation and assumptions about normalcy which challenge many values and beliefs held by social workers who naturally embrace a social model of human growth and development. This will cause tension in some cases and will call for highly developed negotiation skills and knowledge of barriers to multidisciplinary working. Social workers with an understanding of the role of advocate and a strong commitment to human rights will find this work satisfying.

Caring for carers

There are estimated to be one and a quarter million people caring for someone with a mental illness, but fewer than one in five know that they have a legal right to an assessment of their own needs. New rights have been introduced that are aimed at ensuring that carers receive services to match those needs. *The Carers (Recognition and Services Act 1995)* gave carers the right to an assessment of their ability to provide and to continue to provide care. To be eligible a carer has to provide a substantial amount of care on a regular basis. But the carer has to request an assessment, and it is frustrating for a carer to be assessed and have needs identified if nothing is then provided to meet those needs.

The National Service Framework for Mental Health introduced in 1999 tried to influence practice so that carers received an assessment at least annually and have a written care plan which is implemented in discussion with them. A care co-ordinator must closely monitor the care plan, take responsibility for co-ordinating care, and ensure that the plan is delivered and reviewed. A healthy and well supported carer can have a positive effect on the life of the person with mental illness. However, a stressed and poorly supported carer can become physically and mentally unwell and likely to eventually become a client themselves.

A high quality carer's assessment starts from the principle that long-term carers are expert in mental illness. Many simply need to know how to gain access to services, particularly out of normal office hours. Others need a regular break, by arranging respite care to the person being cared for. Some will require financial advice and support to ensure they have full welfare or social security entitlements. Others will want to be put in touch with fellow carers so that they can gain mutual support from people in a similar position. A good carer's assessment looks at the risk of disruption or breakdown in home support. A regular quality assessment can help to maintain family support and family care – the preferred option for many people with mental illness.

ACTIVITY 1.2

List the dilemmas you might face in trying to balance the needs of a mentally ill client and their carer.

Commentary

It is possible to see the inter-relationship between the client and carer that might have evolved over a long time so that mutual dependency makes it hard to disentangle their separate needs. The impact of any intervention planned to offer respite could have the opposite effect and prompt deterioration in the situation. Where children are involved the dilemmas are more complex because of your separate responsibilities and the need to liaise with other professionals. The challenges for

you in implementing the policy direction consistent with your social work values are:

- The need to understand the different needs of users and carers and to enable effective input from each.
- Ensuring that the views of users and carers are actively sought and they are supported to participate equally.
- How to achieve a common purpose between different professional groups in relation to the care programme approach and care management.
- The need to ensure that expectations for staff competency are backed up by training which is relevant to diversity and need.

Community care assessment

The NHS and Community Care Act 1990 together with subsequent practitioners guidance forms the basis for Assessment and Intervention practice with elderly or disabled clients. In 1989 the government White Paper Caring for People emphasised the role of care management as the means by which a persons needs were regularly reviewed, resources managed effectively, and that they had a single point of contact in situations where their needs were numerous or involved significant expense. Research demonstrated that many elderly people were being placed inappropriately in residential care, and that agencies were often duplicating work or delivering home support in a haphazard way. A key part of community care strategy is for different contributions from health, social service, or voluntary providers to be co-ordinated through care management.

The Department of Health has produced detailed advice on care management (DoH, 1991) which is described as the process of tailoring services to individual needs. Seven core tasks are involved in arranging care for someone in need:

1. **The publication of information:** making public the needs for which assistance is offered and the arrangements and resources for meeting those needs. Prospective users and carers receive information about the need for which care agencies accept responsibility to offer assistance, and the range of services currently available.
2. **Determining the level of assessment:** making an initial identification of need and matching the appropriate level of assessment to that

need. If an enquirer requests more than information or advice, basic information is taken about the need in question, sufficient to determine the type of assessment required.

3. **Assessing need:** understanding individual needs, relating them to agency policies and priorities, and agreeing the objectives for any intervention. A practitioner is allocated to assess the needs of the individual and of any carers, in a way that also recognises their strengths and aspirations. In order to take account of all relevant needs, assessment may bring together contributions from a number of other specialists or agencies. The purpose of the assessment is to define the individual's needs in the context of local policies and priorities and agree on the desired outcome of any involvement.

4. **Care planning:** negotiating the most appropriate ways of achieving the objectives identified by the assessment of need and incorporating them into an individual care plan. The role of the practitioner is to consider the resources available from statutory, voluntary, private or community sources that best meet the individual's requirements. The aim is to assist the user in making choices from these resources, and to put together an individual care plan.

5. **Implementing the care plan:** securing the necessary resources or services. The implementation of that plan means securing the necessary finance or other identified resources. It may involve negotiation with a variety of service providers, specifying the type and quality of service required, and ensuring that services are co-ordinated with one another. The responsibility of practitioners at this stage will vary according to the level of their delegated budgetary authority.

6. **Monitoring:** supporting and controlling the delivery of the care plan on a continuing basis. Because circumstances change, the implementation of the care plan has to be continuously monitored, making adjustments, as necessary, to the services provided and supporting users, carers and service providers in achieving the desired outcomes.

7. **Reviewing:** reassessing needs and the service outcomes with a view to revising the care plan at specified intervals. The progress of the care plan has to be formally reviewed with the service user, carers, and service providers, firstly to ensure that services remain relevant

to need, and secondly, to evaluate services as part of the continuing quest for improvement.

ACTIVITY 1.3

What are the benefits of care management and the barriers to good practice?

Commentary

The benefits of care management are that it supports a need-led approach to assessment and the use of resources, tailoring services to individual requirements. It involves a clear commitment to individual care planning, specifying desired outcomes. Care management requires a clear division of responsibility between assessment/care management and service provision, separating the interests of service users and providers. It should result in more responsive services as a result of linking assessment and purchasing/commissioning.

Care management is designed to result in a wider choice of services across the statutory and independent sectors. It should enable partnership practice in which users/carers play a more active part alongside practitioners in determining the services they receive. This could improve opportunities for representation and advocacy and be a way of meeting the needs of disadvantaged individuals more effectively. Greater continuity of care and greater accountability to users and carers should result from these changes. Finally, better integration of services within and between agencies is envisaged as part of government aspirations for closer working between providers.

Policy guidance offers little in the way of addressing the dilemma of meeting potentially infinite demand within finite resources. This is especially so in the context of the increasing age profile of the UK population and individual expectations of service delivery. The implicit principle within the guidance is that users and carers will be empowered. Yet while practitioners are expected to seek the views of both carers and users, most weight is expected to be given to users needs, and ultimately the assessing practitioner is responsible for defining the users needs. The definition of need therefore remains a professional hegemony.

Guidance suggests that assessment should be simple, speedy and based on the principle of what is the least that it is necessary to know. This may not necessarily be the basis for good assessment practice. How is it possible to establish a relationship of trust on what appears to be superficial and brief contact? The policy guidance recommends establishing a balance between the needs of user and carer. It recognises that disentangling these needs would be a difficult task. Yet there is little in the way of concrete suggestions as to how this balance should be achieved especially as the users views are still expected to carry most weight. The tendency to view carers as resources leads to the all-too-easy assumption that the sole purpose of services is to maintain carers in their role.

It can be argued that terms such as 'need' and 'care' places people in a dependent position, reinforcing the perception that they are problematic. This leads to the tendency to focus on a person's deficits and difficulties rather than building upon their strengths and coping strategies. This is especially the case when practitioners are expected to use eligibility criteria – rarely made explicit to the user, to determine the level of need and priority. Integrated and co-ordinated working between agencies and professions is a fundamental aim of community care policy. Yet there are difficulties in putting this aim into practice due to lack of a common culture, values and agendas between agencies. Practitioners tend to rely on their implicit knowledge based on professional training, values and agency culture that differ.

The use of forms and assessment tools involving rather mechanical approaches to assessment can be criticised for simply justifying decisions already made. Consequently assessment tends to focus on physical functioning but the reason for such data collection is not apparent and does not appear to be interpreted or analysed in any meaningful way.

The Single Assessment Process is being introduced as a response to criticisms of the way care management and the aim of multi disciplinary working has evolved. The NHS Plan (DoH, 2000) and the National Service Framework for Older People specifies ways in which assessment of elderly people should be standardised for use by professionals in joint health and social care teams. Agencies are expected to reach agreement on several contentious issues including:

- Agree terminology and reach a common assessment language.
- Agree on shared values.

- Agree the link between medical diagnosis and assessment.
- Agree common assessment approaches.

The SAP has not been rigorously evaluated but early indications suggest that in its desire to achieve effective practice and avoid duplication, the government is making a crude attempt to construct an assessment tool that will not appeal to nurses or social workers. A recent Royal College of Nursing report found widespread dissatisfaction with the single assessment process among nurses who felt they were being used as social care staff inappropriate to their training. Social workers equally fear that the SAP will be medically oriented and eventually marginalise the social aspects of an elderly persons experience.

One of the major barriers to achieving good assessment practice concerns the resources available to develop innovative service options. Social workers often feel like rationers of care and services thus inhibiting them from probing too deeply into an individual's circumstances or spending time to develop a deeper professional, helping relationship. Identifying needs that cannot be subsequently met results in feelings of guilt, disillusionment and low morale.

Personalisation

In 2006 the government published a new Health and Social Care policy (DoH, 2006) which included a range of plans advertised as 'the personalisation agenda'. These plans included increased use of direct payments, more use of voluntary and family support and moves to shift budgets from local councils to individual clients. To some this represents a political shift away from the concept of the post 2nd World War model of a comprehensive, universal welfare state towards a smaller model of individual citizen empowerment and personal responsibility. Social workers already unhappy with a care management role will further feel pressured to become a planning facilitator, a care navigator or a care broker and thus more disconnected from the experiences of clients and part of a market-driven system of resource allocation.

Research demonstrates that many clients express no desire to take over complex budgeting and organising tasks, while social workers will be forgiven for seeing this policy as a smokescreen for cutting services and reducing the quality of care (Ferguson, 2007). In 2009 social workers were allotted a central role in delivering personalised services in the Dept of Health Adult Social Care Workforce Strategy, yet a recent survey highlighted worrying gaps in the skills and knowledge base of social workers. Over half felt they did not have the required knowledge about employing personal assistants, or skills in brokerage (*Community Care*, 2010).

Children and families assessment

The Children Act 1989 provides the legislative foundation on which subsequent policy guidance has been built to inform social work practice in assessment with children and families. *A Framework for Assessing Children in Need* (DoH, 2000) is the latest and most comprehensive guidance to emerge following implementation of the *Children Act 1989*. Since 2001 all referrals to social service departments concerning children in need have been assessed under these guidelines in two ways. An initial assessment where the needs are considered to be relatively straightforward, such as a request for family support, and a core assessment where the needs are perceived to be more complex involving a number of concerns about emotional development or child abuse.

The guidance is a key element of the Department of Health's work to support local authorities in implementing *Quality Protects* – the government's programme for transforming the management and delivery of children's social services. This guidance has been incorporated into other government guidance on protecting children from harm *Working Together to Safeguard Children* (1999). Research into the working of the *Children Act 1989* showed that social workers were conducting child protection investigations but neglecting to assess fully the family's needs for ongoing support (DoH, 1995). Guidance has been driven as much by evidence from research as high profile child abuse cases under the full glare of the media spotlight where complexities are reduced to simplicities.

A recent research project found evidence that social workers find the framework cumbersome, over-reliant on prescribed formats, and expected to be undertaken in unrealistic timescales (Corby, Millar and Pope, 2002). The researchers found evidence that parents involved in these assessments felt their views were not being taken sufficiently into account. Key to parental satisfaction with the process was:

- Feeling that their perceptions about their children were taken into account.
- Reaching agreement about the nature of the problem.
- Maintaining optimism and a degree of sensitivity.
- Using the framework flexibly and creatively to maximise parental empowerment.

The principle underlying the assessment framework is that social workers need a framework for understanding and helping children and families which takes into account the inner world of the self and the outer world of the environment, both in terms of relationships and in terms of practicalities such as housing. This can be called an ecological, holistic, or psycho-social approach. The framework uses a triangular model to distinguish the elements of the assessment framework: the child's developmental needs, parenting capacity, and family and environmental factors. Within each of these elements social workers are expected to gather the following specific information for analysis:

Child's developmental needs

– health
– education
– emotional and behavioural development
– identity
– family and social relationships
– social presentation
– selfcare skills

Parenting capacity

– basic care
– ensuring safety
– emotional warmth
– stimulation
– guidance and boundaries
– stability

Family and environmental factors

– family history and functioning
– wider family
– housing
– employment
– income
– family's social integration
– community resources

Successful implementation of the framework requires you to have a good grasp of the principles underpinning the framework and an ability to translate these principles into practice (Horwath, 2002):

- Assessments should be child-centred and rooted in child development.
- Professionals should recognise and work with diversity.
- Assessment practice means working whenever possible, with children and families and building on the family strengths as well as identifying difficulties.
- The quality of the human environment is linked to the development of the child.
- A range of professionals are the assessors and providers of services to children in need, therefore assessments should be multidisciplinary.
- Assessment is a continuing process. Interventions and services should be provided alongside the assessment.
- Effective assessment practice is dependent on the combination of evidence-based practice grounded in knowledge with finely balanced professional judgement.

You will need to integrate multi-faceted knowledge of child development into your assessments from learning acquired from studies in human growth and development to be able to confidently use this framework (Beckett, 2002). Psychodynamic theory, and Learning theory are especially important tools to employ in this context. Also, two key concepts critical to the interrelationship between the inner and outer worlds are attachment and self-esteem. Children who are securely attached to significant adults in early childhood have been shown to develop good peer relationships and cope well with problems. Social work practice concerned with helping children who have lost attachment figures places great emphasis on providing these children with continuity of good alternative parenting experiences.

It is important to avoid being deterministic about some of these theoretical resources or to assume that adverse childhood experiences can cascade automatically through subsequent generations. Modern research has demonstrated the complexity and diversity of different children's responses to similar experiences. It is important to understand what may act as protective factors in children's lives which can mitigate the effects of negative experiences and promote resilience. And there are children who

with ample social and family support have little capacity to cope with small amounts of stress.

Children vary in their vulnerability to psycho-social stress and adversity as a result of both genetic and environmental influences. Family-wide experiences tend to impinge on individual children in quite different ways. The reduction of negative and increase of positive chain reactions influences the extent to which the effects of adversity persist over time. New experiences that open up opportunities can provide beneficial turning-point effects. Although positive experiences in themselves do not exert much of a protective effect, they can be helpful if they serve to neutralise some risk factors; and that the cognitive and affective processing of experiences is likely to influence whether or not resilience develops (Rutter, 1999).

Evidence based practice requires the gathering, testing, recording, and weighing of evidence on which to base decisions and the careful use of knowledge gained during work with a child and family. This helps the task of determining what is most relevant in a family's situation, what is most significant for the child, the impact intervention is having, and the judgement about when more or less action is required in the child's best interests. It is important to pay equal attention to all three domains in the framework and not be deflected by a child's behavioural symptoms to the extent that parental capacity and environmental factors are neglected.

Recent research demonstrates that assessments can become dominated by the agenda of social services departments thereby undermining the concept of inter-agency co-operation (Howarth, 2002). Also in the drive to complete recording forms within specified timescales anti-oppressive practice is given a lack of attention, while the pace of the assessment is inconsistent with the capacity of the family to cope. In the case of fostering and adoption work research has highlighted practice based on diagnostic assessment of foster carers using psychodynamic theories, contrasted with practice based on task centred, functional analysis which applicants found more useful (Berridge, 1997). The important point is that you can locate and justify your chosen practice orientation and demonstrate how it fulfils the task requirement.

ACTIVITY 1.4

Write down the ways in which you think the guidance will help in your assessment of a child and family you might be working with, and the ways in which this guidance will hinder the assessment.

Commentary

Such a comprehensive guidance framework can seem daunting to social workers working under pressure on their available resources. Time is crucial in many situations and it is often difficult to obtain full information in risky circumstances. Interventions undertaken in one set of circumstances can impact on the quality of subsequent assessment – and vice versa. It is important to consider the purpose of assessment and the relationship between assessment and intervention, which can make it hard to separate their functions. The danger is that social workers will feel impelled to conduct lengthy detailed assessments following the framework rigidly rather than using it as a framework to guide practice across a multitude of different circumstances. The skill will be in focusing on the most important aspects of the framework relevant to particular situations.

Common assessment framework

Government guidance (DfES, 2005) indicates that this should be the main and sometimes only assessment instrument to be used at the first sign of emerging vulnerability in a child or young person, and to act as a marker for referral to another agency or specialist service. Assessments have hitherto been used to make decisions about whether or not a child meets the threshold criteria to trigger delivery of a service. The concept of the Common Assessment Framework (CAF) is that this should lead to a common approach to needs assessment, as an initial assessment for use by statutory or voluntary sector staff in education, early years, health, police, youth justice or social work. It is intended that this will reduce the number of assessments experienced by children and foster improved information sharing and thus help dissolve professional boundaries. However recent research illustrates that such efforts at standardisation and categorisation are highly problematic and likely to fail (White et al., 2009).

The framework is expected to contribute to the wider culture change across the children and young people's workforce by offering (DfES, 2005):

- General guidance on its use.
- A common procedure for assessment.

- A methodology based on the *Framework for the Assessment of Children in Need and their Families.*
- A focus on child development and communication skills with children, carers and parents.
- Gaining consent.
- How to record findings and identify an appropriate response.
- How to share information when a child moves between local authority areas.
- An explanation of the roles and responsibilities of different agencies and practitioners.

The framework needs to be familiar to all staff whose work may not directly focus on the emotional and mental health needs of children and young people, but indirectly contribute to achieving the five outcomes for well-being in *Every Child Matters.* The assessment should be completed with the full knowledge, consent and involvement of children, young people and their parents. It should be child-centred, ensure equality of opportunity, be solution and action focused, and be an ongoing process rather than a one-off event. Using it competently is a skilled practice.

It must be centred on the child or young person and the whole spectrum of their potential needs, rather than the policy focus and statutory obligations of particular services. Outcomes from the CAF should be the identification of the broader needs of vulnerable children without additional support. Earlier intervention is also expected from practitioners looking outside their usual work area for additional support. This should reduce the number of assessments undergone by children and families by improving the quality of referrals between agencies.

The process of the common assessment

Preparation – talk to the child/young person and their parent. Discuss the issues and what you can do to help. Talk to anyone else you need to who are already involved. If you decide a common assessment would be useful you seek the agreement of the child/young person and their parent as appropriate.

Discussion – talk to the child/young person, family and complete the assessment with them. Make use of additional information from other sources to avoid repeated questions. Add to or update any existing common assessments. At the end of the discussion seek to understand better the child and family's strengths, needs and what can be done to help. Agree actions that your service and the family can deliver. Agree with the family any actions that require others to deliver and record this on the form.

Service delivery – deliver on your actions. Make referrals or broker access to other services using the common assessment to demonstrate evidence of need. Keep an eye on progress. Where the child or family needs services from a range of agencies a lead professional must be identified to co-ordinate.

Elements of the common assessment framework:

Development of baby, child or young person

- **General Health** – includes health conditions or impairments which significantly affect everyday life functioning.
- **Physical development** – includes means of mobility, and level of physical or sexual maturity or delayed development.
- **Speech, language and communications development** – includes the ability to communicate effectively, confidently, and appropriately with others.
- **Emotional and social development** – includes the emotional and social response the baby, child or young person gives to parents, carers and others outside the family.
- **Behavioural development** – includes lifestyle and capacity for self-control.
- **Identity** – includes the growing sense of self as a separate and valued person, self-esteem, self-image and social presentation.
- **Family and social relationships** – includes the ability to empathise and build stable and affectionate relationships with others, including family, peers and the wider community.
- **Self-care skills and independence** – includes the acquisition of practical, emotional and communication competencies to increase independence.
- **Understanding, reasoning and problem-solving** – includes the ability to understand and organise information, reason and solve problems.
- **Participation in learning, education and employment** – includes the degree to which the child or young person has access to and is engaged in education and/or work based training and, if s/he is not participating, the reasons for this.

- **Progress and achievement in learning** – includes the child or young person's educational achievements and progress, including in relation to their peers.
- **Aspirations** – includes the ambitions of the child or young person, whether their aspirations are realistic and they are able to plan how to meet them. Note there may be barriers to their achievement because of other responsibilities at home.

Parents and carers

- **Basic care, ensuring safety and protection** – includes the extent to which the baby, child or young person's physical needs are not met and they are protected from harm, danger and self-harm.
- **Emotional warmth and stability** – includes the provision of emotional warmth in a stable family environment, giving the baby, child or young person a sense of being valued.
- **Guidance, boundaries and stimulation** – includes enabling the child or young person to regulate their own emotions and behaviour while promoting the child or young person's learning and intellectual development through encouragement, stimulation and promoting social opportunities.

Family and environmental factors

- **Family history, functioning and well being** – includes the impact of family situations and experiences.
- **Wider family** – includes the family's relationships with relatives and non-relatives.
- **Housing, employment and financial considerations** – includes living arrangements, amenities, facilities, who is working or not, and the income available over a sustained period of time.

Social and community resources

- **Neighbourhood** – includes the wider context of the neighbourhood and its impact on the baby, child or young person, availability of facilities and services.
- **Accessibility** – includes schools, day-care, primary health care, places of worship, transport, shops, leisure activities and family support services.
- **Characteristics** – includes levels of crime, disadvantage, employment, levels of substance misuse/trading.

- **Social integration** – includes the degree of the young person's social integration or isolation, peer influences, friendships and social networks.

ACTIVITY 1.5

Review the above material and make a note of those elements that are less familiar to you.

Make time to discuss these in supervision or with your manager soon to help you understand them and integrate them into your practice.

Assessment as process

Organisational arrangements within social care agencies are driving the way assessment is conceptualised by social workers as we have already noted. It is therefore important that you adopt a wide definition of assessment if your practice is to be empowering and anti-oppressive. It is important to think of assessment as a process rather than a one-off event. There should be a seamless transition from assessment to intervention in a circular process that includes the crucial elements of planning and reviewing. Once completed, the circle begins again at the assessment stage of the process and so on. Think of it as a continuous, perpetual movement, punctuated by a range of activities involving major or minor interventions in the life of service users. Rather than adopting a one-dimensional view of assessment you could also perceive it as an intervention in itself – the very act of conducting an information-gathering interview could have a significant positive impact on a person's well-being. The simple idea that someone cares and is prepared to listen to their story could be enormously comforting to someone lonely, isolated and with low self-esteem.

No discussion of assessment can be complete without addressing the concept of need, as it is a word that frequently appears in much legislation, practice guidance and service providers' documentation. There are universal needs expressed in global documents like the UN declaration on the rights of children, there are special needs which although clearly discriminatory appear to be accepted as a useful signifier for certain groups in society. What this does is to permit rationing to occur under the guise of benign motives. If you consider the idea that every person has special needs, in the sense of their individual uniqueness, and replace this

with the notion of rights then the concept of special needs becomes redundant. In our context of social work the concept of need has a powerful impact on assessment practice. It has been categorised in the following way to help us distinguish the subtleties in meaning and the way need can be defined (Bradshaw, 1972):

- **Normative need** – decided by professionals or administrators on behalf of the community. Standards are set to minimum levels of service with stigma attached.
- **Felt need** – limited by the individual's expression of wants based on their perceptions, knowledge and experience.
- **Expressed need** – these are felt needs translated into service demand but restricted by what the client feels is likely to be offered.
- **Comparative need** – a comparison of need between two areas, or service user groups in order to reach standardised provision. Results in levelling down rather than up.

It is useful to bear these definitions in mind during the process of assessment practice. They can help guide and enable you to move from the role of client advocate by articulating their needs through to the agency representative who is expected to place a boundary or limit on resources. Social workers employed as care managers are to some extent insulated from these twin pressures by being separated from assessment but they too know what is required by clients in particular circumstances, understand the inadequacies of minimum provision and appreciate the negative consequences for service users. One of the aims of an empowering social work practice in keeping with the aspirations of disabled people for example, is to move to a system of client self-assessment. However, the continued emphasis on budget constraints limits the extent to which local authorities are prepared to relinquish their control in the determination of individual need, and self-assessment requires a partnership between social workers and disabled people which threatens that control (Oliver and Sapey, 1999).

Three models of assessment

It is sometimes suggested that social workers can either play a crucial role in understanding the problems of their client, or work alongside the person who has been identified as the client and other significant people in the situation. The task is to arrive at a mutual understanding of the problem and negotiate who might do what to help (Smale et al., 1993). A further distinction is to portray these two approaches as reflecting the questioning model or the exchange model of assessment. A third approach, perceived as a variation of the questioning model, is the procedural model whereby information is gathered to see whether the client meets certain eligibility criteria for services (Coulshed and Orme, 2006). The **questioning model** assumes the worker:

- Is expert in people, their problems and needs.
- Exercises knowledge and skill to form their assessment and identify people's needs.
- Identifies resources required.
- Takes responsibility for making an accurate assessment of need and taking appropriate action.

Whereas the **exchange model** assumes that the worker:

- Has expertise in the process of problem solving with others.
- Understands and shares perceptions of problems and their management.
- Gets agreement about who will do what to support whom.
- Takes responsibility for arriving at the optimum resolution of problems within the constraints of available resources and the willingness of participants to contribute.

The difference between the questioning and exchange model of assessment is in how power is used and its impact on the service user. The latter appears to offer a more empowering experience enabling the person to be fully involved as an equal partner in a process of negotiating the nature of their problem and its possible solutions.

In the questioning model it is assumed that questions can be answered in a straightforward manner and that the worker is able to accurately interpret what the client really wants. The danger is that the complexities of the communication process across boundaries of race, gender, age, disability etc, can be underestimated or even ignored.

In the exchange model the worker concentrates on an exchange of information between themselves and the service user and others involved. A definition of the problem and its resolution or management is arrived at by mutual understanding and sharing of perceptions. The worker tracks or follows what others communicate and is careful not to be influenced by preconceived assumptions. Listening and communication skills are at their optimum effectiveness in this model of practice. The danger is that workers can be misled about the extent of a person's strengths or needs and be drawn towards over-optimistic or over-pessimistic judgements.

The **procedural model** is characterised by questions sometimes framed by pre-printed forms that define the eligibility criteria for services and enable judgements to be made about who should get access to resources. The questions are determined by those setting the criteria for resource allocation – not service users. This process attempts to:

- Identify a particular level of dependency and categorise the client.
- Define the nature of the client's needs in the terms that services are offered.
- The client's definitions of their problems, or that of others, may or may not be included.
- The process is invariably service-driven rather than needs-driven.
- The agency remains central to the definition of problems and the range of available solutions.
- Neither the worker the service user or other involved persons are empowered by the process.

The procedural model is simple and quick to use. It can be controlled easily by managers and eligibility criteria altered to be responsive to changes in policy about resource allocation. Such procedures usually strive towards equitable allocation of scarce resources between competing demands by specifying detailed priorities. Workers often feel they are carrying out policy over which they have little influence. This can be frustrating, but equally they do not always want the burden of responsibility in deciding who gets a service and who does not. There can be a sense of safety in working to a strict set of procedures and guidelines where there is less room for interpretation and individual judgement. The danger is that workers can emphasise the negative aspects of a person's situation and underplay their strengths in order to ensure they fulfil the eligibility criteria for services. This distorts the overall level of demand and results in a deficit model of practice.

ACTIVITY 1.6

List the key features of the three models of assessment described above and describe their advantages and disadvantages.

Creative assessment practice

Accepting that assessment is an imperfect science is a good starting point for creative practice. Also understanding that it is a dynamic process requiring high quality communication skills is very important. Dynamic in the sense that it is not static – information can become out of date, a family's functioning can deteriorate quickly, while the very act of assessment can affect that which you are assessing. Assessment is therefore a purposeful activity. It is the art of managing competing demands and negotiating the best possible outcome. It means steering between the pressures of organisational demands, legislative injunction, limited resources and personal agendas. It includes having the personal integrity to hold to your core values and ethical base while being buffeted by strong feelings.

An assessment should be part of a perceptual/analytic process that involves selecting, categorising, organising and synthesising data. If it is conducted as an exploratory study avoiding labels it can result in a careful deliberation of a service users needs and not just fit them into whatever provision exists. Remember that all assessments contain the potential for error or bias. These can be partly counteracted by following these guidelines (Coulshed, 1991):

- Improving self-awareness so as to monitor when you are trying to normalise, be over-optimistic or rationalise data.
- Getting supervision which helps to release blocked feelings or confront denial of facts or coping with the occasional situation where you have been manipulated.
- Being aware of standing in awe of those who hold higher status or power and challenging their views when necessary.
- Treating all assessments as working hypotheses which ought to be substantiated with emerging knowledge-remember that they are inherently speculations derived from material and subjective sources.

With government policy and organisational changes moving in the direction of more multi-disciplinary team working it is imperative that social work assessment skills in the context of practice with other professionals is both authoritative and creative. The values and knowledge base of different staff from other agencies will be reflected in the way they think about and undertake assessment. Your social work contribution is crucial and depends on having the capacity to work with other colleagues in partnership. Negotiation skills are paramount in order to enable you to challenge and confront when and where necessary to defend clients. Networking is considered a valuable social work attribute and you should be developing expertise in liaison, linking, communicating, and convening meetings.

Multidisciplinary teams can become stressful places to work, particularly when the service is under pressure and energies are drained by resource shortages combined with high demand. It is easier to keep a low profile and grit your teeth in these circumstances rather than open up a painful or uncomfortable issue for discussion. However you will gain respect by voicing concerns about the service or the clients and showing a willingness to tackle difficult issues. Being open, client-centred and demonstrating sensitivity to the team dynamics will be helpful to others who probably feel the same. Your broader understanding of service users in their socio-economic context together with your specific knowledge of child care, mental health or community care legislation will help clarify your distinctive and valued contribution.

Assessment is about making sense of the situation as a whole, and working out the best way to achieve change (Middleton, 1997). Creative assessment ensures that clients are included in the process and feel active in its determination rather than feeling that it is a series of coercive hoops to jump through before receiving a reward. It should be part and parcel of socially inclusive practice that enshrines the policy objective of social justice. These activities demonstrate that assessment can be, and is, inextricably linked to intervention and can be a therapeutic process in itself. The practice will be more creative by doing the following:

- Spending time talking with the client.
- Spending time with them in their usual environment.
- Spending time with them doing things that they enjoy regularly.

- Spending time with them doing some of their regular activities.
- Spending time with them doing something they would not normally do and in an environment they are unfamiliar with.
- Spending time with them around other people both familiar and unfamiliar.
- Spending time talking with other people involved in their life.

Chapter summary

We discussed the way organisational arrangements within social care agencies are driving the way assessment is conceptualised by social workers. It is therefore important that you adopt a wide definition of assessment if your practice is to be empowering and anti-oppressive. A useful starting point is to think of assessment as a process rather than a one-off event. There should be a seamless transition from assessment to intervention in a circular process that includes the crucial elements of planning and reviewing.

It should be apparent that the depth and complexity of the work involved in using official guidance places competing demands on practitioners who face numerous dilemmas such as balancing the needs of clients and carers and individual liberty versus public safety. Time and resource constraints militate against the need for depth and analysis, while assessed needs can be hindered by service provision limits.

We noted how translating guidance into practical, visible and measurable practice is challenging and it is important not to become overwhelmed or deny the possibility of implementing change and rely on cynicism or complacency to excuse inaction. Guidance evolves as a result of research and evaluation of existing practice set against economic and social policy imperatives. Actively contributing to that process is part of ethical social work practice.

The Care Programme Approach is the current policy context which defines the way care is delivered to people with mental health difficulties and influences social work practice particularly in relation to duties under section 117 of the *Mental Health Act 1983*. The care programme approach was introduced in 1991 and its principle aim was to improve the co-ordination of care to people with severe mental health needs. Prior to this some people were not properly assessed, whether in the community or prior to discharge from hospital.

We discussed how the benefits of care management are that it supports a need-led approach to assessment and the use of resources, tailoring services to individual requirements. It involves a clear commitment to individual care planning, specifying desired outcomes. Care management requires a clear division of responsibility between assessment/care management and service provision, separating the interests of service users and providers. Combined with the new Personalisation Agenda it should result in more responsive services as a result of linking assessment and purchasing/commissioning.

The use of forms and assessment tools involving rather mechanical approaches to assessment can be criticised for simply justifying decisions already made. Consequently assessment tends to focus on physical functioning but the reason for such data collection is not apparent and does not appear to be interpreted or analysed in any meaningful way.

One of the major barriers to achieving good assessment practice concerns the resources available to develop innovative service options. Social workers often feel like rationers of care and services thus inhibiting them from probing too deeply into an individual's circumstances or spending time to develop a deeper professional, helping relationship. Identifying needs that cannot be subsequently met results in feelings of guilt, disillusionment and low morale.

We suggested that the principle underlying the Framework for Assessment of Children in Need is that social workers need a framework for understanding and helping children and families which takes into account the inner world of the self and the outer world of the environment. This includes relationships and practicalities such as housing. This can be called an ecological, holistic, or psycho-social approach. The framework uses a triangular model to distinguish the elements of the assessment framework: the child's developmental needs, parenting capacity, and family and environmental factors and has been supplemented with the much-criticised Common Assessment Framework for use across children's services.

Assessment is a purposeful activity. It is the art of managing competing demands and negotiating the best possible outcome. It means steering between the pressures of organisational demands, legislative injunction, limited resources and personal agendas. It includes having the personal integrity to hold to your core values and ethical base while being buffeted by strong feelings. An assessment should be part of a perceptual/analytic process that involves selecting, categorising, organising and synthesising data. If it is conducted as an exploratory study avoiding labels it can result in a careful deliberation of a service users needs and not just fit them into whatever provision exists.

CHAPTER 2

Modern Intervention Practice

Learning objectives

- Describe, compare and contrast a range of classic and contemporary methods and models of social work intervention.
- Apply the appropriate intervention based on skilled assessment and analysis of the client and their personal, psychological and social context.
- Understand the way modern social work practices have become burdened by the demands for efficiency, calculability, predictability and control and how this undermines the quality of the interpersonal helping relationship.
- Develop the capacity to keep the issue of institutional and personal racism constantly in mind so that in every proposed intervention you are actively considering how your practice can resist and challenge overt and covert racist assumptions and beliefs.

Introduction

The role and function of social work intervention in general has been the subject of much discussion throughout the relatively short history of the profession (Giddings, 1898; Richmond, 1922; Titmuss, 1958; Butrym, 1976; Davies, 1981; Barclay, 1982; CCETSW, 1989; Kemshall, 1993; O'Hagan, 1996; Adams et al., 1998; DCSF, 2009). The specific manifestation of that role and function in work which encompasses the whole human experience and developmental life span is necessarily complex. This role gets eclipsed between routinised assessment procedures and high-risk safeguarding and protection work, while the accelerating trend towards care management underplays therapeutic skills. However in the context of multi-disciplinary working, and methods and models of intervention there is evidence of the way a broadly psycho-social model can still be utilised in contemporary social work practice (Brearley, 1995; Copley and Forryan, 1997; Davies, 1997; Howe et al., 1999; Trevithick, 2000; Coulshed and Orme, 2006).

Every intervention should have a purpose and, as much as possible, that purpose should be identified clearly and openly as part of the agreement established with service users, other key individuals and professionals involved. The seemingly routine task of an assessment interview can even be thought of as an intervention in its own right because of the opportunity to gain a greater understanding of people and their situations in a therapeutic way. That is, by using the opportunity to establish a helping, personal relationship as the basis for initiating change, rather than seeing it as an administrative task (Stepney and Ford, 2000; Trevithic, 2000; Walker, 2005).

The choice of intervention open to social workers is necessarily broad because of the wide variety of psychological and social factors influencing the person being helped. The social work literature itself offers a sometimes bewildering array of methods and models of intervention, apart from the wider psychiatric, psychological, and therapeutic texts available to guide the helping process with individuals, families or groups. Public health, education, social and fiscal policy interventions by local and central government agencies also impact on people's welfare generally and need to be taken into account.

One way of conceptualising this mosaic of influences on people and capturing a *meta* view of the panorama of concern is the idea that the variety of influences can be classified into different systems. The notion of a systems approach to formulating interventions was developed 30 years ago and is enshrined in the classic text by Pincus and Minahan which illustrates the variety of systems influencing the service user/client (1973). Within each system of influence are a number of factors, but in the context of this chapter, only those available directly to social workers will be examined in more detail, in order to promote the development of intervention skills.

Before embarking on any one form of intervention though, social workers need to reflect on the ethical questions raised by the choices made and the potential consequences for example, individual counselling or therapy may succeed in helping a troubled young person to develop a sense of self, change their behaviour and gain insight, but in so doing the experience may alienate them from their family. Family therapy may result in the improvement of a child with emotional difficulties, but in the process of the work siblings may be adversely affected or the parental marriage/partnership exposed as problematic (Sharman, 1997). Even though a social worker may not deliver the work themselves, the act of referring to a specialist resource offering specific help means they are sanctioning a potentially powerful intervention in the lives of the person and their family.

A social worker who feels that an adult with mental health problems is bottling up their feelings and needs to learn to express them in counselling may be causing additional stress to that person who is expected within their community or cultural context, to be developing self-control and containment of emotions. However, each intervention comes with its own set of assumptions and potential consequences in terms of generating other stressors. The same intervention could be given to two people with the same problem, but only one of them might benefit. These ethical dilemmas are important to acknowledge and reflect upon before proceeding with any course of action. These points are examined in detail in Chapter 5. The crucial point is to ensure the *most* effective intervention is offered for the *appropriate* problem with the *right* person.

In order to negotiate this difficult terrain to your own personal satisfaction and ethical standards it may be helpful to think about the following as you are embarking on your intervention practice:

- **Good supervision** – this is the foundation of professional social work practice although practitioners often feel they receive too little. On the other hand you might feel that the kind of supervision being offered is really a management/administrative supervision that is experienced as oppressive. Good supervision attends to the issues related to management of the caseload but equally attends to the emotional and relationship issues that invariably affect your practice. It goes without saying that a profession based on the primary helping relationship requires a model of supervision attuned to the discrete psychological processes at work within you as

you experience stressful and potentially distressing situations.

- **Reflective practice** – at its basic this is about learning from our mistakes. But it can be more useful to extend this concept and use it more actively during the process of your direct work with service users. In other words reflecting about what you are doing as you are doing it. It also involves reflecting back on a piece of work ideally with a colleague or supervisor and evaluating what happened and what you might have done differently. We shall return to this subject throughout this book.

- **Whose responsibility?** – at the start of a social work intervention or even before, it is worth spending a few minutes thinking about whether this referral is appropriate for you or your team or your agency. The work may have passed through the variety of eligibility criteria and initial screening measures that are typical of some organisations, yet still on closer examination seem to be inappropriate. The problem is that by the time you realise this you may have already encountered the client and begun to build the helping relationship. It will help if you ask questions of the referrer about their expectations and assumptions about what you can and cannot do. This can save time and trouble and avoid you taking on other agency's responsibilities.

- **Stress management** – contemporary social work practice is typified by staff working to high levels of stress on a regular basis. Sometimes this is mitigated by supportive colleagues and a thoughtful supervisor, however it is worth considering adopting some self preservation strategies as you begin to experience the demands and pressures of the job. An important factor is stress management. There are whole texts on this subject but for now it is important to recognise this need particularly in the context of your direct work because so much else hinges on the quality of this work and the consequences that flow from it. There is considerable pressure to get it right, yet we can acknowledge how this is almost an impossible aim. Managing your stress will be as individual as what stresses you, but learning to say no, taking time out, time management, planning your work, seeking supportive supervision, personal insight and relaxation techniques can all help.

The problem with theory

Social workers are informed by a wide range of social science theory in weighing up and making judgements about human difficulties. In developing a deeper understanding of people's difficulties in your assessment practice with a view to deciding on intervention, you can draw on a range of theories and methods. The skills and values that are part of your individual social work identity will influence, and be influenced, by these. Differing hypotheses result from viewing situations with the aid of these theories. This is healthy although it can be unhelpful if it leads to confusion and drift in your practice. At its best it can help guard against the temptation to claim a single truth in any situation. However you need to integrate all of these factors in order to practice in a coherent manner.

Forming alternative understandings and explanations is a good habit to acquire. However, judgements have to be made, will be demanded by managers and to be expected in legal proceedings where they will be examined and tested. The most desirable practice is where an interpretation is helpful to both worker and client in developing solutions, and where it is rooted in values of respect and anti-oppressive practice. Maintaining a reflexive stance helps you consider the consequences of using particular theories and encouraging service users to develop their own theories about their situations. Also the notion of treating people as wholes, and as being in interaction with their environment is important.

Respecting their understanding and interpretation of their experience, and seeing clients at the centre of what workers are doing, all fit with the central principles of social work (Payne, 1997). You will need more than one model of Assessment and Intervention to enable you to meet the needs of all your clients – if not you will be like a plumber with only one spanner. Having a grasp of different models of practice should enable you with the client to select the most appropriate, and help you maintain a degree of open-mindedness. This process will enable you to plan your intervention by integrating and analysing information and forming a judgement in partnership with your client.

Consumer studies and outcome research into helping relationships in social work, and other professional supportive relationships support the principles underlying the exchange model of assessment. The questioning and procedural models are based on management imperatives about service allocation from finite resources. They all raise questions about the notion of expertise and the use of power-especially in risky situations where a measure of short-term control may result in longer-term empowerment or vice versa. All these models need to be applied in real circumstances in order to allow workers to evaluate their effectiveness and form conclusions about their usefulness. It may be that in practice you find there are elements of each appearing during different stages of a piece of work, or at different times with several contacts with a client. Another important factor is the particular practice context of your work. Each of these models may lend itself to a particular professional function with different service user groups. There are social work teams working in the short or long term across the spectrum of assessment and intervention roles. As always, it is important to be able to reflect on where you and your client are in that process.

ACTIVITY 2.1

Consider the following case scenario. Decide which intervention you might use and describe the process of your intervention.

Paul, a five year old has been looked after for two months at his mother's request following bruising to his right leg and right upper arm. She lost her temper after David had a tantrum. Paul's father is unknown. Kayleigh is two and a half years old and lives with her mother. Previously perceived as a happy child developing normally, her behaviour now seems to be regressing. Their mother, Lucy, is 25 years old, single and expecting her third child in five months. She finds it hard to cope and is asking for help. She has poor health and a past history of physical and sexual abuse. Lucy was in care herself from five to eight years of age and is isolated from family and friends. A review meeting has recommended a comprehensive assessment.

Commentary

The primary aim of this assessment is to assist the decision-making process about Paul's future by assessing Lucy's parenting. This should be made explicit with Lucy. The needs of all family members should be addressed and the elements of the assessment clarified so that Lucy knows what is going to happen, when, where and how. However, you are also intervening at the same time so your choice of working practice needs to be informed by theory that can at least partly, explain the situation. In doing so they can also guide the way forward.

The legal context needs to be explained and the possibility of Paul returning home or care proceedings being commenced. The assessment could be used in evidence but you should avoid any hint of threat or coercion. An empowering approach would explain the rights of Lucy to decline to participate in the assessment, even though this might precipitate care proceedings. The areas for assessment need to be discussed and negotiated so that Lucy's concerns can be acknowledged and valued and what you are expecting her to achieve is made explicit.

Your assessment should include what impact the child protection system has had on the family and acknowledge that their functioning will be affected in that context. A wider focus will include the current role of the grandparents and father of Kayleigh, and what support they might be prepared to offer in future. The details of the plan for assessment and intervention can be incorporated into a written agreement. Lucy should be encouraged to obtain legal or other expert advice throughout the process to ensure she is fully aware of her rights and responsibilities. She should be able to contribute formally to the final report and express any disagreements or alternative interpretations.

A combination of various models for different aspects of the assessment process might be appropriate, as would using other professionals in contact with the family, to contribute their perspective. For example, a psychodynamic model could help you explore with Lucy the effects of past experiences on her current parenting capacity. A task-centred model could assist in mapping out the steps necessary for Paul's return, while a systems model could enable all the important aspects of the family's context to be included. Your model of assessment and intervention will be influenced by your own evolving social work identity and the functional role within the work context. An empowering approach will facilitate the appropriate environment in which to assess Lucy's parenting and ensure practical arrangements such as transport are in place.

Methods and models of practice

The following methods and models of practice are not unique to social work nor are they an exclusive list. Within each are specific skills sets informed by sound theory and research. They have been chosen from the range of modern methods and models available to aid clarity in selection of the most appropriate components of an effective social work intervention (Doel and Marsh, 1992; Payne, 1997; Coulshed and Orme, 1998; 2006, Milner and O'Byrne, 1998; Walker and Beckett, 2003; Walker, 2005). Discussion of the merits of defining methods and models of social work and examination of the distinctions between terms such as practice approach, orientation and perspective, has been avoided for the sake of brevity and in order to avoid adding to the confusion already highlighted in the literature which can detract from the job in hand (Trevithick, 2000).

Crisis intervention

Crisis intervention has become a practice with a theoretical base and can be identified by certain characteristics. Its use can be part of an automatic response from your agency to concerns expressed by a client, member of the public or other agency. It may not feel like an intervention of choice, but neither should it be overlooked as a potentially creative opportunity to initiate long-term changes. Drawing on psychodynamic principles it is aimed at strengthening the person's internal psychological resources through a personal relationship within which you can positively reinforce their coping strategies. Crisis theory is described as a time when a person finds themselves much more dependent on external sources of support than at other times in their life. It has been described as having three distinct phases (Caplan, 1964):

1. **Impact** – recognising a threat.
2. **Recoil** – attempting to restore equilibrium but failing, leaving the person feeling stressed and defeated.
3. **Adjustment/adaptation or breakdown** – when the person begins to move to a different level of functioning.

It is usually a set of interrelated factors and triggers that produce a state of crisis, some of which can be anticipated while others cannot. Rather than see crises as individual failure it is better to think of them as opportunities for interventions when the young person is more likely to respond. Characteristics include:

- Helps the person gain insight into their functioning and better ways of coping.
- Used in conjunction with risk assessment and risk management techniques.
- Is usually short term in nature.
- Relates a person's internal crises to external changes.
- Can help in case of loss, bereavement, reactive depression and trauma.
- Based on the idea that people can return to a previous level of functioning.

Disadvantages

This may be used as the default setting for social work practice as government and employers re-define modern social work to a reactive service administering problems, gate-keeping resources and referring clients on to other services. Done well it offers opportunities for advanced, reflective, psycho-social practice and high levels of interpersonal skill. But if it is used to ration, exclude and constrain then it is more a mechanism of social control.

Community work

Helping people within their own communities is endorsed by valid research as better than removing them to unfamiliar surroundings. The theoretical base of such practice is political and socialist in origins. In its narrowest definition it might exclude statutory work and identify it with voluntary non-statutory sector staff engaged in pressure group action or outreach activity. A broader definition would include it as part of the repertoire of skills required in progressive psycho-social practice. It is characterised by partnership, anti-discriminatory, empowering practice aimed at reducing social exclusion and fostering self-help. It comprises these specific skills (Henderson and Thomas, 1987):

- galvanising
- focusing
- clarifying
- summarising
- gate-keeping
- mediating
- informing

Disadvantages

People who are homeless or in crisis are not often linked to their neighbourhoods, kinship networks or informal support, therefore it is difficult to galvanise them or enable them to accept help offered. The community itself may be hostile to them and their behaviours as well as reflecting racist beliefs and discriminatory practices. Institutional organisation of social work practice is part of the structure of society and welfare which has let many people down by failing to engage creatively with communities as a whole rather than individualising interventions.

Family therapy/systemic practice

Employing a family therapy, systemic or systems model in practice will be characterised by the key notion that individuals have a social context which will be influencing to a greater or lesser extent, their behaviour and their perception of their problem. An important social context is that of the family and this has led to the practice of family therapy as a method of practice based on systemic theory. It offers a broad framework for intervention enabling the mapping of all the important elements affecting families as well as a method of working with those elements to effect beneficial change. It can also be used as a tool to examine organisational characteristics and team functioning as a whole rather than as a set of individual parts. Key features include:

- Convening family meetings to give voice to everyone connected to an individuals problem (e.g. family group conference).
- Constructing a genogram (family tree) with a family to help identify the quality of relationships.
- Harnessing the strengths of families to support individuals in trouble.
- Using a problem-oriented style to energise the family to find their own solutions.
- Assisting in the development of insight into patterns of behaviour and communication within the family system.
- Adopting a neutral position as far as possible in order to avoid accusations of bias/collusion.

Many professionals use this model as an overarching framework to help guide their practice. It is particularly useful to use to clarify situations where there is multi-agency and multi-professional involvement in client's lives. It can help the drawing of boundaries and sort out who does what in often complex, fast-moving, and confusing situations. It also helps avoid the assumption that the individual person is necessarily the main focus for intervention.

Disadvantages

It can be difficult for some families to appreciate the interconnectedness of the problems of individual family members with wider influences. It is a way of viewing the position, role and behaviour of various individuals within the context of the whole system, but in so doing it can appear abstract, culturally insensitive, and disempowering. Used uncritically it can negate the importance of individual work, as well as avoiding location of responsibility in child abuse situations with adult perpetrators.

Psychodynamic practice

The model offers a concept of the mind, its mechanisms, and a method of understanding why some people behave in seemingly repetitive, destructive ways. It is the essential one to one helping relationship involving advanced listening and communication skills. It provides a framework to address profound disturbances and inner conflicts within people around issues of loss, attachment, anxiety, and personal development. Key ideas such as defence mechanisms, and the transference in the relationship between worker and client, can be extremely helpful in reviewing the work being undertaken, and in the process of supervision. The model helps evaluate the strong feelings aroused in particular work situations, where for example a client transfers feelings and attitudes onto the worker that derive from an earlier significant relationship. Counter-transference occurs when you try to live up to that expectation and behave for example, like the client's parent. Key features include:

- It is a useful way of attempting to understand seemingly irrational behaviour.
- The notion of defence mechanisms is a helpful way of assessing people who have difficulty expressing their emotions.
- It acknowledges the influence of past events/attachments and can create a healthy suspicion about surface behaviour.
- The development of insight can be a particularly empowering experience to enable

people to understand themselves and take more control over their own lives.
- The model has influenced a listening, accepting approach that avoids over-directiveness.
- It can be used to assess which developmental stage is reflected in a child or young person's behaviour and to gauge the level of anxiety/depression.

Disadvantages

The conventional criticisms of this model are its genesis in a medical model of human behaviour that relies on expert opinion without too much account of the person in their socio-economic context. In its original, uncritical form it pathologises homosexuality and negates gender power relationships. However modern scholars and researchers in this area of practice have evolved much better understanding and incorporation of anti-discriminatory principles. It is not considered an appropriate way of working with some ethnic minority groups and on its own cannot adequately explain the effects of racism. This is an area of some debate and relates to cultural norms and assumptions about the nature of a person, the mind and behaviour.

Cognitive behavioural practice

Practice with this model is based on the key concept that all behaviour is learned and therefore available to be unlearned or changed. It offers a framework for assessing the pattern of behaviour in people and a method for altering their thinking, feeling, and behaviour. The intervention can be used with individuals and groups. It aims to help them become aware of themselves, link thoughts and emotions, and enable them to acquire new life skills. Using this approach you would decide on the goals/new behaviours to be achieved together with the client, those that are clear but also capable of measurement. The four major behavioural techniques related to CBT include desensitisation; aversion therapy, operant conditioning and modelling. Key features include:

- Using the ABC formula – what are the Antecedents, the Behaviour and the Consequences of the problem?
- Focusing on what behaviours are desired and reinforcing them.
- Modelling and rehearsing desired behavioural patterns.

- Combining behavioural and cognitive approaches to produce better results.
- Gradually desensitising a person to a threat or phobia.

Behavioural approaches have appeal for staff undertaking intervention because it offers a systematic, scientific approach from which to structure their practice. The approach goes some way towards encouraging participatory practice, discouraging labelling, and maintains the client's story as central. The idea of learned helplessness has the potential to bridge the gap between psychological and sociological explanations of behaviour, maintaining the focus on both social and individual factors.

Disadvantages

Usually it is only the immediate environment of the person that is examined. It is not as value-free as it claims. The scientific nature of behavioural assessment rests on *modernist* assumptions about certainty. In other words it does not take account of the unconscious and relies on a simplistic notion of objectivity. There is often in practice a tendency to rush a solution after a limited assessment where the theory is bent so that the individual client changes to accommodate their circumstances rather than the other way round. The potential to use the theory to employ anti-oppressive practice is limited because much of the theory is based on white, male, western norms of behaviour.

Task centred practice

Task centred work is often cited as the most popular base for contemporary assessment and intervention practice, but it may be that it is used as a set of activities rather than as a theoretically-based approach from which a set of activities flows. Key features include:

- It is based on client agreement or service user acceptance of a legal justification for action.
- It aims to move from problem to goal, from what is wrong to what is needed.
- It is based around tasks which are central to the process of change and which aim to build on individual service user strengths as far as possible.
- The approach is time-limited, preserving client self-esteem and independence as far as possible.

- It is a highly structured model of practice using a building block approach so that each task can be agreed and success or not measured by moving from problem to goal.

It can serve as a basic approach for the majority of people and is rooted in the day to day practical stresses and strains experienced by many clients. In this approach the problem is always the problem as defined by the client. It therefore respects their values, beliefs and perceptions. This approach encourages people to select the problem they want to work on and engages them in task selection and review. It lends itself to a collaborative and empowering approach by enabling you to carry out your share of tasks and review them alongside the clients. Time limits and task reviews aid motivation and promote optimism and can be a way of keeping a tight focus in often complex and fluid situations.

Disadvantages

Although this approach has the capacity for empowerment, it can sometimes prohibit active measures by practitioners to ensure it does. Although ostensibly value-free and intrinsically non-oppressive, you should continually reflect on your practice to make this explicit. The coaching role could be open to abuse, or permit you to become overly directive. Task selection can be influenced by your anxieties and statutory agenda and therefore feel disempowering. The emphasis on simple, measurable tasks may focus attention on concrete solutions that obscure the potential advocacy role of practice. The approach requires a degree of cognitive ability and motivation in the person that in some cases will be lacking.

Narrative practice

Narrative therapeutic ideas have developed in recent years among social workers captivated by the notion of storytelling as a means to engage people. Perhaps this development is a reaction against the increasingly technocratic age we live in and where clients are surrounded and constantly stimulated by largely visual and auditory media or communication. Storytelling is advocated by educationalists attempting to reach children in schools, theatres and libraries as a way of preserving some interest in the written word. Ethnic minority communities endeavour to use storytelling in large industrialised countries as a means of recovering their cultural history and maintaining rituals obscured by the homogenised consumer-oriented culture offered by profiteering corporations. Enabling clients to speak with their own voice and to listen with respect and without judgement will help foster a relationship in which difficult issues or decisions can be examined.

Narrative therapeutic ideas recognise the ability people have to ascribe meaning to events that serve to explain but also to influence choices about the possible courses of action. This capacity to generate and evolve new narratives and stories to make sense of experiences involves the use of culturally shared myths legends and fairy stories. Thus therapy is seen as not just offering new perceptions and insights but in the very nature of the conversation taking place. Narrative therapists such as White and Epston (1990) suggest that problems are derived and maintained from the *internalisation* of oppressive ways of perceiving the self. These notions can be reinforced by parents who constantly criticise a child or who only respond negatively to behaviours. Key characteristics include:

- Includes the technique of *externalising* the problem whereby the social worker encourages the person to objectify or personify the problem outside of themselves.
- The person can separate themselves from the problem instead of being seen and related to by others as *the problem.*
- Engage the person in a process of exploring and resisting the problem as an unwanted impediment rather than as an integral part of their psychic constitution.
- Enable a troubled person to begin the process of challenging self-defeating and overwhelming self-concepts.

People who are suffering from psychological distress requiring therapeutic help may be either too young or too old to engage in cognitive and verbal communication about their feelings and experiences. The young ones may be more at ease with activities and play materials to aid expression while the older teenagers will often be difficult to engage and open up having learned the basic defence of silence. Adults can enjoy reminiscence and reflecting back on happy or painful family stories. But they will all know something of fairy tales, myths and legends. Every culture has them and they are usually told during early childhood in a verbal parental or carer ritual as old as time. Earliest school

literature incorporates these stories in education curriculum precisely because they are familiar and accessible.

As part of the healing process literature is an often *underrated* asset. Yet it carries information about families, emotions, morality, relationships and so much else in a way that can enable very damaged children to use devices such as fairy stories to help understand themselves at a deeper level. Fairy stories have the capacity to capture the child's imagination because they usually involve fantastical creatures, transformational experiences or complex predicaments in which the child can immerse themselves and relate to their inner world.

Disadvantages

A person's repressed feelings and worst fears cause inner conflicts that can manifest in acting out behaviour or anxiety states leading to mental health problems. These defences may be a necessary phase through which a child, for example, needs to pass before being able to change. Impatience on your part may be unhelpful. Fairy stories operate at the *overt* level where concepts of right and wrong and other moral dilemmas may seem obvious to you. But the story also operates at a *covert* level carrying important messages to the conscious, preconscious and unconscious mind that will affect the person's sense of culture.

ACTIVITY 2.2

Together with a colleague discuss the above material and see whether you can identify within your own 'style' of work elements of one or several, methods and models.

Consider a recent case and whether it was your style of work or the features of the case that determined your intervention.

Postmodernism and social work

Postmodern ideas have been influencing social work in recent years as practitioners seek ways of resolving the dilemmas inherent in modern practice that is constrained by managerialist values while demand for services increases. Postmodernism seeks to challenge received wisdom about what social work interventions are valid based on apparent empirical certainty. Postmodern theorists have articulated a theory that requires us to continually question the prevailing orthodoxy and to deconstruct theories and practices based on old certainties (Walker, 2004). Replacing these notions with a more flexible, less constrained perspective enables practice to embrace a plurality of intellectual resources from which to guide your work. The growth of the voluntary sector, devolved budgets, and decision making, horizontal management structures and retraction of local authority social services departments, are all stimulating the expansion of postmodernist thinking as creative and innovative ways of delivering social work interventions are being engendered (Walker, 2001).

Postmodern theorists are also highlighting the significance of power relationships within social work practice and arguing for an analysis of how this impacts on intervention practice through the prism of a commitment to social justice and human rights (Leonard, 1997). By attending more closely to the barriers constructed between yourself and service users you can begin to appreciate how professional language is a way of preventing understanding rather than enabling useful communication. Narrative as a root metaphor can replace old modernist certainties derived from the classic theoretical paradigms derived from medical models informing assessment and intervention practice. A more refined social work practice can become a dialogic-reflexive interaction between client and worker using language and the social construction of meaning to define the parameters of the helping process.

If you are interested in a social work practice that seeks to challenge social inequalities and embrace radical ideas based on, for example, feminist or green politics then you can begin with a structural analysis of power in society that produces exploitation of marginalised citizens. The postmodern paradigm advocates the importance of diversity, devolution, decentralisation, and interdependence. An example is offered by Ahmad (1990) who invites social workers to take risks with their own personal world view by revising their perceptions of colleagues, friends, or other professionals and then learn something new about them. An integrated model of social work drawing upon these notions searches for an understanding of the experience of the service user. Explanation or interpretation is still important but in the context of social understanding that is pluralistic where a range of explanations can co-exist and be part of a larger chain of enquiry that challenges discrimination in all its manifestations (McLennan, 1996).

Social work practices have become burdened by the demands for efficiency, calculability, predictability and control. The relentless obsession with cost effectiveness implies that only things that can be counted are important, and that the standardisation controlled by technology ensures predictability. The ensuing conformity and globalisation of practice has been highlighted by Dominelli (1996) resulting in privatisation of welfare services, new organisational structures in social work agencies, and a redefinition of the social work task leading to deterioration in the relationship between social worker and client. This conflict between the bureaucratic context of your practice and the values that attracted you into social work lie at the heart of contemporary intervention practice. Postmodernist thinking offers a potentially liberating perspective to help you locate your practice in the wider social context and within your personal value system.

Anti-discriminatory and anti-oppressive practice

Having reviewed some specific practice interventions, reflected on their advantages and disadvantages and considered their applicability, it is important to locate your use of these theoretical resources in anti-discriminatory and anti-oppressive practice. It has been argued historically in social work that theoretical models have rarely sat easily with the concepts of empowerment and anti-oppressive practice – because they essentially reflect the existing power relationships dominated by white, middle class, heterosexual, male, healthy, employed, Westerners. It is argued that there is a fundamental problem for social workers attempting to practice in anti-oppressive ways because they are part of the superstructure of social control and state sanctioned oppression. Equally it is argued that while government policies emasculate citizens and the economic system is inherently contradictory, there are many opportunities to satisfy your aim of practising in more empowering ways. Some of the features of anti-discriminatory or anti-oppressive practice are:

- Working collaboratively.
- Viewing users as competent.

- Helping users to see themselves as having some strengths.
- Developing their confidence by affirming their experiences.
- Helping them seek diverse solutions.
- Helping users build and use informal networks to increase access to resources.

The use and abuse of power is at the centre of anti-oppressive practice. It is a significant element in every relationship but is not necessarily negative. Rather than becoming monitors of sexism, racism, disablism, or homophobia, you might find it more useful to think in terms of ensuring you and your clients have access to equal opportunities in your environment and in the assessment and intervention plan you formulate. Effective anti-oppressive practice requires a clear theoretical perspective to inform the value base that permits anti-oppressive work (Payne, 1997). To practice in an anti-oppressive way means seeking to bridge the gap between you and the service user in order to facilitate a negotiation of perceptions.

Always be aware that gender is central to power issues and as workers or clients men need to be made aware in every situation of their potential to oppress, how maleness affects their perception of problems, and to be oppressed because of assumptions about masculinity. Feminist social work practice engages both the personal and the social by focusing on the whole person and examining the interconnectedness between people and the structures they live within. It provides a powerful explanatory tool to use in assessing situations involving child abuse and domestic violence for example where social workers inadvertently end up blaming mothers for failing to protect children, instead of understanding the dilemmas and impossible predicament faced by women.

Gender permeates aspects of social, political, and economic life and the organisations that maintain society. Anti-oppressive practice requires the active challenging of dominant masculine discriminatory attitudes, beliefs and practices. In practice this means raising issues about which team member is the most appropriate to work with certain service users. It also means resisting the simple notion that a female worker should necessarily work with a female client. The important point is that the issue is acknowledged and discussed instead of being avoided. A wider theoretical perspective

suggests that your practice should be informed by ideas about how people behave in relation to, and therefore influence, others and the effects of social factors such as stigma, stereotyping and ideology on behaviour in groups (Hogg and Abrams, 1988). In this context empowering practice is both a goal and a process for overcoming oppression.

Similarly anti-racist practice requires an acknowledgement of the combination of institutional and personal racism that privileges white western culture and norms of behaviour whilst denigrating and obscuring black culture. The effects of racism have been measured and quantified as recently as the Macpherson inquiry into the murder of the black teenager Stephen Lawrence, and over the years revealing systematic discrimination against black people in terms of housing, employment, and educational opportunities. In the youth justice system and the psychiatric system young black males are over represented compared to other groups in society, while in the care system black children are likely to face multiple disadvantages. It is important to keep the issue constantly in mind so that in every proposed intervention you are actively considering how your practice can resist and challenge overt and covert racist assumptions and beliefs.

ACTIVITY 2.3

Divide an A4 sheet into two columns. In the first column write down five issues and concerns that are important to you when considering anti-discriminatory practice.

In the second column, list the abilities and skills you currently have or need to be developed, which you think could be used to deal with the issues and concerns you have identified.

Commentary

If one of your concerns was about the use of professional power, you may have been able to recall skills which allow you to use your power productively on service users behalf – for instance where you have done your best to listen and encourage dialogue. If you were concerned about the use of interpreters with clients whose first language is not English, you may have thought about the transferable skills you use when translating professional jargon into everyday speech. Or you may have considered the implications of communicating clearly and simply within one language or across two or more languages.

You may have wondered about your ability to manage difficulties that occur within the service user's cultural context, and your ability to interpret accurately feelings expressed in ways unfamiliar to your culture. You will probably have reflected on your own racial and cultural prejudices, and the way they influence your attitudes and behaviour. This would enable you to anticipate work with your client's own cultural prejudices and fears so that you can establish an open working relationship, rather than one based on mistrust and suspicion. Making these tensions explicit is better than denying or avoiding them.

ACTIVITY 2.4

Read the following case study then list the risks involved in attempting to assess the possibility of maintaining the client in the community and weigh these against the rights of the client to self-determination.

Susan is a 44 year old woman who has been diagnosed as having a persistent delusional disorder. She has been admitted more than once to psychiatric provision, but currently lives on her own in the community with little or no contact with family members. She feels persecuted by various authority figures and has previously threatened police, housing officials and her doctor. Susan refuses to co-operate with the psychiatric consultant, take medication, or participate in the care planning process. She has previously lived in poor accommodation where she was neglecting herself. As her allocated social worker your task is to monitor her mental health; improve her self-care, reduce the intensity of her threatening behaviour, and try to find ways of reducing her emotional distress. Slowly, over time your persistence has enabled Susan to accept an offer of council accommodation, a laundry service, and regular meetings.

Commentary

Susan is still isolated and her refusal to comply with medication constitutes a significant risk. Her link with support services is fragile and she could slip further into self-neglect. There has been no significant reduction in the role played by her delusional thoughts. There is a risk she may carry out planned threats or continue abusive behaviour. Susan has gradually come to accept regular social work intervention. There is now a monitoring system in place co-ordinated by the social worker. So far, she has not carried out any threats to harm others. Susan has accepted permanent accommodation and this might reduce her feelings of isolation and paranoia.

Joint working

Staff from a variety of agencies working to intervene effectively with adults or children and young people are united by a particular case or a particular interagency group but they are disunited by all the natural differences that exist between their professions and agencies. It is these crucial differences that are the blocks to good work. Six key elements hinder interagency collaboration (Murphy, 2004):

- **Perspective and culture** – Each agency can hold a perspective that is substantively different from that of other agencies. Differences in how we see the problem can lead to great differences in how we understand it, and how we then act towards it. Professionals define and explain abuse in different and sometimes conflicting ways and adopt quite different stances about the way work should be undertaken.
- **Roles and responsibilities** – Everyone working with vulnerable people need to know how their role fits with that of others. There is often confusion about the roles and responsibility of other disciplines. Although the different disciplines may acknowledge the same aim – that of safeguarding – in order to do this they come together, maintaining their own separate roles within the wider whole. One of the advantages of interagency training is that it allows an opportunity for the exploration and greater understanding of these different roles and responsibilities.
- **Education and training** – Various enquiries have made several specific recommendations about the introduction of interagency elements in practitioner training and the improvement of training. The review of education and training that followed the *Laming Inquiry* for example, discovered that few practitioner groups maintained standards of interagency working and that those standards that did exist were not held in common between practice groups.

- **Structure and power** – When practitioners undertake complex tasks they usually work within their own professional structure, with a clear understanding of how each part of that structure should behave and what will happen if it fails to do so. When those practitioners come to safeguarding work, they find that this is not the case. Although their agency instructs them to do the work, that work is controlled by the case conference and distant decision-makers. Within this system, practitioners are both instructed to co-operate within the inter-agency framework and to retain the right to independent action.
- **Language and communication** – Information is power and sharing it symbolises some ceding of autonomy. Disagreements exist both as to the content of what is to be shared and about the actual value of talking together at all. What seems essential to communicate for one may seem a breach of confidentiality or peripheral to another. Although most agencies and professional bodies agree that confidentiality may be waived in the face of significant harm, agreement on the threshold of significant harm is difficult, particularly where information is being shared between child and adult oriented agencies.
- **Anxiety** – Anxiety is a constant companion of safeguarding work. It runs through from the highest managers, to practitioners and out to parents, carers and children. This anxiety is part of the reason that agency systems have become so proceduralised. It is not anxiety itself that is the problem, but how that anxiety is dealt with on an interagency and inter-professional basis. Failures at an organisational level to appropriately contain anxiety can permeate all aspects of the agency's work, as well as effecting its relations with the outside world and other agencies.

Resources and intervention

The question of resource allocation (rationing) and its relationship to assessment in safeguarding people is crucial. But resource considerations are unavoidable when making a care plan and considering what type of intervention to make. In this area too it is impossible to separate out purely practice decisions from resource decisions. Knowing there may be a long waiting time for specialist help emphasises the need to acquire further knowledge and skills in this area.

Nevertheless in all safeguarding work you will often encounter those who demand an intervention regardless of whether the resources are available to do it properly. Other agencies will express their particular anxieties about an elderly vulnerable person, a needy child or an adult behaving anti-socially. In fact an intervention carried out without ensuring that the necessary resources are available could be considered irresponsible and unethical. All interventions are likely to do some harm so that they are only justified if there are reasonable grounds for believing that the benefits would outweigh the harm. Realistic consideration of the resources available should properly be part of this calculation.

Sectioning an adult under mental health legislation and depriving them of their liberty will be traumatising however mentally ill a person appears. In-patient care may be of a poor standard and after-care following discharge patchy. This could all lead to a deterioration in that person's well-being and ultimately require more expensive resources to manage. In child care contexts for example, placing a ten year-old child with a foster family is a high-risk intervention due to the psychological trauma of removal from the family home and likelihood of placement breakdown. Any decision about whether this is a suitable plan for a child at risk of abuse should take into account not only the child's needs and wishes, but also factors such as:

- Availability of suitable foster families.
- Availability of skilled long-term support available to foster families.
- Availability of skilled intensive input in support of the child.
- Commitment of agency to provide adequate funding to keep this service in place.

If these things are not forthcoming, it might well be the case that this is simply not an appropriate plan for the child and that other arrangements might be preferable. Every child has the right to a stable and safe family – and that therefore, regardless of resource considerations – this should be the plan. The difficult dilemma is that it is not appropriate – or ethical – to lay down fixed rules for practice unless a specific resource context is specified. Similarly with a client under section in a hospital there may be no follow-up support and a lack of proper resources or community facilities which would mitigate the effects of the primary intervention.

ACTIVITY 2.5

Can you think of instances of interventions which should not be attempted unless adequate resources were secured in advance?

Commentary

You will probably be able to think of other examples, but it seems that some interventions should not be attempted unless the person carrying them out has the necessary skills and training and funding is secured to allow them to bring the process to an appropriate conclusion. What is more they should not be carried out unless adequate support is available to the user of the service, and her carers, during the difficult period while the work is underway.

Endings, closure and doubt

While there are a multitude of books in social work and health care on the subject of loss and bereavement, there is a contrasting dearth of literature on the subject of case closure and the ending of social work input. It is important in the context of assessment and intervention practice that you have an awareness of the potency of ending contact with a service user and the range of feelings generated at this crucial time. Understanding these feelings of loss can help your future practice as well as the current issues for your client. For example you might have planned to end contact at a point in time or after completion of certain tasks, yet find events take over and thwart your planning. This can be the result of workload management decisions, service user choice, resource limitations, you or the client leaving the area, or other agency influences.

Each reason for premature or planned ending can bring a variety of feelings and issues to the surface. Its important to use these feelings in a positive way for clients, so if you are feeling relieved or angry during a final meeting this invariably reflects exactly how the client is feeling. Acknowledging these together with the client demonstrates respect, awareness and compassion, they are authentic and can be discussed openly without making either party feel guilty or responsible. Proper reflective attention to these can be helpful in terms of developing professional practice as well as offering service users a platform to express frustration, anger, happiness or confusion. You may well feel guilty about leaving a client or placing them in residential care despite having a rational, evidence-based justification. Feelings of uncertainty and confusion are not weakness and shedding a tear is not unprofessional. These are quite normal and better out than in – especially in a supervisory context where they can be processed in a supportive way. A model of ending incorporating the following elements is suggested (Coulshed, 1991):

- A discussion in the first meeting that help will not go on for ever.
- Use the experience of ending to confirm what the client has gained.
- Employ a fixed time limit where possible.
- Giving the client certain objectives to achieve in the ending phase of work.
- Explore a person's feelings about the forthcoming ending.
- Introduce a new worker and facilitate expressions of anger/resentment.
- Help the person construct a natural helping network within their community.
- Explore your own feelings and show the client they will be remembered.
- In some contexts a ritual ending and exchange of gifts might be appropriate.
- Write a closing record together.

Chapter summary

In this chapter we have considered the advantages and disadvantages of several examples of contemporary intervention practice. In exploring them in this way we have illuminated difficulties and dilemmas which can be presented when evaluating their effectiveness in taking proper account of service users' needs, rights, strengths, responsibilities and resources. Case studies have been employed to develop further understanding of these issues particularly to highlight the potential for oppressive and discriminatory practice.

We considered how social work intervention begins before client contact and whatever the aim of intervention it may lead to different and quite unexpected consequences. Accepting a wide theoretical panorama from which to choose means you are making every effort to find the right approach for the particular service user you are helping, but it makes the task of selection harder. It also can cause confusion about what to call the possible interventions that spring from the use of particular theories. The pragmatist will seek knowledge sources that fit with their internal concept of what social work should be about.

If you believe that the problems of clients are caused by an unjust economic system that distributes wealth unfairly, then a radical perspective combined with a client-centred approach might appeal to you. On the other hand if you feel that a client's problems stem from an emotionally deprived and neglected childhood you may be drawn to offering an individual psychodynamic intervention. With experience you will begin to see the limited value of these dichotomies and understand that the complexities of people's lives.

We reviewed the contribution postmodernism has made to contemporary intervention practice as it seeks to challenge received wisdom about what social work interventions are valid based on apparent empirical certainty. Postmodern theorists have articulated a theory that requires us to continually question the prevailing orthodoxy and to deconstruct theories and practices based on old certainties. Replacing these notions with concepts of ambivalence uncertainty and a critical stance is harder than succumbing to the quickest and least demanding solution.

Finally we discussed the skills and qualities required for effective relationship-building but warned of the use and abuse of power that is at the centre of anti-oppressive practice. It is a significant element in every relationship but is not necessarily negative. Rather than becoming monitors of sexism, racism, disablism, or homophobia, we argued that you might find it more useful to think in terms of ensuring you and your clients have access to equal opportunities in your environment and in the Assessment and Intervention plan you formulate. Effective anti-oppressive practice should not diminish anyone involved in the helping process.

CHAPTER 3

Risk Assessment and Management

Learning objectives

- Define how risk is conceptualised and applied in complex situations and differentiate between risk, hazard and danger.
- Describe various risk assessment tools and their limitations and how to identify and minimise risks to the social worker, and the risk social workers pose to clients.
- Explain the potential conflict between rights and risk, care and control and illustrate how effective practice achieves a balance between them.
- Work in partnership to identify and analyse potential risk of harm, abuse, or failure to protect.

Introduction

Assessment of risk and its management has always been a dominant theme in social work. As with other aspects of the profession – such as the move to competence and evidence based practice – this has been a reaction to a wider demand for the greater public accountability of professionals in all spheres, and, particularly in social work, several highly publicised failures to protect our clients and the public from dangerous people. Lurid tabloid media stories have over the years initiated public moral panics and fuelled political posturing about mental health, youth justice and child protection policy.

Despite the fact that these failures – mainly in child care and mental health work – represent a minority of social work cases, their impact on practice has been considerable. One death of a child can trigger a wholesale evaluation of the UK child protection system regardless of the specific features of particular cases or the evidence of excellent practice elsewhere. This has led to policy and practice in relation to risk and its management becoming focused on dangerousness (particularly so in work with offenders and mental health) and significant harm (in relation to children and elders). Definitions of both concepts are ambiguous and widely agreed to be determined by social, cultural and historical factors. Apart from the

focus in this chapter, risk as a topic features throughout the whole book as one might expect.

Nonetheless it is important that – in any other than purely philosophical debates – social workers are aware of and work with current definitions – regardless of how open to question they may be. Despite this relativism, there is always a tendency to subscribe to the conventional wisdom within oneself or part of a peer belief system which social workers must be aware of and consider carefully with considerable thought, consultation with managers and involvement of service users.

An interesting aspect of the moral panic about risk, is that the risk to social workers from dangerous people and the adverse attention of politicians and the media has not been of such concern. In terms of its frequency, the risk of abuse and physical threat or attack for social workers is far more prevalent than similar risks to their service users. Social workers – particularly in residential settings – are among those who share the highest risk of assault at work. The recognition of this risk should be a primary consideration for all social workers, their managers and the organisations within which they work.

As in other areas of practice – such as community care – the consequence of such pressures has been an obsession with the production of checklists such as eligibility criteria, assessment schedules and risk assessment scales. The tendency has been for practice to become narrowly focused on *aspects* of the individual (such as dependency or dangerousness) rather than on the *whole* person-in-context. This is counter to – and in extreme cases can threaten – the established values and practice of social work which emphasise individualisation, respect for the person and a holistic approach which takes full account of social and cultural context.

There is some evidence that effectiveness in assessment and intervention can be enhanced by the use of well validated assessment scales – for example in relation to risk and its management with offenders or suicidal individuals.

Additionally, in terms of accountability, social workers must be able to demonstrate that they are aware of and make appropriate use of all available aids to best practice. However, the consensus from research presently is that such tools are useful adjuncts to competent professional judgement, not substitutes for it.

In relation to the assessment and management of risk there is a need therefore to resist the reductionist tendency to focus exclusively on assessment of risk conceived as 'danger' and intervention as 'risk control'. Ironically the danger of such practice is that in pursuing the ultimately unattainable goal of entirely risk free practice workers may:

- Overlook the risks attached to intervention.
- Neglect the rights of individuals in order to control the risks they pose to themselves or others.
- Lose sight of the individual-in-context, their strengths and the creative potential for development and growth this brings.
- Overlook the risk to the social worker.

As in other areas of practice, the skill of social work lies in intervention which is:

- Optimally non-intrusive.
- Compatible with the promotion of individual potential and personal responsibility.
- Balances both rights and risks, and care and control.
- Recognises risks to social workers.

ACTIVITY 3.1

Try putting an item on the agenda for your next team/group meeting to discuss ways in which social workers pose a risk to clients/service users, and how those risks could be minimised.

Two approaches to risk

As social work develops it's understanding and practice in relation to risk, two contrasting approaches have emerged which have been described as:

1. The 'safety first' approach which can be paraphrased as CYB – cover your back.
2. The 'risk taking' approach which subscribes to the view that risks are an inherent part of social life and that if individuals are to be fully engaged in social life, some risk is inevitable.

Both terms are problematic:

- Competent social work should not be entirely defensive and preoccupied with covering your back.
- Risk taking has connotations of an advocacy of taking risks which is counterintuitive to many and easily misconstrued as irresponsible in view of the vulnerability of many service users.

For these reasons risk control and risk management are terms used here and some of the implications identified.

Risk control

- **Definition:** risk is negative – danger, threat.
- **Priority principles:** professional responsibility and accountability.
- **Practice:** identification (assessment scales) and elimination (procedural, legalistic).
- **Benefits:** apparently unambiguous (clear categories of risk); routinised, standardised, quality assured (check lists); defensible (evidence based); publicly understood (politicians, public and media).
- **Drawbacks:** risk is seen as static, unchangeable; context neglected; strengths unacknowledged; labelling, stigmatising, stereotyping; opportunities for development missed; practice is rule driven; assessment tools are imperfect; impossible to eliminate risk entirely; risks to social workers ignored.

Risk management

- **Definition:** positive – risk is part of life, balancing risks and benefits is part of an individual's development, being self-determining and personally responsible.
- **Priority principles:** self-determination, anti-oppression.
- **Practice:** solution-focused, partnership practice, empowerment.
- **Benefits:** in keeping with values and practice of modern social work; emphasises *process* of maximising benefits as well as minimising risks, rather than *procedure* of identifying and eliminating risk; builds on strengths; developmental rather than judgmental.
- **Drawbacks:** relies heavily on highly developed professional competence and judgement; requires commitment of client to partnership; requires intellectual/cognitive competence of client; involves ambiguity and uncertainty; is poorly understood by public; requires

supportive management practice and organisational policy; risks to social workers ignored.

As understanding and practice in relation to risk develops it becomes clear that there needs to be an integration of the best of both approaches. Eliminating or totally controlling risk in social work is impossible.

It is undesirable to think of risk and the social work task in relation to it in this way because evidence and intuition suggests it is impossible and thus resources are wasted. Risk is part of social life and the real world of everyday experience and should not be perceived as only of interest to specific client groups. Practice which is effective in terms of promoting individual responsibility and social competence can not be reductionist – it must recognise the person-in-context and build on strengths. Social work agencies have responsibilities in law in relation to certain client groups and you need to be very aware of legislative imperatives determining the scope of your powers. Individual social workers must neither neglect these responsibilities nor accept 'unlimited liability' – whether or not there are legal requirements.

It is very important to remember that the social and individual costs of control can outweigh the social and individual benefits thus highlighting your assessment and analytical skills. Social work routinely brings its practitioners into contact with dangerous people and entails professional judgements which are potentially castigated by management, your work organisation, professional association and the media.

Minimising risk is possible

Competent social workers must do so by being aware of the meaning of risk and its role in the personal development and social life of service users. Understanding the function and then appropriately employing well validated risk assessment scales where they are available is useful in some cases. Ensuring practice is evidence based and in accordance with statute, government guidance and agency policy will provide you with a safe framework within which to practice.

Having the ability to handle stress and crisis situations or managing 'decision calls', is something that cannot be taught, but is learned through practice, reflection and skilled supervision. It is important when anxieties are

escalating not to be rushed, ensure immediate safety of all parties involved, be appropriately assertive, be sure a decision has to be made and by whom, share responsibility, involve where possible and support the subject of the decision, report back to referring agency, ensure continuity, debrief and reflect with a supportive manager/ supervisor.

The Skills for Care and the Children's Workforce Development Council produced guidance on effective supervision in 2007 yet in 2010 the Social Work Taskforce found evidence of many social workers not receiving monthly supervision. Further guidance due in 2011 will specify minimum levels of supervision especially for newly qualified social workers when national standards for employers will be published. Supervision is not a luxury it is a critical priority and could mean the difference between life and death in some cases.

By clearly identifying specific risks and the contexts in which they might occur you can begin to sort out priority areas for more of your attention and intervention. This will be helped enormously by fully engaging clients and significant others as far as possible in risk assessment, management and recording accurately is crucial. Differences will happen and these need to be openly acknowledged and recorded too. Multidisciplinary sharing of risk management with other involved professionals is advised and expected but you must be prepared for difficulties and the potential for conflict and disagreement. Everyone will claim to be making a professional judgement but these often sit on top of considerable personal anxieties and strongly held beliefs while clearly recording risk assessment and management plans, relating them to specific legal requirements as appropriate is necessary. You should always ensure the availability of supervision and recording key decisions from it. Finally never forget that managing risk to self is a priority of professional practice.

The recording of risk assessment and management plans, and relating them to specific legal requirements as appropriate should be a matter of routine, and many assessment schedules/forms will contain guidance on the statutory grounds for your intervention. It is important to ensure the availability of supervision and recording key decisions from it, otherwise you will be vulnerable to charges of a cavalier approach to your work and open to disciplinary procedures. However you also have a professional duty to object to and refuse to comply with activity that is not in your view in the best interests of the client. Professional codes of practice and trades union advice and support, is available to help you cope with and manage these situations.

Social workers are sometimes harmed in the normal course of their working lives physically or emotionally, and several have been killed by clients, therefore managing risk to self should be a priority of professional practice. Try to resist being drawn into a situation where your own internal pressure to help and support others in distress combines with ineffective management to produce a dangerous situation. What follows is intended to provide you with a discussion of some of the important issues in practice with these client groups. For more specific theoretical and practice guidance you will need to consult other sources. Throughout the text and in the bibliography you will find pointers to specialist texts that deal more comprehensively with specific client groups.

The social construction of risk

Risk is an inherent part of safeguarding children and young people. Definitions of concepts such as risk, dangerous and significant harm are ambiguous and widely agreed to be determined by social, cultural and historical factors. There is no absolute definition of dangerousness that is independent of any social and cultural context. Similarly, the definition of significant harm is relative. The legal debates about the acceptability of physical chastisement (smacking) of children, is an example of this. In some European states this is illegal: it is currently not in England and Wales although there is an ongoing debate about whether it should be so. Many consider such parental behaviour to be physical abuse with the potential for significant harm to the developing child, others believe that sparing the rod spoils the child. This lack of absolutes and the ambiguity it brings has profound implications for safeguarding practice in relation to risk. This is epitomised in the tension between care and control.

ACTIVITY 3.2

Make some brief notes describing several disadvantages of viewing risk solely as danger and intervention as about risk control.

Commentary

Ironically the danger of such practice is that in pursuing the ultimately unattainable goal of entirely risk free practice workers may:

- **Overlook the risks attached to intervention:** Removing a child allegedly in danger from its family opens the child up to other dangers which can be equally damaging such as developmental or emotional trauma, or scapegoating in foster homes.
- **Lose sight of the individual-in-context, their strengths and the creative potential for development and growth this brings:** Focusing too narrowly on one aspect of the individual (e.g. dangerousness) may limit opportunities for interventions that can enable clients to build on their strengths to become less dangerous.
- **Overlook the risk to the worker:** Over-eagerness to control risks posed to others can expose workers to unacceptable levels of risk to themselves. This can result not only in serious harm to the worker, but add to the guilt and other problems experienced by the client involved in violence against the worker.

The benefits of the risk management perspective are that they are in keeping with the values of modern practice emphasising the process of *maximising benefits as well as minimising risks* rather than a procedural approach to identifying and eliminating risk. The advantage is that this builds on strengths the drawbacks are that it relies heavily on highly developed professional competence and judgement and requires the commitment of the client to partnership. It also requires intellectual/cognitive competence of the client.

That this involves ambiguity and uncertainty, is poorly understood by the public and requires supportive management practice and organisational policy. Risks to workers are virtually ignored. As understanding and practice in relation to risk develops it becomes clear that there needs to be an integration of the best of both approaches. Eliminating or totally controlling risk in child protection work is impossible. It is undesirable to think of risk and the task of safeguarding children in relation to it in this way because:

- Evidence and intuition suggests it is impossible and thus resources are wasted.
- Risk is part of social life.

- Practice which is effective in terms of promoting individual responsibility and social competence cannot be reductionist – it must recognise the person-in-context and build on strengths.
- All agencies have responsibilities in law in relation to certain client groups. Individual workers must neither neglect these responsibilities nor accept unlimited liability – whether or not there are legal requirements.
- The social and individual costs of control can outweigh the social and individual benefits.
- Safeguarding children routinely brings its practitioners into contact with dangerous people and entails professional judgements which are potentially castigated by management, organisations and the media.

It is possible to minimise risk. For example by appropriately employing well validated risk assessment scales where they are available. Other ways of minimising risk would include being aware of the meaning of risk and its role in the personal development and social life of service users. Ensuring practice is evidence based and in accordance with statute, government guidance and agency policy. Managing decision calls – don't be rushed, ensure immediate safety of all parties involved, be appropriately assertive, and be sure a decision has to be made and by whom. The capacity to share responsibility, involve where possible and support the subject of the decision, report back to referring agency, ensure continuity, and debrief as soon as possible with your manager/ supervisor is important.

Risk assessment in child care

Government policy

There is a very extensive body of government policy and practice guidance in relation to risk assessment in child care and government guidance on assessing children to safeguard and promote their welfare is continually evolving in the light of research and the inspections carried out by the Social Services Inspectorate and since 2006 by the Office for Standards in Education, Children's Services and Skills (OFSTED). Their task is to regulate and inspect to achieve excellence in the care of children and young people, and in education and skills for learners of all ages.

In 1988 an influential guide was published by the DoH and formed the basis of local authority practice in this field (DoH, 1988). The DoH

subsequently commissioned 20 research studies on child protection, the results of which were published in Child Protection: Messages from Research (DoH, 1995). In 1998 the government's eight objectives for children's social services were set out in the Quality Protects initiative. Since when further publications have emerged including the draft consultative document *Framework for the Assessment of Children in Need and their Families* (1999) from the Department of Health. A comprehensive summary of these publications, recent research and policy development is to be found in The *Children Act Report – 1995–1999* (DoH, 2000). This report can be found at www.doh.gov.uk/scg/chactrep.htm and is essential reading for those with a special interest in child care.

Several recent reports on assessment in child and family work affirm that many of the general issues about assessment which we have discussed already, apply specifically to child care and child protection. Perhaps the most significant is the effects which have been found of the over-emphasis on risk control which followed the Children Act and various child protection failures. One report concluded that child protection appeared to have a de-skilling effect on social workers who were only expecting to respond to families in crisis, and where children were at risk of significant harm. Social workers therefore gained little experience beyond this in developing work with families (SSI, 1997).

It described a very worrying picture, with departments continuing to respond to child protection and looked after children cases to the exclusion of support to other families of children in need. Therefore too narrow a focus on danger can lead to neglect of the wider picture whereas a strategy of risk management which takes the wider context into account is more likely to effectively meet need. This has been recognised in the most recent practice guidance in *Framework for the Assessment of Children in Need and their Families (2000)* which requires that any assessment of a child and family will take account of three interacting domains:

1. The child's developmental needs.
2. The parenting capacity of the child's carers to respond to those needs.
3. Relevant wider family and environmental factors.

This is part of a growing recognition that since the *Children Act (1989)* practice has focused too narrowly on assessment of risk rather than need (of which risk is only a part). In 1996 a national commission of inquiry into the prevention of child abuse recognised the need for a more holistic approach. It included in its definition of child abuse not only direct and acute forms (such as violence) but also indirect forms such as poor housing, family health and poverty (1996, HMSO). Nonetheless the narrow view has persisted and has led frequently to a failure to provide supportive services to children and families in need such that:

- Over half the estimated 160,000 children subject to child protection enquiries each year receive no further services.
- Interagency work is often relatively good at the early stages of child protection enquiries, its effectiveness tends to decline once child protection plans have been made.
- Discussions at child protection conferences tend to focus too heavily on decisions about registration and removal rather than on focusing on plans to protect the child and support the family.

The first of these points reminds us of the issue discussed earlier about the tendency that has developed over the recent past to view social work assessment as separate from intervention.

Risk assessment in mental health

Government policy

As with child care, partly as a result of highly publicised cases of murder and assault by psychiatric patients, there has been a considerable volume of government policy and practice guidance in mental health. As in child care, risk and dangerousness have increasingly become the focus of policy and practice during the past decade, to some extent threatening the multi-agency, holistic approach to need which has also been a feature of government policy during this time. The *Code of Practice for the Mental Health Act 1983* (DoH and Welsh Office, 1990) asserts that a broad range of contextual factors – in addition to the health and safety of the patient – should be taken into account in any decision on compulsory admission. These include:

- The patient's wishes and view of their own needs.
- Their social and family circumstances and cultural background.

- The needs of the patient's family.
- The need for others to be protected from the patient.

The Code provides specific guidance on risk assessment related to the protection of others, it includes the need to take account of:

- Reliable evidence of risk to others.
- Relevant details of the patient's medical history and past behaviour.
- The degree of risk and its nature. Too high a risk of physical harm, or serious persistent psychological harm to others, are indicators of the need for compulsory admission.
- The willingness and ability to cope with the risk, by those with whom the patient lives.
- Consideration of any prognosis of future deterioration of mental health.

This apparently holistic approach continued in the DoH guidance on multi-agency collaboration in mental health care *Building Bridges* (DoH, 1995). This stressed that the Care Programme Approach had not been intended to be a bureaucratic system, but was intended to ensure that people in the community received the treatment, care, support and monitoring they needed to stay as well as they could, and to remain safe. However, at the same time doubts had arisen about the effectiveness of the CPA in this regard as a result of several highly publicised murders by psychiatric patients. Many see the *Patients (in the Community) Act 1995* – which amends the *Mental Health Act (1983)* extending powers of authorities to cover people in the community – as the culmination of this.

The government strategy document *Modernising Mental Health Services* (DoH, 1998) was published partly in response to public concern about safety and risk in relation to people with mental health problems. It stressed the need for services to be safe, sound and supportive. This increasing concern about risk and dangerousness is despite research which has shown a 3 per cent annual decline between 1957 and 1995 in homicides committed by people defined as mentally ill (Taylor and Gunn, 1999). In 1999 the SSI published the results of its inspection of 15 social services authorities reporting that it was very concerned about several aspects of risk assessment procedures. It found:

- Only one authority had an agreed risk assessment procedure.

- A complete lack of risk assessment in some authorities.
- Different models of risk assessment being undertaken within the same agencies.
- Lack of coherence between in-patient risk assessments and implications for discharge.
- Lack of acceptance by different professionals that everyone has a contribution to make in undertaking risk assessments (SSI, 1999, *Still Building Bridges.* p 6. DoH)

Risk and dangerousness in mental disorder

There is considerable research evidence from the UK and abroad – much of it from longitudinal studies with very large samples – which suggests that assessing risk in this field is particularly difficult. Predictors of actual suicide (as opposed to self-harm) are highly unreliable – a recent study in the UK found that the majority of people who committed suicide were not seen as high risk. Also, predicting violence is very difficult – over-prediction of violence especially from men and ethnic minorities, is common and where accuracy is greater it is because of the greater accuracy of predicting who will not be violent. Violent women are underpredicted by professionals. There is also little research about the protective factors in individuals' lives that serve to reduce the risk to self and others. However there are a number of other findings that do provide useful guidance for assessors:

- Whilst the link between mental disorder and violence is contested, where mental disorder occurs with substance or alcohol misuse violence is more likely, and in addition it is more likely where delusions are present, and where the diagnosis is anti-social personality disorder.
- Aspects of social networks and social support have been shown to be associated with increased violence in people with a diagnosis of mental illness e.g. if they are financially dependent on others.
- People with a mental disorder are far more likely to be a risk to themselves.
- Risk of suicide among those with schizophrenia is 8.5 times that of the general population, opiate dependence increases the risk by between 14 and 20 times and a history of self-harm combined with drug abuse among women increases their risk by 87 times.

ACTIVITY 3.3

Think about a recent news item, film or story you have read in which mental health features. Was the portrayal of mental illness positive or negative and what effect might this have on public perception?

Commentary

The research evidence suggests that even individuals who fit into high-risk categories, may actually pose no risk to others, and – as in risk assessment generally – it is important to have an holistic approach. In particular, it is inadequate to have a static conception of violence as a characteristic of an individual regardless of the changing factors of clinical process and social context (Parsloe, 1999). Be prepared to question your assumptions and re-consider the likely impact of recent therapeutic interventions.

Risk assessment with elderly people

Government policy

There is a relative dearth of government policy and practice guidance in relation to risk work with elderly people. Whilst the *National Health Service and Community Care Act (1990)* lays out policy and practice guidance in relation to adult service users generally who are mainly older people and people with mental disorder, it is does not deal specifically with risk assessment related to elders. As part of the reform of health services at that time GPs' contracts were changed to require that primary care groups offered annual assessment to all people over 75 in their area. These developments led to a growing body of mainly medical literature dealing with assessment, some concerned with issues of risk and assessment (Beales, Denham and Tulloch, 1998). As we shall see there was a Law Commission report on mental incapacity in relation to elders and a subsequent Green Paper (1997) which made no recommendation for substantive changes in the law, despite intensive lobbying by pressure groups such as Age Concern.

There have been a series of reports from the Social Services Inspectorate into aspects of community care provision for elders (DoH/SSI, 1996, 1997a, 1997b) and one dealing with community care for black and ethnic minority elders (1998). These reports provide valuable insights into progress and problems in implementing the National Health Service and Community Care Act in relation to elders.

The relative lack of statutory guidance is due in part to elderly people – being adults – are to some extent covered in such guidance as is available in relation to vulnerable adults generally, for example, the Mental Health Act 1983. There is a well documented and enduring ageist tendency within social work and other professions which has historically relegated work with elders to the least prestigious realms of the profession where the least well qualified work in some of the least well resourced environments. This has led to the neglect until comparatively recently of the risks faced by elders, and the role of social work in protecting them. The statutory framework for protective work with elders specifically is minimal in comparison with the extensive legislation available to guide practice in child care and mental health.

Despite this there is an extensive body of academic literature and research on elder abuse – much of it American. However recent UK publications which provide valuable evidence-based practice guidance include Bennett and Kingston (1993) Pritchard (1995) Eastman (1994) McReadie (1995). More recently Professor Olive Stevenson has drawn informative comparisons between child protection and elder care (Stevenson, 1996 and 1999) and provides us with a concise overview of the issues in risk work with elders in Parsloe (1998).

Most risk assessments are done as part of a more general assessment of need. It seems very important that the interaction of need with risk be at the heart of the process. In this way, the implications of the assessment, including the elements of risk, will be considered creatively, with a search for imaginative solutions to the tensions between autonomy and protection. The principle of needs-led assessment has been distorted and impoverished by current resource constraints and the mental set of workers caught up in over bureaucratic systems (Stevenson, 1999). The fundamental tension, which we have noted in relation to risk work generally, between care and control in relation to older adults can be reconceptualised in terms of the balance between autonomy and protection.

Autonomy vs. protection

It is accepted in our society that part of being adult is the right to autonomy. Within the bounds of law and the mores of social life, autonomy is perceived as a definitive characteristic of adulthood in democracies. This is not so in relation to children who are defined as ill-equipped because of the incompletion of the developmental process, to exercise autonomy and bear the consequences and responsibilities which this brings. Much of the risk work arising with elders involves individuals who by dint of dementia or other degenerative disease, are incapable of fully exercising autonomy because they are either insufficiently aware of the consequences of so doing or physically incapable of coping with them.

Social workers and other professionals therefore have to balance the ethical and statutory requirements to protect vulnerable adults whilst recognising their right to autonomy. Unlike in child care and mental health there is very little in UK social policy and legal statute to guide workers in managing this dilemma. This lack of guidance was recognised by the government in 1997, when it stated that there was a clear need for reform of the law in order to improve the decision making process for those who are unable to make decisions for themselves or who cannot communicate their decisions. Despite acknowledging that elderly people were some of the most vulnerable people in our society this did not lead to reform. Thus you are left with the dilemma. There is some limited guidance, however, from the Law Commission's enquiry that led to the Green Paper in which they proposed four principles for assessment in this situation in relation to mental incapacity. These are that assessment should take account of:

- A person's ascertainable past and present wishes and feelings.
- The need to permit and encourage the person to participate.
- The views of other people concerned with the person.
- Whether the required action or decision can be achieved by less restrictive methods.

You will inevitably draw the conclusion that this very limited official guidance points to the value of the holistic social work assessment of risk which we have described, and for which social work, because of its integration of knowledge, skills and values is particularly well equipped. It seems very important that the interaction of need with risk be at the heart of the process. In the relative absence of specific policy, practice and statutory guidance we will now draw on what we have learned of the social work process to identify some practice guidance in relation to risk work with elders.

Implications for practice

The particular dilemmas of risk work with elders centre around the tension between autonomy and protection. As we suggested in the introduction to this chapter, the social construction of risk is an aspect of assessment work that cannot be ignored if assessment practice is to be effective. Ageism in caring organisations and the professions who work in them, reflects the socially constructed ageism of wider society in terms of the procedures and practices adopted. Awareness of this has a key role to play in effective assessment of risk in working with elders.

Ageism and assessment practice

Ageism as with any other prejudice involves the ascription to individuals of the socially ascribed, stereotypical characteristics of a group. In relation to elders in western society this involves attributing to individuals the largely pejorative stereotypical attributes of inevitable decline, incompetence and dependency. Ageism can affect assessment both in terms of organisational procedures and professional practice.

The referral may be allocated to an untrained worker as is routine organisational policy with older people – thereby denying the client properly qualified assessment. The elderly person may not wish to have been referred in the first place and may not be asked her permission for a visit and/ or assessment – thereby invading her privacy and denying her autonomy. In view of the elderly person's age and diagnosis of dementia, assessment may focus on the aspects of their personality and capability damaged by the dementia – not on the whole person-in-context. Thereby this fails to take account of factors such as a supportive social network which if mobilised, could mitigate the currently limited effects of her condition.

Preoccupation with the symptoms of the elderly person's condition may lead to the neglect of their wider personality much of which might remain intact – leading not only to neglect of her strengths but to denial of her uniqueness and individuality. An assumption of inevitable decline and complete dependency based upon

the stereotypical characteristics of advanced age and of dementia may lead to a neglect of the possibility of rehabilitation.

Focusing on the hazards of the current situation and an eagerness to eliminate, rather than manage risk can lead to neglect of the hazards of intervention – particularly in this case those involved in the removal to residential care including loss of independence and autonomy through admission to residential care. Awareness of the impact of ageism on assessment is therefore essential to effective practice, but what does research tell us about which elderly people may be most at risk of losing their autonomy and independence?

ACTIVITY 3.4

Consider and reflect on the above material and discuss with a colleague your attitudes towards elderly people. Be honest and open.

High risk factors for elderly people

A review of research evidence on risk factors that provides a practically useful summary and concise typology of risk shows that high risk factors include advanced age, recent hospital discharge and recent change of home. Medium risk factors include recent bereavement, living alone and social class. Low risk includes lack of social contact, childlessness, and never having been married. Beales and Tulloch (1998) in discussing this typology raise several caveats in relation to this, which mostly reflect the kind of limitations shared by all such risk assessment schedules we mentioned in relation to child care and mental health.

Whilst it is useful to be aware that most elders at high risk will be of advanced age, it is equally true to say that most people of advanced age are not. Age alone is therefore an unreliable indicator. Overly narrow focus on age and disability which such assessment schedules frequently encourage leads to a preoccupation with hazards and a neglect of strengths in Brearley's terms. For example, living alone and never having married may well point to an independence of character that can in fact enable the individual to manage debility and its hazards better.

Recent bereavement whilst posing potential hazards, need to be seen in context. We know that most informal care of severely disabled elders is carried out by spouses who are themselves aged. Whilst bereavement will inevitably lead to a period of grief – it may also signal the end of a distressing and physically demanding responsibility and an opportunity for a renaissance of energy and social contact. Gender and ethnicity are often ignored in such schedules as in this one, despite the fact that these are influential factors in debility, disadvantage and the social context within which they occur. This brief discussion of risk assessment typologies once again reminds us of the limitations of procedural, check list approaches to assessment and the pressing need to resist the reductionism they can entail in favour of the process approach we have advocated throughout.

Elder abuse and assessment

New guidelines issued by the Department of Health to ensure the protection of vulnerable adults (POVA) were introduced in 2006 as a way of alerting everyone involved in adult care services of the prevalence of abuse and the need for better strategies for stopping it. However rather like the child protection system the POVA system relies on convictions against abusers to enable them to be added to a list of risky individuals. As with child abuse, this means a huge amount of abuse is being undetected due to the victims fear of disclosure.

As we pointed out at the beginning of the chapter on assessment with particular client groups, this book is not intended as a specialist text. We have referred to some of the most recent of these. The extent of elder abuse in the UK has been disclosed as much greater than previously believed and still remains, despite this, a low priority for social policy and legislative action (DoH, 2007). Both the belated recognition of its extent and the lack of government action are symptomatic of the endemic ageism of our society. Elder abuse is not only widespread both in residential and domestic settings, but is multi-faceted and often not recognised as such by its perpetrators – both organisational and individual. Abuse may be physical, verbal, emotional and financial and may take the form of neglect which may not be immediately dangerous but which can result in significant harm in the longer term.

Abusers frequently don't recognise what they are doing as abuse because they do not regard aged people as fully adult, rather perceiving them as dependants who require protection from themselves. Such ageist attitudes can result in relatively minor forms of abuse such as referring an elder to social services without their consent, and to major forms of brutality such as tying elderly people in chairs to prevent them moving around in under-staffed residential facilities. In one such case recently not only did the staff involved in perpetrating such brutal abuse in an NHS hospital claim it was acceptable practice, but senior managers seemed to assert that because it was common practice with elders it did not actually constitute abuse.

Thus, elder abuse is as much a social construct as any other aspect of risk work we have discussed. Ageism is so endemic that it prevents people from recognising the brutality they have inflicted on elders actually constitutes abuse. How much greater, therefore, is the danger posed to effective assessment by professionals who themselves are exposed to the pervasive ageism of our culture? As in risk work with any other group, attention to the person-in-context – not narrowly focusing on the attributes of the client which allegedly put them in danger, is the foundation of effective practice.

In the light of this it is clear that holistic assessment of the whole context of elders at risk is essential if it is to be effective, either in promoting their continued autonomy or protecting them from harm. Many of the issues raised in relation to elders at risk thus reflect our discussion of risk work in general, and in risk work specifically with children and people with mental distress. This affirms – perhaps justifies and legitimates – the point we consistently make in this book. This is that the social work process is a well tried and tested one, which has value and relevance beyond the politically driven moral panics which have shaped practice in relation to client groups with a higher political profile than elders. A moral panic the results of which – in terms of overly narrow definitions of risk and danger – have been detrimental to professional practice and those it serves.

Towards holistic risk assessment

ACTIVITY 3.5

Review this chapter and consider some of the fundamental principles we discussed. Now apply these to your practice environment and make notes of how you might integrate them in your work.

Commentary

It is suggested that social work has a distinctive contribution to make to risk work because it has a socially-informed, user centred perspective which can counterbalance diagnostic and behavioural approaches (Davis, 1996). These have become overly concerned with attempting to eliminate risk at the expense of other important aspects of assessment practice. According to Davis there are four essential components of risk work which stress the values underpinning practice which is person centred and empowering, whilst being aware of the need to protect. These are:

1. Practice principles.
2. Interpersonal encounters.
3. Practice locations.
4. Organisational support.

Many of the elements she points to in terms of practice principles and interpersonal encounters we have addressed earlier in this session and we will list them only briefly to remind you of the issues involved. Davis's points about the practice environment of risk work which can be more or less supportive of it, are addressed in a little more detail as we have not specifically discussed this before.

Practice principles

- Empowerment of clients through choice and opportunity.
- Recognition of individuality, self-determination, personal responsibility, autonomy.
- Counterbalances loss of client autonomy in reactive over-protectiveness and control.
- Attention to competence, its limits and creative ways of working with all levels of it.
- Involvement of service users, practitioners and managers in reviewing principles.

Interpersonal encounters

- Quality of assessment is linked directly to the establishment of relationship, trust, and empathy this takes time – there are no short cuts.
- 'Risk consuming work' – getting to know individuals, building trust and confidence.
- Allowing time for mistakes, failure and return to the task.
- Listening closely to the person in distress – even if apparently irrational.

- Enable expression of feelings whilst calmly pursuing purpose of minimising risk.

Practice locations

Aspects of practice environments which are supportive to competent assessment practice include minimising the negative risks of harm and harassment so that workers and service users both feel secure in working with risk is very important. Physical safety must be ensured through adequate arrangements for protection and care should the need arise – including physical aspects of working environments and working practices. Maximise opportunities for positive risk taking for change and empowerment would include multi-disciplinary, co-working and partnership practice. Policy and practice which reflect agreed practice principles is crucial especially as SSI reports have disclosed that many authorities and organisations involved in risk have no policy and practice guidance specifically relating to and supporting it.

Provide support for clients in risk taking from other service users as well as staff so that support from existing informal and well as professional networks can be offered in supporting clients taking on the challenge of positive risk taking. Support for staff engaged in stressful work with competent and regular supervision and consultancy, co-working and forums for peer support, all contribute to developing a culture of positive and creative risk taking which is not based on 'covering your back'. Forums to address separate and shared concerns of service users and staff are necessary. Whilst confidentiality is a major concern in building trust, the isolation for both professionals and service users which can characterise risk work can be reduced through group work. This can itself be a powerful method of building trust between agencies, workers and service users.

Organisational support

Workers who fear organisational blame become anxious and defensive encouraging entirely negative interpretations of risk, the pursuit of risk elimination and the growth of a 'cover your back' culture can contribute to professional isolation and a fear of encouraging positive risk taking for fear of failure. Supervision is essential to effective practice, it is a venue for both self-reflection in terms of striving for the integration of knowledge, skills and values which we have stressed as being essential, for accountability and for confidence building. Managers should review assessment practice and support required with workers and clients, expanding the managerial role to include not only monitoring and ensuring accountability, but also the development of an appropriate organisational culture and commitment to its shared values and practices both among workers and clients.

Interagency policy and practice should support and promote social work assessment. It is not only a legal requirement in some cases, but is essential to effective practice. Differences of professional culture and organisational policy and practice can inhibit this and lead, again to defensive practice. There is a need to work with these differences, understand and manage them in the interests of effective assessment. This will involve working towards a shared value base, policy and practice in relation to creative – not defensive – assessment practice.

Chapter summary

The increasing focus on risk assessment in modern social work practice has led to policy and practice in relation to risk and its management becoming focused on dangerousness, particularly so in work with offenders and mental health and significant harm in relation to children and elders. We noted that this puts undue pressure on work that is already highly sensitive in many cases and paradoxically may provoke the very behaviour that it seeks to prevent. The risk of abuse and physical threat or attack for social workers is considerable and social workers – particularly in residential settings – are among those who share the highest risk of assault at work. We argued that the recognition of this risk should be an important consideration for all social workers, their managers and the organisations within which they work.

We then went on to discuss what is meant by the 'social construction of risk' and how this knowledge contributes to effective practice. Describing Brearley's framework for risk assessment enabled us to usefully differentiate between risk, hazard and danger. We explored tension and potential conflict between rights and risk, care and control and illustrate how effective practice achieves a balance between them. The benefits of the risk management perspective are that they are in keeping with the values and practice of modern social work; emphasises process of maximising benefits as well as minimising risks, rather than procedure of identifying and eliminating risk; and builds on strengths.

We noted however that the drawbacks are that it relies heavily on highly developed professional competence and judgement and requires commitment of client to partnership. It also requires intellectual/ cognitive competence of the client. It involves ambiguity and uncertainty, is poorly understood by the public, and requires supportive management practice and organisational policy.

Throughout the chapter we have stressed the need to work in partnership with colleagues and service users to identify and analyse potential risk of harm, abuse, or failure to protect and explored how such general principles and practices underpin effective risk work with three particular client groups. Finally we discussed Davis's four components of effective risk work – practice principles, interpersonal encounters, practice locations and organisational support and, in particular, how practice environments can contribute to positive practice and the minimisation of risks not only to clients but to social workers.

CHAPTER 4

Safeguarding and Protecting Vulnerable People

Learning objectives

- Understand the importance of balancing the tensions between care and control in safeguarding practice.
- Appreciate the ethical complexities in protecting vulnerable people and the principle of self-determination.
- Develop competence in using the relevant National Service Frameworks and legal provisions to safeguard vulnerable children, young people, women, elderly persons and adults with mental health problems.
- Describe how changing patterns of service delivery in health and social services are influencing professional relationships.

Introduction

The importance of understanding the link between abuse and a person's behaviour, attitudes, parenting capacity and mental health problems is paramount. In Britain at least one child dies each week as a result of adult cruelty, elderly people are abused and neglected regularly, and many women face systematic violence from partners or husbands. Much of the guidance and knowledge discussed in this chapter can relate to all these three domains in which abuse takes place.

It has been estimated that about 5,000 minors are involved in prostitution in Britain at any one time.

Nearly 23,000 children were being looked after by local authorities for the year ending 2007. About 60 per cent of these children had been abused or neglected with a further 10 per cent coming from 'dysfunctional families' (ONS, 2008). In 2007 there were over 300,000 children in need in England. Of these 69,100 were looked after in state care while the rest were in families or living independently. One quarter of all rape victims are children. 75 per cent of sexually abused children do not tell anyone at the time. Each year about 30,000 children are on child protection registers. Children with learning disabilities are at a greater risk of experiencing all forms of abuse and neglect. Recorded offences of gross indecency with a child more than doubled between 1985–2001 but convictions against perpetrators actually fell from 42 per cent to 19 per cent. Fewer than one in 50 sexual offences results in a conviction. In 2007–08 there were 20,000 recorded sex offences against children (NSPCC, 09).

The prevalence of abuse

Social workers have instinctively been conditioned to link the words abuse with adults behaviour towards children yet recent research evidence has exposed another aspect of abuse which is beginning to impact on how we perceive our society and culture. The abuse of elder people has been estimated at 2.6 per cent of all adults over the age of 66, equating to approximately 227,000 people. Abuse of elder people includes physical, sexual, psychological mistreatment and includes abandonment and financial abuse. It can take place in a person's own home or in private or local authority care homes. Using a broader definition of abuse caused by neighbours and acquaintances increases the prevalence rate to 4 per cent with a total number of 342,400 annually (DoH, 2007).

Solid data about the prevalence of child abuse is difficult to obtain but a reliable indication is that about 750,000 children will have been abused by the time they reach 18 years of age, with 400,000 having been sexually abused (Cawson et al., 2000). This NSPCC research suggests that about 30 per cent of girls have been sexually abused and about 15 per cent of boys. Reductions in the length of time children spend with their names on child protection registers seem to imply that child abuse is decreasing – which is not the case, rather they illustrate the shorter time spent on registers consistent with the reported increase in de-registrations. In other words the government target for shorter registration periods may be being achieved, but the consequence is that risk is being hidden.

The problem with child abuse is the often hidden nature and secrecy surrounding it combined with societal ambiguity about state intervention in family life. Crude structural and organisational changes to the way child protection services are delivered are the institutional knee-jerk response to improving the safeguarding of children and young people in the wake of the damning *Laming Inquiry Into the Death of Baby P* (2008) *Victoria Climbie* (DoH, 2003) and the *Bichard Report of the Deaths of Holly Wells and Jessica Chapman* (Home Office, 2004). *Every Child Matters: Change for Children* (2004) established the new framework for building services *around children* in which previously separate services must work together in an integrated way.

Above all, these changes aimed to provide professionals with consistent ways of communicating about children's welfare. In many ways it is the most important because organisational change of itself cannot bring about shifts in entrenched attitudes, beliefs, customs and vocabulary. And despite repeated child abuse inquiries citing poor communication between agencies as one of the major reasons why children have not been properly protected, it remains difficult to get right. Recent research also highlighted the paradox of the disproportionate investment in management performance recording templates, rigid timescales and IT systems resulting in a reduction in safety of systems and children rather than an increase in safety (Broadhurst and White, 2009).

Despite the hyped publicity and modern media circus exploding around high profile child deaths, historically expectations of child protection staff have tended to be lower than they are nowadays. Up until 1914 around 250 children every year died in child protection cases that were known about – more perished without coming to the attention of professionals. By 1970 the number of deaths in child protection cases had shrunk but the impact of the cruel death of Maria Caldwell and the blaming of professional staff started a trend in public discourse that endures today. Ironically, the better social workers have become at protecting children and preventing their deaths, the more bitter the public and political outcry has become when this fails to happen (Ferguson, 2007). Poor inter-agency communication is usually cited in subsequent internal investigations and public inquiries.

Rather than trying to design ever more elaborate bureaucratic data systems, Reder et al. (1993, 2003) suggest that agencies need to put greater effort into understanding the *psychology of communication* in order to improve it. This means more than superficial and tokenistic exercises hosted by agency managers, but a fundamental re-appraisal of the knowledge, values and personal beliefs held by every member of staff engaged in work with children and young people so that integrated working is actualised. The mental health and emotional well-being of children can be both a consequence of child abuse and a precursor. You must consider this aspect of your work in safeguarding children as much a priority as learning new procedures, computer data systems and legislative guidance.

Integrated working does not mean absence of disagreement-indeed the evidence suggests closer proximity with other agency staff *accentuates differences* between professionals. But this need not be a problem provided you work hard to appreciate each other's perspectives and not be so certain of your *omnicompetence*. Thinking about yourself as an *equal part of an integrated system*, rather than as an individual agency representative is a crucial re-conceptualisation to make. Disagreement may actually be healthy and force staff to compromise or continue seeking a solution. At another level such differences between professionals may reflect the dynamics in the family situation which produce splits. The mental health of a young person at risk of abuse can find expression in other family members through a process of identification and projection (Walker, 2005).

Equally you should be wary of rushing too quickly to agreement and consider whether the multi-agency group are avoiding or denying some unanswered and complex issues because of the risk of exposing an argument. This could reflect the emotional dynamics within the family. Self awareness is one of the keys to managing the stress and strain inherent in working together to safeguard children. This requires skilled and highly developed supervision skills from line managers and a willingness to expose your practice to scrutiny and to engage in reflective practice (Walker and Thurston, 2006).

Stages of the safeguarding process

It is possible to discern and identify the stages through which a safeguarding case may pass. Many cases do not pass beyond the investigation and initial assessment stage. Very few will reach the stage of legal proceedings. At each stage the system asks whether the person has suffered, or is likely to suffer, significant harm. If the answer is yes, the case proceeds to the next stage. If no, the child or adult drops out of the system. At the same time, if the person is considered to be in extreme danger, at any stage of the process, a legal order may be requested (usually by social services from a magistrate's court) that can remove the person for a short period of time to a safer environment. The series of stages within any safeguarding system is as follows:

1. Observation and recognition
2. Referral
3. Investigation and initial assessment
4. Conference
5. Assessment and review conference

Observation and recognition

The Laming Inquiry (2003) discovered several occasions when Victoria Climbié should have been included in the protection system but was effectively excluded by the practitioners who dealt with her. Dingwall et al. (1995) argue that there are certain belief systems that prevent practitioners from recognising the signs of abuse. The most influential of these is *the rule of optimism* which leads to a belief on the part of an individual practitioner that child abuse would not happen in their class, patient list or caseload. A second factor that might hold a practitioner back from acting on a suspicion of significant harm is called *cultural relativism*. This is where the practitioner suspects that something is wrong, but this is excused as normal in that culture, family or community.

In Victoria Climbié's case, the poor relationship between Victoria and her great aunt was reframed as normal in West African families. At some time a threshold will be crossed when the practitioner will begin to suspect abuse and further evidence may then lead to subsequent referral. Often it is difficult for the practitioner to judge if that threshold has actually been passed, in which case it is advisable for the staff member to get help both from within her own agency and from the outside system. Paradoxically, practitioners who have had their awareness of child abuse or elder abuse increased by study or by training, can express fears that they will employ a *rule of pessimism* and see abuse in every person that they work with (Murphy, 2005).

Referral

The referral stage is often the first stage of interagency co-operation and communication, and can set the scene for the interactions that subsequently occur. Referrals can be made to social services, the NSPCC or to the police. When the referral is made a conflict of expectations sometimes arises. The referrer often comes from a non-social work agency, or is sometimes a member of the family or the public. Making such a referral is an unusual, often stressful event, during which they require reassurance and time to discuss their concerns. But the duty social worker needs to elicit the maximum amount of hard information about the case in order to judge whether it is an appropriate referral or not.

Investigation and initial assessment

The first task of the investigation is to access as much information about that particular person and their family. Social services databases and records should always be checked. Access to education, health, probation and police information will also be requested. Any specialist mental health involvement needs to be highlighted and investigated to ascertain the background and explanations for disturbed behaviour. In Britain, police checks reveal if any member of the household has been convicted of serious crimes against children (Schedule 1 offences). If it becomes known that the family had regular contact with any other agency relevant information from their databases would also be sought.

Most agencies have safeguards against disclosure of confidential information to third parties. However, the needs of the child, via the child protection procedures, supersede these safeguards, and relevant information is usually forthcoming. In practice, the test of relevancy and the breaking of confidentiality for some practitioner groups is still an area of some difficulty (Kearney et al., 2000). The risk of sabotaging sensitive therapeutic work addressing the child's emotional well-being is balanced with the need to obtain reliable evidence to put into court. The gathering of all this information could take a substantial amount of time. There could be a considerable time delay between referral and actual investigative interview. This delay can increase anxiety in the child or adult of concern and the referrer (Murphy, 2005).

Following the gathering of information the investigating social worker interviews sometimes jointly with the police, the referrer, the child, the child's parents or carers, the alleged abuser, the child's brothers and sisters and any other person with relevant information to disclose. Although the interviews with relevant adults may be quite direct and detailed, the interviewers are conscious of the need to form a close working relationship or partnership with the adults who care for the child concerned. When interviewing children, great emphasis is now placed on not leading, suggesting or influencing the child's story in any way (Home Office, 2001).

In British child protection systems, the medical examination commonly occurs in cases of physical and sexual abuse, and sometimes in the cases of neglect, organised and professional abuse. The child always has the right to refuse to be medically examined, and the parent, in some circumstances, also has the right to refuse on their behalf. In practice this refusal seldom occurs. There are three reasons for the investigative medical examination:

- To inform other agencies about the likelihood of abuse having occurred.
- To gather forensic evidence for use in legal proceedings.
- To assess the immediate medical needs of the child or adult.

There can be significant differences between the medical examinations involved in physical and in sexual abuse. In physical abuse, the medical will frequently be undertaken by a hospital paediatrician. Signs of physical trauma can last for some considerable time but as far as forensic evidence is concerned, the medical examination needs to occur as soon after the abusive event as possible. In child sexual abuse the examination will usually be done by a police surgeon. Forensic evidence in child sexual abuse needs to be gathered as soon as possible, often within 72 hours of the last occasion of abuse.

These investigative medical examinations have been criticised in the past for having been too intrusive (thereby re-abusing the child) and for being too inconclusive, thereby not giving the system any clear messages on which to work. However experienced practitioners can make the medical examination a non-intrusive, positive experience for the child concerned (Murphy, 2005). They can however, tend to focus on physical forensic matters and neglect the associated mental health and emotional issues.

The definition of significant harm is not precise but this can mean the term can be adapted to different circumstances. It is the *harm* which has

to be significant – not the act that caused it. Thus a sustained series of privations, not individually harmful as in the case of neglect over time, could amount to significant harm as far as the person's development was concerned. Not all harm will be significant, nor will significant harm in one context necessarily be significant in another. Ultimately it is a matter for the court to determine whether the harm is significant for the particular person in question (Butler and Roberts, 1997). The problem is that mental health and emotional well-being are difficult concepts for the criminal justice system to comprehend and measure. This is where your extra expertise and knowledge can significantly benefit the client by helping the court understand what psychological impact has occurred.

ACTIVITY 4.1

Discuss a recent safeguarding assessment with a colleague/supervisor and reflect back on how you did it. In retrospect how do you feel you assessed the mental health and emotional well-being of the client?

Identify three areas for improvement and the means for doing so.

The Children Act 1989

The Children Act Report (DfES, 2002) discovered that '30 per cent of updated child protection plans were unsatisfactory . . . However all agencies accepted that they have a fundamental responsibility to ensure that children are safeguarded, and in most cases this was backed up with a firm commitment by senior managers to ensure that their agencies did so'. The DoH (2003) developed a straightforward document – *What to do if You Are Worried a Child is Being Abused*, which progresses the child care practitioner through a number of flow charts highlighting the appropriate approach to take if you suspect abuse is occurring and how to work alongside other professionals.

Social workers have an opportunity to engage with CAMHS specialist staff who often assist with facilitative interviews as part of Section 47 assessments. This is an important role where they can add their expertise into the process particularly with young children, traumatised children and disabled children. *The Children Act* aimed to consolidate a number of child care reforms and provide a response to the evidence of failure in children's services that had been mounting in the 1980s (DHSS, 1985). The Act provides the legislative foundation on which subsequent policy guidance has been built to inform planning and intervention in safeguarding children and young people. There is a specific legal requirement under the Act that different authorities and agencies work together to provide family support services with better liaison and a corporate approach.

The guidance is a key element of the Department of Health's work to support local authorities in implementing *Quality Protects* – the government's programme for transforming the management and delivery of children's social services. This has been incorporated into other government guidance on protecting children from harm – *Working Together to Safeguard Children* (1999). This has subsequently been augmented with the *Every Child Matters* (2003) programme of reforms aimed at developing more effective child protection work and the new *Children Act 2004*. The duties under the terms of the *Children Act 1989* are straightforward and underpinned by the following principles:

- The welfare of the child is paramount.
- Children should be brought up and cared for within their own families wherever possible.
- Children should be safe and protected by effective interventions if at risk.
- Courts should avoid delay and only make an order if this is better than not making an order.
- Children should be kept informed about what happens to them and involved in decisions made about them.
- Parents continue to have parental responsibility for their children even when their children are no longer living with them.

Section 17 – lays a **duty on local authorities to safeguard, promote the welfare and provide services for children in need**. The definition of 'in need' has three elements:

1. The child is unlikely to achieve or maintain, or to have the opportunity of achieving or maintaining, a reasonable standard of health or development without the provision for the child of services by a local authority or;
2. The child's health or development is likely to be significantly impaired, or further impaired, without provision for the child of such services or;
3. The child is disabled.

The Act further defines disability to include children suffering from mental disorder of any

kind. In relation to the first two parts of the definition, health or development is defined to cover physical, intellectual, emotional, social or behavioural development and physical or mental health. These concepts are open to interpretation of what is meant by a 'reasonable standard of health and development', as well as the predictive implications for children having the 'opportunity' of achieving or maintaining it. However it is reasonable to include the following groups of children within this part of the definition of in need and to argue the case for preventive support where there is a risk of children developing problems (Ryan, 1999):

- children living in poverty
- homeless children
- children suffering the effects of racism
- young carers
- children separated from parents
- young offenders
- refugee and asylum seekers

Some children from these groups may be truanting from school, getting involved in criminal activities, or have behaviour problems at school or home. Agency responses tend to address the presenting problem and an intervention to address this rather than the underlying causes. Assessment of the needs of individual children and families therefore is often cursory, deficit-oriented, and static. It should be more positive, enabling, build on strengths and be undertaken alongside family support measures. Mental health and emotional well-being needs should be fully explored.

Care orders can be made in respect of children under section 17. This results in the child being placed in the care of the local authority which then assumes parental responsibility for that child. Parents still retain parental responsibility for the child but this is shared with the local authority. The grounds for a care order are:

- The child concerned is suffering significant harm, or is likely to suffer significant harm.
- The harm or likelihood of harm is attributable to:
  - The care given to the child, or likely to be given if the order were not made, not being what it would be reasonable to expect a parent to give them.
  - The child is beyond parental control.

Section 26 – provides for a **complaints procedure** through which children and young people can appeal against decisions reached by social workers. There are informal and formal stages to the procedure with an expectation that an independent person is included at the formal stages. When these procedures have been exhausted a Judicial review can be applied for within three months of the decision being appealed against. The three grounds for succeeding with Judicial Review are:

- **Ultra vires** – the social services department did not have the power to make the decision.
- **Unfair** – the decision was reached in a procedurally unfair manner, or by abuse of power.
- **Unreasonable** – all relevant matters were not considered, the law was not properly applied, or there was insufficient consultation.

Section 27 – requires Local Education Authorities and other organisations to **assist in functions** derived from Section 17.

Section 31 – enables staff to apply for a **care order or supervision order** if the child is suffering, or is likely to suffer, significant harm or the likelihood of harm, is attributable to the care being given the child not being what would be expected from a reasonable parent. The court decision is based on the balance of probability which means a parent can lose the care of their child even though in a preceding criminal court they were found not guilty because the standard of proof is beyond reasonable doubt.

Section 43 – enables staff to apply for a **child assessment order** from a court following parental lack of co-operation in a child protection assessment. The worker in situations like this, and in full care proceedings, has a crucial role in balancing the need to protect the child with the future consequences on them and their family of oppressive investigations and intervention.

Section 44 – enables staff to apply for an **emergency protection order** where they need to investigate suspected child abuse and access to the child is being refused. The order allows immediate removal of the child to a place of safety for eight days.

Section 46 – permits the police to **remove and detain** a child for 72 hours without reference to a court where they have reasonable cause to believe a child would otherwise be likely to suffer significant harm.

Section 47 – gives the local authority a **duty to investigate** where they suspect a child is suffering or is likely to suffer significant harm. Guidance suggests the purpose of such an investigation is to establish facts, decide if there are grounds for concern, identify risk, and decide protective action.

There is a very extensive body of government policy and practice guidance in relation to assessment in child protection. Research on assessment in child and family work affirms that mental health and emotional well-being apply specifically to child care and child protection. However it is clear that the over-emphasis on risk control which followed the Children Act 1989 and various child protection failures preceding it have obscured the mental health aspects in these complex situations. One report concluded that child protection appeared to have a de-skilling effect on staff who were only expecting to respond to families in crisis, and where children were at risk of significant harm. Workers therefore gained little experience beyond this in developing work with families to prevent the development of child and adolescent mental health problems (SSI, 1997; Thompson, 2005).

Social work departments find the policy emphasis is on reacting to child protection and looked after children cases to the exclusion of support to other families of children in need. Therefore too narrow a focus on danger can lead to neglect of the wider picture whereas a strategy of risk management which takes the wider context into account is more likely to effectively meet need. Or the policy emphasis swings towards more early intervention designed to prevent abusive situations developing.

Since the Children Act 1989 practice has focused on assessment of risk rather than need (of which risk is only a part). In 1996 a national commission of inquiry into the prevention of child abuse recognised the need for a more holistic approach. It included in its definition of child abuse not only direct and acute forms (such as violence) but also indirect forms such as poor housing, family health and poverty (HMSO, 1996). Nonetheless the narrow view has persisted and has led frequently to a failure to provide supportive services to children and families in need such that:

- Over half the estimated 160,000 children subject to child protection enquiries each year receive no further services.
- Interagency work is often relatively good at the early stages of child protection enquiries, its effectiveness tends to decline once child protection plans have been made.

- Discussions at child protection conferences tend to focus too heavily on decisions about registration and removal rather than on focusing on plans to protect the child and support the family.

Case illustration

The following case study examines the skills that could be used when developing a safeguarding children plan and reviewing its progress. As a practitioner you have inherited the case from a colleague who has moved job leaving a risky situation in which the mother is finding it difficult to trust anyone.

Ms B is a depressed young Albanian Muslim woman with three children under five years of age exhibiting disturbed behaviour and a 10 year old at primary school with poor attendance. The family are refugees and have experienced severe trauma in recent years. Her partner, who is ten years her senior has been involved with drug and alcohol abuse and is suspected of abusing her. She is terrified her children will be removed because she is unable to care for them properly or protect them from the violence of her partner. Ms B is hostile to social workers, health visitors and teachers who have expressed concerns about the welfare of all four children. She feels persecuted, does not want any involvement and resents any interference in her life. The child protection plan summary could look something like this:

- Younger children to attend nursery daily.
- Ms B to play with the younger children once a day.
- Ms B to attend domestic violence survivors group.
- Ms B to take 10 year old to school.
- Partner to attend anger management course.
- Partner to attend drug counselling.
- Family network to visit Ms B weekly.

ACTIVITY 4.2

Together with a colleague consider the case illustration and map out an action plan, including alternatives and the reasons for them.

Commentary

Whilst the main focus of intervention must be on the care and safety of the children, practitioners also need to engage Ms B by addressing her own needs for safety and protection. She is aware that her partner will harm her if she asks him to leave

so she is stuck in an impossible dilemma. If he stays the practitioner will allege she is failing to protect the children, if she tries to make her partner leave she will endanger herself as well as the children. If staff acknowledge this dilemma in an uncritical way without blaming Ms B or by pretending that there is a simple solution, then they are more likely to begin the process of gaining her confidence and working collaboratively rather than coercively.

The context of her culture and religion are important factors in seeking to understand the complexities of her situation. The social worker needs to be open and direct about this without giving the false impression of knowing how she feels or by signalling discomfort or embarrassment at such sensitive matters. Consideration should be given to employing an interpreter or translator even though she may be able to make herself understood, as this will signal a respectful approach and provide a cultural connection that will be emotionally supportive.

Engaging Ms B in a conversation about her experiences as a wife and mother in Albania and comparing her life with how it is now will open up a rich seam of information which simultaneously can serve a therapeutic purpose. Getting Ms B to list her worries and concerns about the children will enable her to demonstrate that she is a capable mother and help you appreciate the emotional aspects of her experiences. Attempts to engage her partner need to be made but not at the risk of inflaming the situation or putting her and the children at greater risk.

You can then help her consider ways of tackling these worries in small, practical ways before addressing the major issue of her complex relationship with her partner. The review needs to examine every element of the plan, check whether it is happening, which agency is responsible for what element, what impact the intervention is having on each child's development and whether additional needs have emerged or alternative interventions need to be considered. The review should check whether the plan is addressing and meeting each individual child's developmental needs, mental health and emotional well-being, as well as their collective needs as a sibling group.

It also needs to examine the parenting capacity of Ms B on her own and conjointly with her partner. The wider family context should be explored to see what pattern of relationships exist with a view to encouraging increased supportive contact. If no immediate family exist then a wider definition of 'family' could identify religious, spiritual or social support networks. In a safer environment the children's behaviour may regress and deteriorate so it is important to distinguish these temporary healing experiences from sustained developmental problems due to continued abuse.

Ms B may not be able to manage every aspect of the plan because it feels overwhelming. For example the survivors group may be poorly organised by unskilled people who cannot meet her particular needs. She may be the only Muslim and the target of racist abuse within the group. Thought needs to be given to finding the right group for her particular needs rather than just the first available resource. However she may be succeeding in getting the older child to school and she must be genuinely congratulated for this.

By establishing a solid platform for her to feel supported, empowered and capable of defining her children's needs she will be more likely to feel strong enough to deal with her violent partner. If the situation became more risky then the practitioner would need to confront Ms B with the likely consequences of inaction on her part. However this needs to be done alongside offering maximum support by all agencies involved in a co-ordinated package. Effective review and closure will more likely happen if a collaborative relationship with Ms B has developed which will enable her to seek further help in future if required.

The Children Act 2004

The *Children Act 2004* offers recent guidance on how to develop your individual practice to safeguard children and provides a legislative spine for the wider strategy for improving children's lives and therefore their emotional well-being. This covers the universal services which every child accesses, and more targeted services for those with additional needs. The Act defines children and young people to mean those aged 0–19 but also includes those:

- Over 19 who are receiving services as care leavers under sections 23c to 24d of the *Children Act 1989*.
- Over 19 but under 25 with learning difficulties within the meaning of section 13 of the *Learning and Skills Act 2000* and who are receiving services under that Act.

The overall aim is to encourage integrated planning, commissioning and delivery of services as well as improved multi-disciplinary working, removing duplication, increasing accountability and improving the co-ordination of individual and joint inspections in local authorities. The legislation is enabling rather than prescriptive and provides local authorities with a considerable amount of flexibility in the way they implement its provisions. The Act set the seal on a series of developments for safeguarding Children and Young People's welfare that have radically changed the shape of provision and created a new organisational context for their protection:

Section 10 – came into force in April 2005 and placed a **duty on local authorities and relevant partners to co-operate in order to improve the well-being of children in their area**. Well being covers: physical and mental health, emotional well-being, protection from harm and neglect, education, training and recreation, the contribution made to society, and general well-being. These terms are not well defined and neither is the linkage between the separate elements. This could lead to very different perceptions from the variety of agency staff involved with the same child. The notion of co-operation includes working together to understand the needs of local children, agreeing the contribution each agency should make to meet those needs, effective sharing of information about individual children at a strategic level to support multi-agency working, and the commissioning and delivery of services.

Schools and GPs have only recently been included in the specific list of 'relevant partners' in the Act mandated to co-operate. This had caused serious concern among child care organisations who feared the government's drive to increase the autonomy of schools would undermine the coherence and collaboration explicit in safeguarding policy. The National Youth Agency was disappointed that Youth Work is relatively ignored in this legislation despite evidence of the effectiveness of youth workers in safeguarding young people and managing mental health and emotional well-being. The government believes that other guidance implicitly expects all agencies to co-operate in safeguarding children and young people:

Sections 11 and 28 – introduced **a general duty of care on services to safeguard and promote the welfare of children**. This applies to the

Children's Services Authority, Schools, District Council, Strategic Health Authority, Primary Care Trust, NHS or Foundation Trust, Police authority, Probation Board, Youth Offending Team, Prison Governor and Connexions. The duty to co-operate is meant to lead to integrated services through: Children's Trusts, National Outcomes for Children and Young People, The Common Assessment Tool, Information Sharing Databases and Safeguarding Children's Boards.

Safeguard means prevention of and protection from maltreatment. Promoting welfare means ensuring children and young people have opportunities to achieve physical and mental health; physical, emotional, intellectual, social and behavioural development. However current guidance on section 11 fails to establish a clear line of accountability between Children's Trusts and Safeguarding Children Boards or to make explicit how the two bodies relate to each other on child protection matters.

Section 12 – provides for **the creation of a database to facilitate a new Identification, Referral and Tracking system**. This was one of the key practical measures to emerge following the 2003 Laming Report and is an information system designed to enable all staff concerned about any child or young person to access a database to ascertain who else might be involved and contact them if necessary. However the aim of encouraging better inter-agency communication may well be at the cost of reducing the much-valued confidentiality desired by young people in contact with sexual health, HIV and mental health services. There is no guarantee this information system will actually deliver better inter-agency communication and a real prospect of placing some young people at greater risk of harm if young people are deterred from seeking help because of fears that their confidential details will be exposed.

The system should only contain the child's name, address, gender, date of birth, a unique identifying number, plus the name and contact details of any person with parental responsibility or day to day care of the child, education provider and primary care provider. A flag will indicate that a professional working with a child has a cause for concern. The nature of the concern would not be described on the system. This has attracted criticism because there are no published threshold criteria for *what constitutes reasons for concern*. The fear is that this is likely to lead to a variety of definitions from staff in different

agencies and result in defensive practice whereby minor concerns are flagged to ensure legal cover causing unnecessary work. Guidance suggests that concerns need to be flagged when:

- A practitioner feels that others need to know the important information that cannot appear on the database.
- That this information may affect the types of services made available to the child or young person.
- The practitioner has completed an initial assessment under the Common Assessment Framework and wants to discuss their findings.

Security of this database has been questioned because of fears that a lack of staff training combined with the sheer numbers of staff able to use the system will invariably lead to a breach of security. Also users need to ensure compliance with the *Data Protection Act* 1998 and the *Human Rights Act* 1998 where client's rights will sometimes conflict with child protection procedures. Children and young people when consulted about this accept that information should be shared between agencies if it will help them gain access to the services they need. But they want to be consulted, know with whom it is being shared, and to be reassured that the information is accurate, will be used properly and kept safe.

The government has proposed that a lead professional should be designated to act upon information placed on the database, operate as a gate-keeper, decide whether information was merited and co-ordinate service responses. The recommendation is that this person should be someone from the agency with most day-to-day contact with the child. For most children this person will be their school teacher but teachers are resisting taking on this scale of responsibility.

Sections 13 to 16 – provide for the establishment of **Local Safeguarding Children Boards** which will replace the previous Area Child Protection Committees (ACPCs). Their responsibilities include:

- Developing local procedures.
- Auditing and evaluating how well local services work together.
- Putting in place objectives and performance indicators for child protection.
- Developing effective working relationships.
- Ensuring agreement on thresholds for intervention.

- Encouraging evidence based practice.
- Undertaking part eight reviews when a child has died or been seriously harmed.
- Overseeing interagency training.
- Raising awareness within the community.

With Safeguarding Children Boards put on a statutory footing their expanded role will cover monitoring of practice, training and service development. The majority of this membership will be drawn from Police, Education, Social Services and Health. Health can be particularly well represented from paediatrics, hospital trusts, the Primary Care Trusts and Child and Adolescent Mental Health. The Probation Service, the Crown Prosecution service, CAFCASS, the Magistrate's Court, the NSPCC and other voluntary organisations are all likely to be represented (Murphy, 2004).

Sections 17 and 26 – introduce **a new children and young people's plan (CYPP)** which from April 2006 is the strategic, overarching plan replacing the Behaviour Support Plan, Children's Services Plan, Early Years Development and Childcare Plan, Education Development Plan, ACPC Business Plan, Teenage Pregnancy Strategy and Youth Services Plan. The CYPP should set out the improvements that local authorities intend to make to meet the five outcomes for children and young people identified in *Every Child Matters* (2003):

Enjoying and achieving – this means getting the most out of life and developing broad skills for adulthood; attending school and achieving national educational standards; achieving personal, social, development and enjoying recreation.

Staying safe – being protected from harm and neglect and growing up able to look after themselves. Being safe from maltreatment, neglect, violence, sexual exploitation, bullying and discrimination. Protected from crime and anti-social behaviour. Learning and developing independent living skills.

Being healthy – enjoying good physical health and mental health and living a healthy lifestyle. Being emotionally and sexually healthy and choosing not to take illegal drugs.

Making a positive contribution – to the community and to society and not engaging in anti-social or offending behaviour. Making decisions and supporting community development and enjoying positive relationships. Choosing not to bully or discriminate, develop self confidence and manage challenges.

Economic well being – overcoming socio-economic disadvantages to achieve their full potential. Engage in further education or training and prepare for employment, family life and independent living. Access to decent homes, transport and sustainable incomes.

National Service Framework for Children, Young People and Midwifery Services

The NSF is a 10 year programme intended to stimulate long-term and sustained improvement in children's health. It aims to ensure fair, high quality and integrated health and social care from pregnancy right through to adulthood. Overall, the NSF sets national standards for the first time for children's health and social care, which promote high quality, women and child-centred services and personalised care that meets the needs of parents, children and their families. The standards require services to:

- **Give** children, young people and their parents increased information, power and choice over the support and treatment they receive, and involve them in planning their care and services.
- **Introduce** a new Child Health promotion programme designed to promote the health and well-being of children from pre-birth to adulthood.
- **Promote** physical health, mental health and emotional well being by encouraging children and their families to develop healthy lifestyles.
- **Focus** on early intervention, based on timely and comprehensive assessment of a child and their family's needs.
- **Improve** access to services for all children according to their needs, particularly by co-locating services and developing managed Local Children's Clinical Networks for children who are ill or injured.
- **Tackle** health inequalities, addressing the particular needs of communities, and children and their families who are likely to achieve poor outcomes.
- **Promote** and safeguard the welfare of children and ensure all staff are suitably trained and aware of action to take if they have concerns about a child's welfare.
- **Ensure** that pregnant women receive high quality care throughout their pregnancy, have a normal childbirth wherever possible, are involved in decisions about what is best for

them and their babies, and have choices about how and where they give birth.

Standard five of the NSF states that 'all agencies work to prevent children suffering harm and to promote their welfare, provide them with the services they require to address their identified needs, and safeguard children who are being, or who are likely to be, harmed'. The responsibility for contributing to this new multi-agency integrated framework rests with:

- **Primary care trusts** who are responsible for improving the health of their whole population.
- **Strategic health authorities** who are the performance managers.
- **NHS trusts** are required to designate a named doctor and nurse to take a professional lead on safeguarding children.
- **Ambulance trusts**, **NHS Direct** and **NHS walk-in centres** must have similar arrangements in place.
- **Local authorities** must ensure there is a designated professional for safeguarding children in **social services**, **housing** and the **education department**.

Safeguarding and promoting the welfare of children should be prioritised by all agencies, working in partnership to plan and provide co-ordinated and comprehensive services. Agency roles and responsibilities should be clarified to ensure that harmed children are identified and assessed as soon as possible by appropriately trained staff with suitable premises and equipment. Under the NSF an up to date profile of the local population must be compiled to facilitate needs assessment and to provide integrated services to meet that need.

ACTIVITY 4.3

Obtain a copy of your agency safeguarding children procedures and practice guidelines, or make sure you know where it is held. Make a note of the contents to see where child and adolescent mental health is mentioned.

Examine it carefully and make sure you know how and to whom you should refer in cases involving child protection.

National Service Framework for Older People 2001

The National Service Framework for Older People is the framework for the provision of

equitable services for older people led by the NHS. It has eight standards:

1. **Stopping** age discrimination and preventing local authority providers using age to limit access to services.
2. **Providing** person-centred care using the Single Assessment Process and integrated commissioning.
3. **Access** to intermediate care in a person's own home or designated care settings.
4. **Hospital Care** which is appropriate, specialist and which respects dignity and privacy.
5. **Slowing** the rate of strokes in the community and provide prompt specialist services.
6. **Reducing** the number of falls that result in serious injury and better treatment and rehabilitation.
7. **Access** to integrated mental health services especially for depression and dementia.
8. **Promoting** health and active life expectancy.

Echoing concepts in Children's safeguarding the NSF for older people (DoH, 2001) introduced the single assessment process (SAP) which aimed to provide a unified structure to the assessment of client's needs and avoid duplication by different agencies involved in their care (McDonald, 2010). Just as in safeguarding children, the SAP is designed to be enhanced via specialised or complex assessments:

- **Contact assessment:** is used to screen people to identify support needs from different services.
- **Overview assessment:** is used to support multiagency working by addressing the person's physical, social, mental and environmental needs, including any carer involvement.
- **Specialist assessment:** is used where there is a need to obtain more information about the cause of a problem and the services required to tackle it.
- **Supported assessment:** is used by any professional or agency as part of the process of self-directed support.

However evidence thus far (Challis et al., 2004) suggests that the SAP is facing problems in implementation due to a lack of trust and coherence between agencies, differing perceptions about a person's needs; and an assessment model that reflected administrative imperatives. It seems that older people prefer regular contact from professional staff rather than infrequent assessment visits with bureaucratic forms with a rigid set of questions and pre-coded answers. In the context of pressures to discharge older people from hospital by the *Community Care (Delayed Discharges) Act 2003*, which imposed financial penalties on social care services, the evidence suggests deterioration in inter-agency relationships (CSCI, 2005).

National Service Framework for Mental Health 1999

The National Service Framework for Mental Health introduced in 1999 focused on the mental health needs of working-age adults up to 65 and is based on the premise that one adult in six suffers from a mental health problem at any one time. The guidance included in the framework covers mental health promotion, assessment and diagnosis, treatment, rehabilitation and care, and encompasses primary and specialist care and the role of partner agencies. Working in partnership is a key strand – partnerships between those who use services and those who provide services, between different practitioners and professional groups, between the NHS and local government; and within the community, voluntary organisations, and independent sectors. The guidance approaches mental health service delivery from a corporate or holistic perspective which looks at the spectrum of care and need, and attempts to meet that need across a range of sectors.

The care programme approach

The care programme approach defines the way care is delivered to people with mental health difficulties and influences social work practice particularly in relation to duties under section 117 of the *Mental Health Act 1983*. The care programme approach was introduced in 1991 and its principle aim was to improve the co-ordination of care to people with severe mental health needs. Prior to this some people were not properly assessed, whether in the community or prior to discharge from hospital.

The care programme approach to work in mental health was designed to complement the principles underlying care management in the *NHS and Community Care Act 1990*. This means people should have an individual care plan based on a thorough needs led assessment which is designed taking account of the views and aspirations of the service user and carer. This plan should be implemented within multi-agency provision and co-ordinated by one professional who should be responsible for monitoring and reviewing the plan. A care plan is a written statement specifying the objectives for the future agreed between practitioners and users and their carers or family, and outlining the means by which those objectives are to be met.

Research shows that only minimum involvement of users and carers takes place under the care programme approach reflecting prejudiced and discriminatory attitudes to vulnerable people with mental health problems (Carpenter and Sbaraini, 1997). In order to more fully involve users and carers and to develop an integrated care programme approach the following elements of good practice have been identified:

- Ensuring that planning meetings involve carers, users, advocates, and professionals.
- Recording users and carers views on services in the community or in hospital.
- Identifying and recording separately everyone's views on problems, needs, and aims, and noting disagreements.
- Formulating action plans to meet needs rather than accept existing services and agreeing a contract clarifying monitoring and review arrangements.
- Providing specific information about rights and services, including medication and complaints procedures.
- Making sure an explicit agreement is obtained by the signature of everyone involved.

ACTIVITY 4.4

Make a list of the factors you think make it difficult to ensure the care programme approach is effectively implemented in this area of social work practice

Commentary

Your list should address the evolving nature of the relationship between users and carers which may not remain static but will not be noted unless regular and sensitive review takes place. The process can be very time consuming and highlights lack of appropriate provision in the community. GPs are generally ill informed about the care programme approach and few are involved in developing or reviewing it. The approach may not of itself benefit multi-disciplinary team working and the recent introduction of other AMHP staff involved in assessment may further water down a social dimension to the CPA. The fear is that new guidance accompanying the 2007 Mental Health Act is aimed at more compulsory treatment with less social work involvement.

New Horizons

The New Horizons policy guidance issued in 2009 aims to foster a better cross-government programme of action to:

- Improve the mental health and well-being of the population.
- Improve the quality and accessibility of services for people with poor mental health.

This is the latest in a long line of policy pronouncements which have failed to deliver significant change in the much neglected area of mental health. Latest estimates for example show that 0.1 per cent of the NHS budget is put into mental health promotion, the cost to the overall economy of mental illness is £77 billion, non-pharmaceutical treatments are in short supply and rely on brief cognitive based therapy, while the mental health aspects of drug and alcohol abuse, domestic violence and crime and disorder are neglected (Mental Health Foundation, 2009). The New Horizons policy aims will be tested against the evidence of their success assessed by a variety of measures, instruments and data. For the busy social worker this evidence will need to be set beside your own experience and that of your clients, who will ultimately be the best judge of whether mental health services have improved.

ACTIVITY 4.5

Make a list of the advantages and disadvantages of working in partnership with professionals from other agencies in the area of mental health.

Commentary

Your list will highlight the challenges in working jointly across professional boundaries, often using identical theoretical resources, but trying to maintain your professional distinctiveness. Many agencies work with mentally ill people but what is your role with this client group? Shared responsibility can relieve the burden of stress but can also involve negotiating disagreement. The different power and status of some professionals becomes apparent in partnership practice.

The Care Programme Approach (CPA) assessment is a core activity for all workers in mental health services. In adapting this framework to your client's individual needs it is important to link assessment with the appropriate intervention. This is to ensure that you:

- Evaluate the individual's strengths.
- Assess the level of risk.
- Identify the need for specialist assessment.
- Determine whether intervention from mental health service is appropriate.
- Identify the person's level of need.
- Establish an information base.

Working effectively with black and ethnic minority communities is highlighted throughout the National Service Framework for Mental Health. Standard one notes that some black and minority ethnic communities have higher diagnosed rates of mental health problems than the general population and calls for specific programmes of service development for these communities. Standards two to six discuss the need for performance assessment to include the experience of service users and carers, including those from black and ethnic minority communities.

ACTIVITY 4.6

What do you think are the factors influencing the higher rate of compulsory admission to psychiatric hospital for black and ethnic minority people?

Commentary

Here you will be able to review the social context of mental health, cultural variations in emotional expression, and the wider effects of racism in producing higher levels of stress and disadvantage among black and ethnic minority people. This is then compounded by practice in psychiatric services that are perceived to be institutionally racist and insensitive to individual needs. The development of psychiatry and theories of human growth and development constructed in the 18th and 19th centuries were based on white ethnocentric beliefs and assumptions about normality. The western model of illness regards the mind as distinct from the body and defines mental illness or mental health according to negative, deficit characteristics. In non-western cultures such as Chinese, Indian and African, mental health is often perceived as a harmonious balance between a person's internal and external influences. Thus a person is intrinsically linked to their environment and vice versa.

The western model of mental illness tends to ignore the religious or spiritual aspects of the culture in which it is based. However, Eastern, African and Native American cultures tend to integrate them (Fernando, 2002). Spirituality and Religion as topics in general do not feature often in the social work literature, yet they can be critical components of a person's well-being offering a source of strength, and hope in trying circumstances. Clients for whom family and faith backgrounds are inseparable may need encouragement to feel comfortable in multi-faith settings. Social workers need to address this dimension as part of the constellation of factors affecting black people, bearing in mind the positive and sometimes negative impact spiritual or religious beliefs might have on their mental health.

Interagency working

The much vaunted aim of joint working and closer collaboration has echoed throughout much of the past 30 years of public reports where people have been killed when problems in communication between agencies have occurred. In fact it appeared much earlier in the 1945 inquiry report into the death of Denis O'Neill – often cited as the first child killed while subject to child protection agency involvement.

Guidance suggests that staff should receive more comprehensive safeguarding training that equips them to recognise and respond to a person's welfare concerns. Thus the policy aspiration to foster closer collaborative working between agencies involved in safeguarding people faces serious obstacles.

The principle reason given for failures in interagency co-operation is that one key individual within that system failed to fulfil their part of the process which resulted in a breakdown in the protective intervention. It is not the individual within the system but the structure of the system itself that is of key importance. That one individual within a system can be blamed for a child's injury denies the whole concept of collective interagency decision-making and responsibility. Agencies can fall into the convenient practice of finding a scapegoat reflecting a societal individualistic culture and the adversarial legal system: 'In Britain, when things go wrong, the system encourages a blaming of individual agencies and practitioners' (Murphy, 2000).

ACTIVITY 4.7

Make an effort to link up with a practitioner from another agency and meet to discuss the above.

Draw up an action plan to present to each other's teams to tackle the barriers to better collaboration.

Commentary

If better communication is to happen it is essential that the practitioner or agency concerned behaves in an assertive way by explaining the reasons behind a judgment or opinion to the rest of the interagency group. You must never attempt to take over another agency's role or sphere of activity. It is helpful to use the technique of predicting positive or negative outcomes for the proposed courses of action. Where possible, aim for compromise if not consensus. Where there is a sense that one side has forced a decision through, the probability of positive interagency co-operation being achieved around that decision is extremely low.

By being pro-active about potential problems and difficulties much goodwill can be generated and mis-conceptions dealt with before they occur during stressful situations. Acknowledging the powerful feelings aroused during this stressful work in a safe environment away from the front line with a neutral facilitator can be very helpful in reducing all sorts of barriers to better communication. These training experiences are not add-on extras or self-indulgent experiential exercises. They are the real process by which learning takes place, practice improves and clients are better safeguarded.

Skills and knowledge for safeguarding

This is an attempt to enhance integrated practice in safeguarding people. The main elements of the common core in which people who work with vulnerable people need to know about and become proficient in are:

- **Effective communication and engagement** – includes establishing rapport and respectful, trusting relationships; understand non-verbal communication and cultural variations in communication; active listening in a calm, open and non-threatening manner; summarising situations to check understanding and consent; outline possible courses of action and consequences; ensuring people feel valued; understand limits of confidentiality and relevant legislation; report and record information.

- **Human growth and development** – includes observing behaviour in context; understand developmental processes and mental health issues; evaluate circumstances in a holistic way and distinguish fact from opinion; know when to refer on for further support; demonstrate empathy and understanding; support the person to reach their own decisions; take account of different life styles; distinguish between organic disability and poor parenting producing delayed development; understand attachment patterns and the inter-relationship between developmental characteristics and being clear about your role and how to reflect on practice to improve it.

- **Safeguarding and promoting the welfare of the person** – includes ability to recognise overt and subtle signs that people have been harmed by considering all explanations for sudden changes in mood or behaviour; involve parents/carers in promoting welfare and recognising risk factors; develop self-awareness about the impact of child abuse; build confidence in challenging oneself and others; understand legislation, guidance and other agency roles; share information in the context of confidentiality; appreciate boundaries of your knowledge and responsibility; Respond appropriately to conflict, anger and violence and understand that assumptions, values and prejudice prevent equal opportunity.

- **Supporting transitions** – includes recognising changes in attitudes and behaviour; empathise and reassure to help the person reach a positive outcome; consider issues of identity and the effects of peer pressure; understand key areas affecting emotional well-being such as divorce, bereavement, puberty and family break-ups, primary to secondary school, unemployment, leaving home; disability and increasing levels of vulnerability; knowledge of local resources and how to access information.

- **Multi-agency working** – includes effective communication by listening and ensuring you are being listened to; work in a team and forge sustaining relationships; share experience through formal and informal exchanges; develop skills to ensure continuity for the person; know when and to whom to report incidents or unexpected behaviour changes; understand how to ensure another agency responds while maintaining a focus on the persons best interests.

- **Sharing information** – includes making good use of available information such as a common assessment; assess the relevance and status of different information and where gaps exist; use clear unambiguous language; respect the skills and expertise of others while creating a trusting environment and seeking consent; engage with people and their families to communicate and gain information; share confidential information without consent where a child is at risk; avoid repetitive questions and assessment interviews; appreciate the effect of cultural and religious beliefs without stereotyping; understand the Fraser principles governing young people's consent; distinguish between permissive information sharing and statutory information sharing and their implications.

Chapter summary

Changes to the organisation and delivery of safeguarding services have followed legislative change and policy guidance that has evolved over many years in relation to vulnerable elderly people and those with mental health problems, as well as children.

Children's Trusts are becoming the core focus for the delivery of joined-up services for children and young people whereby staff from every agency will be expected to work collaboratively in multi-disciplinary teams or networks.

The Education Act 2002 and Extended Schools Programme together with general duties to safeguard children and young people under the *Children Act 2004*, means that teachers and other education service staff will be expected to play a much bigger and more active role in child protection than previously. They also need to improve knowledge and skills in the emotional well being of young people.

Social workers working with vulnerable people need to learn about, understand and engage critically but positively with other agency staff responsible for client protection. Different values, knowledge bases and skills in perceptions of the needs of people, who are or may be at risk of significant harm, need to be acknowledged.

Part Two:
Challenges and Dilemmas in Practice

Chris Beckett

CHAPTER 5

Shifting Roles in Assessment and Intervention

Learning objectives

- Recognise the different roles that social workers play, often in the context of a single job: advocacy roles, direct work roles and executive roles.
- Recognise the conflicts and contradictions that can occur between these roles (for example the conflict between 'gate-keeper' and 'advocate').
- Develop an understanding of the 'control agent' role and social work's involvement in control, sometimes justifiable in terms of protecting the vulnerable.
- Recognise the impact of the control agent role on social work practice generally, and on the way that social workers perform other roles.
- Recognise the different relationships that service users have with social work agencies as a result of the different roles that social workers play.

Introduction

This chapter begins a new part of the book in which I will look at some of the difficulties and dilemmas that arise when we try and apply practice principles in the world of social work as it actually exists, a topic which is a particular interest of mine. In the next chapter, Chapter 6, I will look at the challenges that arise as a result of working with limited resources. In Chapter 7, I will look at the intervention thresholds that social workers apply as they try and achieve consistency and equity. In the present chapter I will look at the diversity of roles that are played by social workers and the conflicts that can occur between them.

Social work is not a homogeneous activity. What is meant by 'social work' varies considerably between agency contexts and service user groups. For example a social worker employed by a small voluntary agency working with homeless adults will play a very different set of roles from a social worker in a community mental health team, or an 'intake' social worker working in a children's social care team, or a social worker who manages a residential home for the elderly. Social workers in different specialisms can and do sometimes find themselves at loggerheads with one another, because of the different roles that they play in relation to the same service users. I think, for example, of the sometimes tense working relationship between a mental health social worker and a child and family social worker who are both working with the same family, one primarily concerned with the parents, one primarily concerned with the children. They may have very different priorities and very different perceptions of what needs to be done.

But what I particularly want to look at in this chapter is the diversity of roles that a social worker must play *within* a single context. One social worker's daily work may include advocating on behalf of service users, helping to manage an agency's limited resources, negotiating agreements with different agencies, listening to a service user's problems, investigating allegations of abuse and giving evidence in court. These roles do not always sit very easily or comfortably together.

Diversity of roles

The literature on social work tends to draw quite heavily on the literature on psychotherapy and counselling. Most books on social work theory (see for instance Payne, 2005; Beckett, 2006; Howe, 2009) will tell you about psychodynamic approaches, cognitive behavioural therapy, Carl Rogers, systemic family work and solution-focused therapy. There are good reasons for this, because social work, like psychotherapy, deals with personal change, and not surprisingly draws on the same body of ideas about the psychology of change. But the prevalence of this material in the social work literature might lead an unsuspecting reader to assume that social work was an activity closely allied to psychotherapy or counselling. Sometimes it can be, but at other times it is something very different indeed, and social workers perform a whole range of roles which differ fundamentally from those performed by counsellors or therapists.

We can group the roles played by social workers into three broad areas:

1. **Advocacy:** We are acting as direct advocates when we speak out on someone's behalf. We are acting as indirect advocates when we support someone in speaking out for themselves. In either case the aim is to help give voice to needs or demands or points of view that might otherwise go unheard. Social workers are not the only professionals who act as advocates. Doctors, nurses and teachers will all at times act as advocates for those they work with. Lawyers of course specialise in advocacy and indeed in some contexts are simply known as advocates. There are also many specialist advocacy services which employ advocates, or recruit volunteer advocates, who may not be either lawyers or social workers by training. But advocacy has always been an important part of the role of most social workers, and takes many forms, from writing letters to utility companies, to helping set up campaigning groups.

2. **Direct work:** Direct work is work in which the interaction between social worker and service user is intended, *of itself*, to be a service. The interaction between social worker and service user is central in almost all areas of social work, of course, but in many cases the interaction is not in itself the service that the social worker is delivering, but is rather a means to an end. For example a social worker may have a conversation with an elderly person about her care needs. In this case the conversation is *not* in itself the service. The service will be a package of care services. The conversation is a vital part of ensuring that this package does actually, as far as possible, meet the needs and wishes of the service user, but it is not direct work in the sense that I am using the term here. Direct work is occurring when the interaction itself, rather than some other

service, is offered as a means of supporting personal change. Direct work is the social work role most akin to counselling and psychotherapy, for psychotherapists and counsellors also offer conversations intended to be services in themselves. But it also includes a wider range of work than psychotherapists or counsellors normally engage in, including work in which the social worker is more of an educator, or a mediator.

3. **Executive roles:** I have coined the term 'executive roles' as a catch-all to cover the many ways in which social workers provide a service not through advocacy or through direct work, but by drawing on various external resources to bring about change in the environment of the service user. For example social workers commission care packages, arrange placements, engage in court work, co-ordinate the activities of other professionals, develop and maintain services and act as gate-keepers for material resources. In most areas of social work, these executive functions, very different from the work undertaken by counsellors or psychotherapists, may take up all or most of the working day, and it could be argued that the executive roles are the most distinctive of all social work roles, even though they are probably the least discussed in social work texts.

Actually the executive roles are so diverse that it makes sense to further subdivide them. Table 5.1 summarises the main ones.

ACTIVITY 5.1

Thinking about social work as you have practised it, or have seen it practised, which of the roles (summarised below) predominate. What proportion of a social

Table 5.1: Varieties of Executive Role

Gate-keeper: distributing limited resources.

Care manager/care co-ordinator: commissioning services from others.

Responsibility holder: taking responsibility for the well being of people who lack the maturity or capacity to take full responsibility for themselves.

Control agent: using powers conferred by law to exercise control over people who are at risk, or are placing others at risk.

Multi-agency co-ordinator/keyworker: co-ordinating the activities of other professionals.

Service developer: developing, enhancing and/or and maintaining a service (this could include, for instance, the role of social workers acting as home finders, trainers or managers, or indeed lecturers like the authors of this book).

worker's time is typically spent on each of them? Bear in mind that activities such as recording or interviewing service users, or meetings with other agencies, are not really roles in themselves but may be linked with several different roles. (If you are filling out an eligibility form then that is to do with the gate-keeping role; if you are making a note of some key points that emerged in a direct work session with a child, then that is to do with direct work.)

The roles are:

- *Advocacy*
- *Direct work*
- *Executive roles, including:*
  - *gate-keeper*
  - *care manager/care co-ordinator*
  - *responsibility holder*
  - *control agent*
  - *multi-agency co-ordinator/keyworker*
  - *service developer*

Commentary

You may find that it is sometimes difficult to tease out the separate roles, which are often closely interwoven. For example: if you spend 45 minutes with an elderly person completing an assessment of needs, you could say that that the time you spent was primarily to do with care management, but depending on the circumstances, the interview may have had an important direct work component as well and may have raised issues for which advocacy might be appropriate.

Conflict of roles

The difficulty of playing so many different roles is that at times they can come into conflict with one another or get confused with one another. The gate-keeper and care management roles, for instance, can be difficult to combine with the direct work role. Most therapists would agree that a therapeutic relationship works best when unencumbered by other things. If your therapist or counsellor is also your access point to a variety of services, or is in a position to provide you with financial assistance then this can create a number of difficulties:

- Are service users entering into a direct work relationship with the social worker because they actually want to, or are they doing so because they believe that this is the way to gain access to services or material assistance?

- If entering into a direct work relationship is required to gain access to other services is this ethical?
- If the worker undertaking direct work is also the care manager, they will probably need to share information about the service user with others. Can they separate out the information that they have obtained in a 'direct work' role from the information they have obtained as a care manager? (In other words: is it possible to provide the level of confidentiality that counsellors and therapists can normally offer?)
- The social worker's judgement on whether services and material assistance are given or withheld are likely to be influenced by their understanding developed in the course of their direct work. This creates an additional layer of complexity to the power relationship between client and counsellor.
- If the social worker, in their care manager capacity, decides that it is not appropriate to accede to a request for a service or material assistance, this is likely to have a significant impact on their relationship with the service user in a direct work context.
- Conversely, fear of upsetting the working relationship, may make it difficult for social worker to make fair and objective decisions about whether or not to provide material assistance or services that are asked for.

ACTIVITY 5.2

You are working with a service user who we will call Linda. (You can imagine whatever context you like!) You are doing some work with her on building her self-esteem and helping her to cope more assertively with others. You have established a good working relationship with her and feel that you are making progress. She has told you that she trusts you and that she feels that you 'really listen to her'. During one session she tells you that she is aware that your agency is able to give financial help in some circumstances and she asks you for a cash grant.

You are aware that the funds available for this purpose are very limited and you are not sure that the purpose for which Linda is requesting the grant can really be regarded as very high priority. What sort of position would this put you in?

Commentary

Different people would deal with this in different ways. However we would suggest that, for you to say no to the request might create some difficulties for your direct work with Linda. Equally, if you said yes, simply in order to avoid creating these difficulties, this in itself has some implications. Are you going to have to say yes to every such request? Would this be fair to other service users? Is your direct work going to be the same once it has been established that, as well as offering the opportunity to talk and reflect, you are also a source of material help? A lot of social workers would seek to sidestep these issues by passing the decision about the financial help to a manager (and in many agencies this sort of decision would *have* to be made by a manager – something we will come back to in the next chapter), but even so the problems do not entirely disappear.

Another conflict that can occur is between *advocacy* and gate-keeping roles. At the time of the introduction of the 1990 *NHS and Community Care Act* (which still provides the main legal framework for adult social work) the tension between these two roles came to the fore because local authorities were required, firstly, to carry out 'needs led' assessments of adult service users (that is: they were asked to make an assessment of what the client's needs were without pigeonholing people into the services that were actually available), and secondly to manage a substantial community care budget.

In pursuit of the former aim, government guidance and staff training programmes encouraged social workers to look holistically at service users, to consider all their needs and to find creative ways of meeting those needs. If, to give an illustration, an elderly man asked for a place at a day centre, then social workers were encouraged not just to consider him 'a day centre case', but to explore what needs a day centre was supposed to meet, to consider whether there were other ways in which these needs might be better met and to consider whether he might have other needs which a day centre would not meet – and consider how these needs too might be met.

What was really being suggested, then, was that social workers – or others acting as care managers/ care co-ordinators – should not merely act as officials arranging access to various services, but should act as a kind of advocate for the service user, getting a picture of the service user's needs *as the service user saw them* and then working on behalf of the service user to get those needs met.

At the outset, not surprisingly, many authorities went wildly over budget and, as a result, complex new screening procedures involving eligibility criteria became part of the process, dampening down initial hopes of a more creative, user-led service. But this raised the question as to whether social workers, or care co-ordinators, in this field, can carry out genuine needs-led assessments and act as advocates for the service user in trying to get these needs met and yet *simultaneously* take responsibility for rationing resources and therefore limiting access to services? Bateman (2000) suggests six ethical principles for advocacy of which the first two are: 'Always act in the client's best interests' and 'Always act in accordance with the client's wishes and instructions', but those involved in gate-keeping resources cannot put the best interests of one client before everything else but must set the interests of one client in the balance against the interests of others. (The ethical principle involved in gate-keeping is not unconditional support for a *particular* service user, but equity *between* service users.)

Some specialist advocacy services can concentrate entirely on advocacy but local authority social workers have no choice to reconcile these two roles as best they can, whatever the tension between them. Is it really feasible for one person to carry out both roles at the same time? There are arguments both ways on this, and I will be exploring them further in the next chapter. For the moment we will just note that there are, at the least, tensions between acting as a whole hearted advocate for a service user within the system and, at the same time, acting on behalf of the system to protect it against being overwhelmed and to help it distribute its resources as fairly as possible. These tensions occur in most, if not all, areas of social work, and not just in social work under the *NHS and Community Care Act*.

But perhaps the most difficult of role conflicts relate to tensions between social work's control agent role and its other roles. It is the control agent role, and the way it impacts on other roles, that I will now explore.

ACTIVITY 5.3

Before going any further you might like to take stock by considering your own experience of social work and asking yourself what are the most difficult role conflicts that you have encountered?

Social work and social control

The dichotomy between what I have called the control agent role and other aspects of social work is sometimes presented as *care* versus *control*. I will therefore begin by noting that this is something of a false dichotomy. In life, control can often be caring. A parent who made no attempt to control her toddler next to a busy road would not be very caring, to give an obvious example.

But the control agent role *is* (of course) central to the 'social control' aspect of social work, an aspect that many social workers are uncomfortable with, sitting uneasily as it does with the social work values of promoting empowerment and self-determination. The control agent role often *feels* oppressive and this makes it seem difficult to reconcile with the idea of anti-oppressive practice. It is sometimes necessary to remind ourselves that, for example, to leave a small child in a situation where she is at risk of being used by adults for sex would be much *more* oppressive than to use statutory powers to intervene and prevent the abuse from happening. Or, to give another instance, in the case of a man who is having terrifying paranoid delusions as a result of an acute psychotic illness – and who has shut himself off from family and friends and all other sources of help as a result of those delusions – it might be much more oppressive to leave him to suffer than it would be to use the powers given by the *Mental Health Act 2007* to take him to a hospital and get him treatment. The latter might even involving asking the police to break down his door and remove him by force, and could therefore feel very oppressive and brutal indeed. If it was done unnecessarily, it would *be* oppressive too (see Kinney, 2009). But if done appropriately, it could be that when he was well again this service user would thank you for doing it nevertheless, or would at any rate have a better quality of life as a result of your actions.

We should bear in mind too that the control agent function is not the only aspect of social work that is connected with social control. It is simply the most obvious one. In fact many would argue that the 'therapeutic' direct work role played by social workers, psychiatrists and others is *also* sometimes about social control. Critics of social work from the political left have pointed out how 'explanations in traditional social work reduce complex social problems to individual psychological ones' (Payne, 2005: 233, discussing McIntyre, 1982) as a result 'blaming the victim' and making the client responsible for problems which are really social and political in origin. Parton (1991) draws on the work of Foucault (1977) to discuss how this process of defining problems in terms of individual psychology has the effect of increasing the power of various professional groups to regulate the behaviour of others, legitimised by discourses drawn from 'human sciences' like medicine, psychology and psychiatry. So the control agent role is not the only area of social work in which issues of oppressive practice arise, but it is certainly the most obvious area, and it is the area which we will now discuss in more detail.

More on the control agent role

Historically, social workers have exercised a wide range of statutory powers, across several specialisms, in a way what sets them apart almost all of the other 'caring professions'. For example Section 47 of the *National Assistance Act 1948* (as amended by the *National Assistance Amendment Act 1951*) allowed local authority social services departments to apply to a magistrates' court for an order authorising them to remove a elderly person 'in need of care and attention' from their home and to take them to a hospital, residential home or some other 'suitable place' if:

- The person is 'suffering from grave chronic disease or being aged, infirm or physically incapacitated, is living in insanitary conditions', and
- 'Is unable to devote to themselves, and is not receiving from other persons, proper care and attention', and
- The person's removal from home is necessary, 'either in their own interests or for preventing injury to the health of, or serious nuisance to, other persons'.
- The Community Physician has supplied evidence in writing to the local authority to this effect.

The *Mental Health Act 1983* placed social workers in a unique position of authority which was not found in any other social work specialism, or any other profession. Social workers 'approved' under the Act were the professional group given the task of deciding whether people should be detained, and even given treatment, against their will. It is only recently, under the *2007 Mental*

Health Act, that other professionals (Approved Mental Health Professionals, in place of Approved Social Workers) can be given equivalent powers.

Social workers in drug and alcohol services also work in an area where there is a control agent element, for service users of such agencies may be required to submit to tests, including urine tests, in order to get a service (for example: in order to become eligible for referral to a treatment unit). Social workers along with other professionals in youth offending teams are also engaged in control, since they make recommendations to courts about orders and are involved in implementing those orders and reporting to the courts if offenders fail to comply.

But it is the control agent role exercised in children and families social work that is most widely known to the public at large, and the one that rouses the strongest and most ambivalent passions. After all, albeit only with the approval of a court, social workers take children away from their families, violating one of the most sacred taboos in our society: the sanctity and privacy of the family.

The fact that these powers are widely known mean that social workers have power even when they do not have a court order, as it were, in their back pockets. The multi-disciplinary arrangements under *Working Together* (DfES, 2006) create an environment – case conferences, core groups, strategy meetings – in which parental behaviour is placed under scrutiny and parents are expected to comply with the child protection plans put in place by the multi-agency system. Such plans do not, in themselves, have statutory force but almost every parent will be aware that failure to comply places them at risk of being taken to court. And we should note that, while this is a multi-agency system, only social workers can take on the key worker role of co-ordinating the overall effort.

There is no doubt that, among the caring professions, social work does have a particularly strong 'control agent' strand. Because we are uneasy about this, we are inclined to downplay it and minimise the extent to which our activities are actually about exercising control. This is a mistake. The exercise of control is often entirely justifiable, but unless we acknowledge when are doing it, we cannot have the conversation about when it is justifiable and when it is not, and we may exercise control unnecessarily. As Kerstin Svensson observes:

Does the positive understanding of being a social worker help conceal the controlling and normalising actions taken? Which actions can be performed in the name of good social work when control is ignored, separated and rewritten? Are actions actually good because they result from an individual's good character? Who decides which characteristics are good in social work? If we do not keep questions like this alive in everyday social work, there is a risk that social work will contain much more control than we are aware of.

Svensson, 2009: 246

ACTIVITY 5.4

Looking at the area of social work with which you are most familiar, consider to what extent a control agent role is part of the social work task. Do you think social workers are always aware of the extent to which they are engaged in control? How do you think the existence of the control agent role impacts on the relationship between social worker and service user?

The control agent role and direct work

The control agent role undertaken by social workers is important. Some people cannot take full responsibility for managing their own lives, either because of their own capacity (people who cannot think clearly as a result of mental illness or dementia, people with profound learning difficulties . . .) or because of their powerless position (children, frail elderly people who may be unable to stand up to abusive carers . . .) or both. It is appropriate that powers should exist to intervene in order to protect such people, and/or to act to prevent them from endangering others, in certain clearly defined circumstances. However, in all areas of social work, the existence of the control agent role has the potential to cast a shadow over other roles. This is particularly the case in relation to the direct work role, since direct work – and certainly direct work of a counselling or therapeutic kind – is generally agreed to work best in an atmosphere of trust, confidentiality and what Carl Rogers called 'unconditional positive regard' (Rogers, 1967: 47).

Rogers suggested that it was important in a therapeutic relationship to convey 'a warm acceptance and prizing of the other person as a separate individual' (Rogers, 1967: 38). It is important that social workers attempt to give this message to service users in *any* context – social workers are certainly not there to pass judgement on anyone's value as a human being – but it is much harder to give this message convincingly when you are also (for example) involved in a court case where you are arguing that this person is not parenting her child adequately. In such a context it is, of course, also much harder to *receive* such a message. While it should still be possible for the social worker to convey to the service user that she is respected as a person, it is perhaps asking too much of both service user and social worker to expect them to establish the kind of context that is necessary for direct work of a therapeutic kind. And if this is the case in respect of the extreme situation in which the social worker and service user are on different sides of a court case, then we need to ask ourselves also whether it may be the case too in somewhat less extreme situations:

- The social worker is key worker under child protection procedures and has recommended that a child's name be made subject to a child protection plan.
- The social worker has expressed some concerns about the service user's parenting. The social worker has not invoked child protection procedures or legal proceedings, but the service user is aware that these possibilities exist.
- The social worker has not expressed any concerns about the service user's parenting, but the service user is aware that the social worker is employed by a child protection agency.

These examples come from children and family work and I suggest that conflict of roles is particularly acute in this area because, in this field, social work agencies are simultaneously placed in the position of being the agency on whom primary responsibility is laid for exercising control over families, *and* the agency primarily responsible for *bringing about change* in families. Nevertheless the clash between control agent and other roles is undoubtedly felt in other specialisms as well.

ACTIVITY 5.5

(a) Suppose that you are a parent under a great deal of stress. You have on several occasions felt a murderous rage towards your children and you are genuinely frightened that you may hurt them. How willing would you be to disclose these fears to an independent counsellor? And how willing would you be to disclose them to a child protection social worker?

(b) Suppose that you have recurring mental health problems and have been detained in a mental hospital in the past. Suppose you become aware that certain frightening and delusional ideas are becoming more and more insistent in your mind. How willing would you be to disclose this to an independent counsellor? How willing would you be to disclose this to a social worker who had applied for you to be detained under section in the past?

Commentary

(a) People can and do disclose such feelings to social workers, but you will probably agree that many people would be more reluctant to talk to a social worker about such things than they would be to talk to an independent counsellor, because of a fear that the social worker would take away the children, or a fear that in some other way the social worker would *take over*.

(b) Clearly if detention under the Mental Health Act had not been a positive experience, you would be extremely wary what you told the social worker who had put you in that position.

Implications for assessment

Most of us are wary what we tell people who we perceive to have power over us and are reluctant to disclose private, personal information about ourselves unless we trust the person we are talking to and are confident that the information will go no further without our permission. Since part of the assessment process consists of information-gathering, assessment is unavoidably compromised when the person carrying it out is perceived to be in a position of power, or is perceived not to be able to keep the information to herself even if asked to do so. Both these circumstances apply when the social worker is acting in – or could move into – a control agent role. (We should note in passing that these circumstances apply too if the worker is acting in a gate-keeping role). We cannot expect completely open communication under such conditions and we should be very careful not to leap into labelling service users as 'unco-operative', 'unwilling to engage', 'anti-authority' and so on, if they are cautious about, or resistant to, sharing information.

When working with a child protection social worker, a service user – parent or child – *should* be able to be confident that her social worker will not gossip about her case to friends or to other clients. But, that aside, she cannot be given any guarantee of confidentiality as this would normally be understood, for the worker can give no undertaking that she will not disclose information about the case to other people. On the contrary, she is obliged to record the substance of what a service user says to her in files to which others have access. She is obliged to discuss the content of her conversations with the service user with her supervisor (who in turn must pass on any concerns she may have to *her* own supervisor). In the event that the social worker is told things that raise child protection issues, even only tentatively, then she will have to discuss these with professionals from other agencies. If the matter comes to a case conference or a court, the social worker is obliged to include any salient information from her files in her reports. So, for instance, if a parent tells the social worker that she sometimes feels like killing her child, she may later have to hear the social worker talk about this in front of a dozen professionals in a case conference, or read it in a statement prepared by the social worker for a court.

In an introductory handbook on counselling, Milne (2002: 10) writes: 'Generally speaking, whatever theories the counsellor is familiar with . . . the basic requisites are the same. These are that the counsellor provides an environment of privacy, safety and assured confidentiality, is non-defensive and shows respect for the client at all times.' This is clearly not an environment which a child protection social worker can create, at least in respect of privacy, safety and assured confidentiality.

Nor is loss of privacy by any means the only implication of disclosing a piece of information to a social worker. A teenager who is being sexually abused might wish to find a professional with whom she can discuss the situation and decide, within the safe confines of that professional relationship, what she ought to do next. However a social worker cannot offer that safe space (and nor actually can any other professional involved in the child protection system). Having heard an allegation of sexual abuse the social worker has no choice but to act on it. There are people to whom the social worker *must* talk, systems that *must* be set in motion . . . The teenager will find that, having spoken of her abuse to a social worker, the question of what to do next is largely taken out of her hands. It is a very far cry from a truly confidential counselling service such as is offered by, say, the Samaritans, set out in the following statement:

Statement to Callers About Samaritans' Confidentiality Policy

Samaritans would like to reassure its callers about our confidentiality policy.

At Samaritans we believe that everything our callers tell us, including the fact that they have contacted us, is confidential to Samaritans.

This means we can't talk to anyone outside of the organisation about anything we hear.

Samaritans' concept of complete confidentiality means that we do not disclose information that has been divulged by a caller, even if the caller remains anonymous.

Why do we have a confidentiality policy?

We believe our confidentiality policy encourages people to talk to us.

If people thought their information would be passed on to another source, there is a strong chance that they would not be honest about how they are feeling.

It is the act of speaking the seemingly unspeakable that can offer huge emotional release, reduce distress and help people to think through their options and see another way forward.

By taking away confidentiality, we risk someone not talking at all. By taking away the opportunity to talk, emotions can spiral out of control and there is a danger of closing the gap between thought and action, between suicidal feelings and the possibility of a suicide attempt.

Samaritans, 2010

The basic conditions for a counselling relationship quoted above from Milne (2002) included *safety*. If you make a disclosure only to find that you have started off an intrusive process over which you have no control, this is likely not to feel safe at all. Indeed Roland Summit (1983) went so far as to describe a specific 'Child Sexual Abuse Accommodation Syndrome' under which children who have disclosed abuse experience such a frightening loss of control as a result that they then retract the allegation as a means of re-establishing some control.

One could make out a good case for requiring social workers to caution their clients at the beginning of an assessment in the manner of the police: 'You have the right to remain silent, but anything you say will be taken down and may be used in evidence.' Even though a caution like this is not given in so many words, it is important to be honest with service users about the true position and important to be aware that service users are understandably cautious about what information they are prepared to share and what information they will keep to themselves.

Of course the control agent role does not impact only on the service user's handling of the assessment relationship. It also inevitably impacts on the social worker. A child protection social worker investigating alleged abuse clearly cannot necessarily go at the client's own pace. Inconsistencies must be challenged, awkward questions asked. A social worker investigating abuse cannot simply be accepting of the service user's 'world and himself as he sees them' (Rogers, 1967: 38) but must be suspicious and even confrontational. (Social workers are frequently criticised, followed child abuse tragedies, for not being sufficiently suspicious, or challenging, notably in the case of 'Baby Peter'). The same is true to varying degrees for social workers operating in other areas: in drug and alcohol services, for example, or in agencies that work with adult offenders, or in aspects of mental health work.

ACTIVITY 5.6

Before reading further you might like to pause and consider your own experience of social work. How is the assessment process affected, in your experience, by the existence of social work's 'control agent' role? How do service users respond to questioning by social workers?

Implications for intervention

The control agent role casts a shadow over the assessment process in social work, because it creates an understandable reluctance on the part of service users to engage in open communication. Open communication is not just important for assessment purposes but for any direct work intervention. We have already discussed the ways in which, because of her control agent 'hat', the social worker cannot adopt the conventional stance of the counsellor or therapist on going at the client's own pace and

respecting the client's own choices, and cannot offer privacy, confidentiality and safety in the way that these are normally understood. A child who discloses abuse will find that a process of intervention starts to unfold from that point, whether she wanted it to do so or not. In the mental health field a client who admits to the recurrence of delusional ideas may likewise find that processes are set in motion over which she has no control.

Can a social worker in a control agent role also undertake useful direct work? My suggestion would be that it is still possible for a social worker in a control agent role to undertake useful direct work with a service user, but that it is important to be clear that this is very different to direct work as this is generally understood. The temptation for a social worker can be to minimise this difference and to draw a veil over her control agent role, in an effort to give a sense of confidentiality and safety for the client *which is in fact spurious*. Helen McClaren (2007) found, in an Australian study, that a large proportion of social workers did not honestly forewarn service users that they would be obliged to report and act upon disclosures of abuse, either for fear of upsetting the service user, or to avoid feeling uncomfortable themselves.

This is a strategy which is likely to backfire, though, since if the social worker has not been honest from the outset about her dual, or multiple, roles, then the sense of betrayal will be all the greater on the part of the service user at a later date when the social worker has to suddenly switch to a control agent role. In any case, it is unethical for a social worker to lie to service users, even if this is allegedly to spare the service user's feelings. It is commonly said that information is power. Misinformation, by the same token, is profoundly disempowering. If the fact is that you will have to breach confidentiality if any child protection issues come up, then the service user needs to know that. Whether our current system is too preoccupied with information-sharing is another question (see, for example, Munro, 2007): the fact is that we must operate in, and be honest about, the system that actually exists.

However by being very clear from the outset about her different roles and her responsibilities, it is often possible for the social worker to establish a working relationship of trust and respect, albeit of a limited kind, and to be able to work with a service user on specific problems.

Establishing clear ground rules, in other words, is key to working successfully in a context like child protection or mental health where the social worker may have no choice but to hold a control agent role while at the same time trying to enable the service user to make changes in their life. These ground rules – and it is helpful to put them in writing because people do not always retain everything they hear, specially when distressed – should include a statement about the limits to confidentiality and about the circumstances under which the social work might intervene using statutory powers. A social worker in this context cannot offer unconditional confidentiality but can offer openness and honesty. These are qualities which, in my experience, are very much valued by service users. The message can be reinforced by ensuring that the service user is kept up to date with what is going on and by, for instance, sharing case recording with the service user so that she can see for herself what is going into the file.

Some ethical considerations

If combining a control agent role with elements of a direct work role is difficult for social workers, we should be careful not to forget that it may be much more difficult for the service user on the receiving end. I suggest that if counselling or therapeutic work is to be included in a Child Protection plan, or any other kind of care plan with which a service user is required to comply, then service users should have some choice as to who they do that work with. If they feel uncomfortable about doing the work with the social worker who, as key worker, is also monitoring their performance, then this should be respected. Since the social worker cannot offer what is normally regarded as an environment conducive to counselling, the service user should not be labelled as unco-operative if she does indeed feel that what the social worker can offer is not for her.

One strategy to deal with dual roles is to split the task, with one social worker taking on most of the control agent functions while another worker offers the direct work role. If both workers are from the same agency, however, it is unlikely that they will not talk to each other and co-ordinate their efforts and it remains important to be honest about this, otherwise the kind of 'spurious safety' and 'spurious confidentiality' that we mentioned earlier is simply being reproduced in another

form. Even if the two are from different agencies the multi-agency system means that they are likely to be linked in the same information-sharing and decision-making network. If tasks are to be split, then the nature and limits of that split should be made clear and not used manipulatively and dishonestly in a sort of social work version of the 'good cop bad cop' routine.

When social workers embark in direct work akin to counselling and therapy they sometimes forget that this sort of work is a highly personal matter. What is helpful to one person is profoundly unhelpful – even damaging – to another. Few of us would be willing to enter into a counselling or therapy as a client (even in an entirely 'safe' and 'confidential' context) without being able to choose who we entered into it with. I suggest that a social worker should never use her 'control agent' powers to force a service user to enter into a counselling or therapeutic work relationship.

Roles and relationships

I will conclude this chapter with one final point about the different roles that social workers play and their consequences. We have seen that being a social worker is not a single homogeneous activity, but involves playing different roles that may not sit easily together. One result of this is that being a service user is not a single experience either. The existence of the control agent role, as well as the power that social workers acquire through their other roles (for example the power to access resources that is characteristic of the gate-keeper role) mean that service users may have one of a number of different kinds of working relationship with social workers, as summarised in Table 5.2.

In recent times, social work discourse (both in academic texts and in government publications) has focused a great deal on the need to make services more responsive to, and more led by, service users themselves. The impetus for this has tended to come from disability services and mental health services, two fields in which it is often entirely possible to envisage service users having a 'service requester' relationship with social care agencies (subject to issues about capacity that apply in some cases). In this sort of context, it does indeed make sense to move towards services which service users can shape for themselves, just as we shape other aspects of

Table 5.2:   Varieties of Service User Relationship with Agency

---

Service requester: the service user has engaged with the agency entirely of their own choice, and is free to end the relationship whenever they choose.

Supervisee: the service user is subject to some control by the agency, explicitly legitimated by the service user's perceived capacity to harm others (this might be the case with a parent whose children are subject to a child protection plan, or a person with mental health problems thought to pose a risk to others, or a young offender subject to a supervision order).

Protectee: the service user is subject to some control by the agency, explicitly legitimated by the service user's perceived vulnerability and lack of ability to protect themselves (this might be the case with a small child on a care order, or an elderly person suffering from dementia, or a person with profound learning disabilities).

Nominal service requester: although ostensibly able to choose whether to work with the agency or not, the service user does not actually feel that he or she has a choice, whether as a result of fear of the consequences of not going along with what the agency wants, or for fear of losing needed support.

---

our lives to suit our needs. We can choose what kind of TV set we want, and do not expect to have a TV foisted upon us that is not to our liking. Why should the same not be true of social care services that impinge on our lives in much more personal ways that any TV set?

However when it comes to service users who have a 'protectee' or 'supervisee' relationship with agencies, the issue becomes more complex, for, as Hugh McLaughlin observes, where there are issues of risk to vulnerable people, 'there is a point in social work practice whereby the social worker is expected to act on their own professional assessment of the situation, informed by agency policy, legal mandates and research, irrespective of what the service user's choices or views are' (2009: 1109). In other words, the analogy of choosing a TV set no longer applies, and a different set of working relationships come into play. As McLaughlin notes, the representative service users who participate in social work courses are rather less likely to come from the groups which tend to have more of a 'protectee' or 'supervisee' relationship with social work agencies:

> *Within social work education ... courses are required to involve service users in all aspects of the new social work degree and post-qualifying framework. But which service users are expected to be involved? For example, are courses to encourage those convicted of sexual crimes to become involved in admissions or parents whose children have been compulsorily removed to assess child-care assignments?*
>
> ibid, 2009: 1109

I do not want to imply here that 'protectees' and 'supervisees' are, so to speak, a different species

from 'service requesters', for people typically move between these different relationships (a person who suffers from psychotic illness may be a protectee during acute psychotic episodes, but a service requester at other times, for instance). The point I wish to make is that the exercise of control means that, at any given point in time, many service users are not service requesters, and that is misleading to talk about them as if they were.

As we have seen, sometimes the exercise of control can be justified (as least to the satisfaction of most commentators) in terms of protecting the vulnerable, and if this is indeed the case, it is not necessarily unethical on the part of social workers to work with some service users as protectees or supervisees. I do suggest, though, that we need to honest with ourselves about our exercise of these powers and be very conscious of the *fourth* category in my table, the 'nominal service requesters', for this category will not even be visible to us as social workers if we go into denial about our controlling role. If we do not realise how powerful we may seem to others, and what effect this has, we may very easily fail to see that people who apparently work with us out of free choice, do not in fact feel that they have a choice at all.

Being honest with ourselves and with service users about the roles we play and the limits of each, it seems to me, is the key to the business of juggling different roles which may not always sit easily together. Social work tends to speak a great deal about advocacy and direct work, and not very much at all about controlling and gate-keeping. This silence does not make these less palatable roles go away. On the contrary, it lets them undermine our other roles even more than would be the case if we spoke more honestly about them.

Chapter summary

This chapter has looked at the difficult combination of roles that social workers typically have to play and considered the contradictions that exist between them. I suggested that the main roles could be categorised as:

- *Advocacy*
- *Direct work*
- *Executive roles, including:*
  - *gate-keeper*
  - *care manager/care co-ordinator*
  - *responsibility holder*
  - *control agent*
  - *multi-agency co-ordinator/keyworker*
  - *service developer*

I considered the conflicts that can arise between the direct work role and the care management and gate-keeping roles, potentially resulting in one undermining the other. I also discussed the conflict between advocacy and gate-keeping roles, before moving on to look at the control agent role in particular, cautioning against a simplistic assumption that the control agent role is necessarily oppressive or that other roles necessarily are not.

Looking at the control agent role in more detail I briefly considered what it involves in different areas of social work, including child and family social work, which is probably the area of social work where the statutory powers of social workers are most widely known.

I then considered the ways in which a control agent role clashes with the direct work role. I discussed the implications for assessment, pointing out that information-sharing is inevitably compromised by the existence of a social worker's statutory powers. The same is true in respect of social work intervention. A social worker with 'control agent' responsibilities cannot offer the privacy, confidentiality and safety that would normally regarded as appropriate in a counselling or therapeutic relationship. Useful direct work *can* still take place in this context, but only if the ground rules are clearly spelled out.

The chapter concluded with a brief discussion of the different relationships that service users are placed into in relation to social work agencies, as a result of the different roles played by those agencies, with some service users having an entirely voluntary relationship, others being subject to some control as a result either of their perceived vulnerability or the risk they are perceived as posing to others. There is also a large category of people who, while nominally free to choose whether to work with an agency, in fact feel they have little choice. Honesty with ourselves and others about roles would help to minimise the likelihood of people falling into this group, and would make it easier to juggle different roles effectively.

CHAPTER 6

Working with Limited Resources

Learning objectives

- Recognise the central importance of decisions about resources, both time and money, in social work assessment and intervention.
- Understand some of the philosophical principles and dilemmas involved.
- Understand the fundamental difference between public services and private organisations, and the reasons that rationing (or targeting) of resources is typically unavoidable in the former.
- Recognise the traditional split of responsibility for resources and casework between management and practitioners, and consider alternatives such as 'social work practices' and individual budgets for service users.
- Recognise possible areas of waste in social work organisations and develop an understanding of the concepts of economy and efficiency.

Introduction

The existing social work literature, both on assessment and on intervention, often seems to place surprisingly little emphasis on the issues associated with managing within limited resources. Yet one of the main purposes of many social work assessments is to determine a service user's eligibility for the allocation of specific resources and to determine the priority to be given to the service user's case vis-à-vis the cases of other service users.

Some of the most difficult ethical judgements made by social workers concern the allocation of resources. As Russell Hardin observes, 'ought implies can. If it is impossible for you to do something then it cannot be true that you ought to do it' (1990: 529). Since the limited time and resources available to us means that we cannot do everything we might like to do, professionals such as social workers 'must be concerned with the fairness of their services and with making a reasonable trade-off between competing, honourable ends' (1990: 540).

When a social worker in a children and families team undertakes an initial assessment or core assessment of need, she is not simply assembling a picture of a family's needs, she is also determining whether those needs fall within the brief of her agency to meet, and, if so, how those needs should be measured against the competing claims of other service users for the limited time and resources of her agency. The same is true of an assessment carried out by a social worker in a team whose brief is the social care needs of elderly people. The social worker will be required to come to a view as to the service users' eligibility or otherwise for varying levels of service provision. Both of these examples relate to formal assessment processes, but even the most informal decision-making processes carried out by social workers require constant judgements to be made about resources. Even simply deciding how to allocate one's limited time between different cases is a resource allocation process that is no different in principle from deciding, say, how to allocate limited funds available for domiciliary care.

Nor are resource issues relevant only to our thinking about the assessment process. Responsible planning of interventions cannot take place in some theoretical vacuum, but must take into account the availability of resources. Clear, realistic thinking about resources is not, as we might sometimes feel, a distraction from the *real* business of social work, but a core part of the job in all of the following ways:

- Decision-making about the allocation of resources is one of the main purposes of assessment in many circumstances.
- Negotiation over scarce resources where there are competing claims is a crucial social work role and an essential part of care planning.
- Making decisions about the best way of deploying resources are a key responsibility of any social work agency, statutory or voluntary.
- Any responsible intervention requires that adequate resources are properly secured in order to be able to carry the intervention through.
- Even in allocating her time between different cases on her caseload, or between different tasks, a social worker is involved in deciding

between competing claims on resources (as noted above).

Social work's involvement in rationing

The language of government guidance requires us to target resources at those most in need . . . Targeting is rationing dressed up in more acceptable language.
Bamford, 1993: 35

Social work – like other public services – are *necessarily rationed*, though words like 'targeting', 'eligibility' and 'prioritisation' tend to be used. This is true both in the state sector and the voluntary sector because supply is limited by the resources available and cannot expand to meet demand unless additional resources are provided. If you were running a commercial organisation (let us say a biscuit factory) increased demand on your services would generate new income for you and – in due course – allow you to take on additional staff or purchase additional manufacturing plant to meet the demand. But if you are part of a team of social workers delivering, say, a children and families social work service to a given neighbourhood, then, even if demand increases, you will have to continue to manage among yourselves all of the referrals on children and families that come from that neighbourhood. Increased demands on the services of your social work team will not generate new income and, unless you can persuade your employers to provide you with additional resources, you will still have to manage the new demand within the team.

So, although additional demand is good news for a private company, for a public service it may be an additional source of stress and create increasing difficulties in providing an adequate service. As Norman Flynn (2007: 5) observes, 'one characteristic makes the management of public services different in principle from managing private services: the fact that they are not actually sold to people at a price that yields a profit and are not withheld from people who cannot afford them.'

However we are living in a time when public services are constantly being encouraged to imitate private business. Social work students born in the 80s or 90s probably get irritated by the frequent references in social work texts written by middle-aged academics (like the authors of this book) to how different things were back in the 70s. The 1970s were certainly no golden age (however they may sometimes seem in memory

to those who were young then) but it really is the case that a fundamental change occurred at the end of the 70s in terms of the political context within which public services operated, including health, education, the police, housing and social security, as well as social work and social care.

In discussing the new era that began with the election of Margaret Thatcher's government in 1979, writers on social policy speak of 'new public management' (NPM) or 'new managerialism' to describe the ethos under which managers of public services have been expected to make their agencies more 'businesslike' and more like commercial organisations. Among the characteristics of this approach listed by Massey and Piper (2005: 5) are the following (I have not used their exact wording, except in the passages given in quotes, and have added my own examples and comments in brackets):

- A concern about the growth of government (this may include rhetoric about 'rolling back the state', 'cutting red tape' etc.).
- An interest in privatisation and in marketisation, the latter referring to the tendering out of public services (many services formally provided directly by local authority social care agencies are now commissioned from private providers).
- Emphasis on improving the efficiency, effectiveness and economy of public services.
- Breaking up of large bureaucratic organisations into 'discrete single-purpose agencies' (for example: the breaking up of the NHS into autonomous 'trusts', the facility for schools to become 'academies', free of direct control by local education authorities).
- Emphasis on 'the role of the individual citizen as a consumer of services' and on delivering 'greater value, choice and accountability to the individual citizen' so that the concern is 'to empower citizens as individuals, but not as a "collectivity"' (this includes describing citizens as 'customers' or 'consumers' of public services).
- 'Explores new structures of government and service delivery based on the best practice of the private sector and involves the private sector wherever possible' (for example as sponsors of the academies discussed above).

All this is now such a familiar and accepted part of the discourse of all the major political parties in the UK, that some readers may be surprised to learn that this approach to the delivery of public services is only a few decades old. The trouble is that the constant emphasis on making the public sector (including social work and social care services) more like the private sector, misses out on the core difference.

The need to ration represents a fundamental point of difference between public services and private companies but, for whatever reason, there is a widespread reluctance to acknowledge this and a tendency to speak and act as if this was not the case. An example which I often use (because it is a very influential document in the social work field) is Lord Laming's report on the Victoria Climbié tragedy. In this report, Laming criticised social services departments for seeming to 'spend a lot of time and energy devising ways of limited access to services, and adopting mechanisms to reduce service demand' (2003: 11) and yet he also specified that no case should be allocated to a social worker 'unless and until his or her manager ensures that he or she has the necessary training, experience and time to deal with it properly' (2003: 377). How do you manage workloads without managing demand? Given that their resources are finite and their staff human, social work agencies have no choice *but* to limit access to services – and can only hope to do so as fairly and as humanely as possible.

Rationing in voluntary organisations

Most of the discussion in this chapter will relate to statutory agencies. Certainly it is in the statutory services that we characteristically see elaborate bureaucratic filtering mechanisms intended to ration out resources on the basis of risk and need. These tend to be much less evident in social work agencies run by the voluntary sector, especially in the smaller local agencies. But rationing does occur in the voluntary sector too. The reason that rationing is less evident in the voluntary sector is that voluntary agencies are not required to provide a universal service and can therefore control their workload in other ways. For example:

- By dealing only with a small and specific client group (*for example: a mental health day centre that offers an open door service to people with mental health problems in a small market town*). Because they do not have to make service users jump through elaborate hoops, in the form of assessments of need and eligibility, such services may feel much more user-friendly than many statutory services.

- By taking on a fixed number of cases at any given time (*for example: a family assessment unit that takes on x number of families for an agreed period of time*), after which they are simply 'full' and do not take on any new work until a vacancy arises. Because they can control the type and/or amount of work that they take on in ways like this, voluntary agencies may be able to do a much more thorough job than statutory agencies. And, unlike statutory agencies, voluntary agencies operating on this kind of basis can proceed with their work without there being a risk that at any moment an even higher priority piece of work will come along requiring them to drop what they are already doing.

- Service level agreements under which voluntary agencies to take on tasks on behalf of statutory agencies specify the type and volume of work to be taken on.

For these kinds of reasons voluntary agencies may be able to offer better services in many respects than statutory ones, but it is important to bear in mind that it is the existence of the statutory services (as a 'safety net' to pick up those cases which fall outside their brief) which makes possible this distinctive role for voluntary agencies.

ACTIVITY 6.1

In the contexts where you have seen social work practised:

1. What mechanisms existed to determine how resources should be allocated between different cases?
2. What proportion of social work time was taken up with servicing these mechanisms? For example by writing reports for and attending panels whose purpose was to determine how resources were allocated – or filling out forms intended to establish eligibility.

The manager-practitioner split

On the whole, books about social work practice do not discuss resource management very much and this reflects the traditional division that occurs, not only in social work agencies but in other public services too, in which resource decisions are made by managers while casework decisions, such as decisions about intervention strategies, are made by practitioners. The traditional division, in which managers deal with resources and practitioners deal with casework,

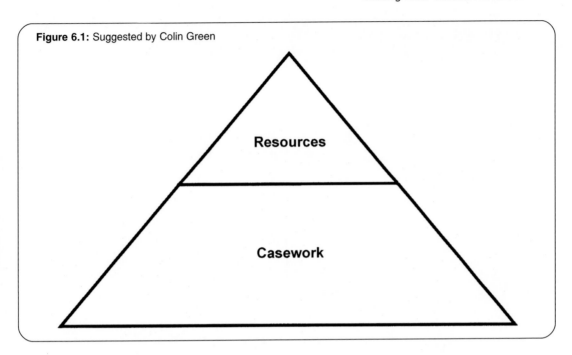

Figure 6.1: Suggested by Colin Green

has some advantages for those involved. Being a little cynical, one could say that it allows front-line practitioners to blame their managers for not making resources available to service users ('I'd provide this service to everyone if it was down to me, but all my managers seem to think about is money!') and it allows managers to blame practitioners for pieces of casework that go wrong and/or to dissociate themselves from the day to day contact with human distress. The Climbié report, for instance, comments (in paragraph 1.26) on the ways in which senior managers attempted to distance themselves by saying, for instance, that their role was 'strategic' and that they were not responsible for the 'day-to-day realities'. (Lord Laming, 2003: 5). But in fact resource decisions and casework decisions are closely inter-related: neither type of decision can really be made without reference to the other.

It is worth asking the question as to whether the traditional split of responsibilities between managers and practitioners, which could be represented by Fig. 6.1, is necessarily the best way of running a social work agency. As we've seen, it does have the benefit to both front-line staff and managers of reducing anxiety by allowing responsibility for some painful decisions to be pushed away onto others. McCaffrey (1998) relates this division to the psychological defence against anxiety known in Freudian and Kleinian psychology as 'splitting', and suggests that it is likely to be harmful because it allows front-line workers and managers respectively to project negative, uncomfortable aspects of their job onto one another. McCaffrey suggests that it would be better therefore to try as far as possible to 'heal the unconscious splits' which 'would mean that the rationing task *and* the clinical task must be held in mind at the same time' (McCaffrey, 1998: 103). In short: responsibility for managing within resources *and* responsibility for case work decisions should be taken on board by the agency at every level, as represented by Figure 6.2.

There are various ways in which this could happen. The green paper *Care Matters* (DCSF, 2006) included a proposal, taken up in the subsequent white paper, for 'Social Care Practices'. These would be autonomous organisations of social workers, analogous to GP practices, which would take responsibility for the cases of children in care contracted out to them by the local authority. It was envisaged that:

Each practice would hold a budget, provided through the contract with the authority, and would use it for individual social workers to fund the placement, support and activities that they believe 'their' children should have. Social workers would be given the autonomy and the freedom from a complex management structure needed to be able to put the child above everything else.

DfES, 2006: 35

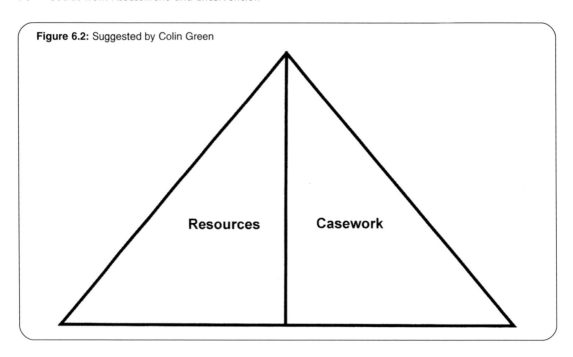

Figure 6.2: Suggested by Colin Green

Resources | Casework

Opinion has been sharply divided in the social work community about the merits of this proposal (see McGregor, 2010a, b) and, at time of writing, just five pilots are under way in various parts of England and have been running for less than a year. It is too early to really be able to judge the merits or otherwise of such a model. However it does seem to offer an example of an approach which gets away from the traditional split of responsibilities. The following describes one of the pilots, Evolve YP, set up by a group of social workers in Staffordshire:

- Fifteen people, including admin staff and a cleaner, run the practice, which offers services to 150 looked-after children and care leavers aged 12 to 21.
- Ten of the staff form a board of partners who own 52 per cent of the practice in line with government rules. They include the practice lead, who acts as a link to the council, a senior practitioner, three social workers, four personal advisers and an office co-ordinator.
- Everybody is responsible for their own caseload – the average is 15 for each social worker – but staff ensure work is shared out equally. 'You aren't just allocated a case', says social worker Paula Beesley. 'Allocations are discussed by the board and decided based on capacity and the needs of the young person.'

- It's a relatively flat management structure, but if there's a dispute the final decision rests with Donna Fallows (practice lead) who holds a full caseload as well as being the practice lead.
- The main advantage is that practitioners do not waste time chasing managers for a signature because board members can sign for each other. 'All that time spent on filling forms, waiting for managers' signatures – we don't do that anymore,' says Fallows.
- 'We're doing what we feel is right rather than thinking, "what would a manager say?" or "what would the head of service say?"' adds Beesley.

McGregor, 2010a

It may be that devolving responsibility for budgets to front line staff budgetary responsibilities to front line staff might actually promote creativity. On the other hand it is also possible to argue that in many situations the split between resource and casework decision-making are a necessary division of labour which results in a useful creative tension. And it is possible to argue that a division of labour makes everyone's task more manageable. As McCaffey (1998: 105) comments: 'Splits are to some extent inevitable and, up to a point, can be helpful in allowing different groups or disciplines to carry bearable amounts of anxiety.'

ACTIVITY 6.2

Before continuing, you might like to try and list the advantages and disadvantages of splitting resource decisions from casework decisions. In your opinion, do the advantages outweigh the disadvantages or vice versa? Would your view vary depending on the type of context and the service user group?

Individual budgets and direct payments

But if we are going to devolve budgets to practitioners, why not go one step further and devolve them to service users? Why not give service users their own budget and leave them to commission their own services rather than have to rely on a social worker do it for them? This is the idea behind Direct Payments and Individual Budgets (DoH, 2009a, b) which allow service users to organise their own care and recruit and employ their own carers.

Many service users welcome the freedom to put together their own package of care and the direct payments model seems to fit very well with the emphasis in social work on promoting user empowerment and self-determination, even though it means dispensing with part of the service normally offered by social workers. It allows the service user to purchase social care in much the same way that we purchase holidays, or houses, or TV sets or other things that we want or need in life. (As I observed in the previous chapter, we do not expect to be submitted to an assessment of our needs when we buy a TV set, or to have an expert decide what kind of TV we need!)

Of course this model is only empowering if service users are adequately safeguarded against exploitation by (for instance) relatives who might divert funds for other purposes. And it is only empowering if service users actually want to use it and do not feel that having to make their own care arrangements and employ their own carers is one more burden (Scourfield, 2007). In much the same way, some entrepreneurially minded social workers might welcome the autonomy of running their own social care practices, but others might feel that they would prefer others deal with financial matters and leave them to assess needs and identify ways of meeting them.

Competing for resources

Social work assessments of need are integral to the resource allocation process. It is assessments, and how those assessments are presented, that typically determine how large a 'slice of the cake' is allocated to each service user. In some contexts there are panels to which social workers come to present their reports and argue the case of their respective service users, in other situations it will be an individual manager who decides between competing claims presented by social workers who have carried out assessments.

It is worth considering what sort of dynamic these mechanisms create within a social work agency. Social workers who have carried out assessments are often effectively bidding against one another to obtain access to a limited pool of resources. Inevitably practitioners learn to manipulate the system to maximise the benefits to the particular service users about whom they feel most strongly. As a result the bidding process is far from being a rational way of distributing resources. For instance, service users whose social workers are skilled performers or manipulators may win out over other service users, regardless of real need. What is more, the bidding process creates a strong temptation to exaggerate the needs of some service users to obtain resources for them. This may be to their advantage in some respects, insofar as it may give them access to services that they otherwise would not have received but it may well be to their own considerable *disadvantage* in the long run if this means being labelled in some way. An extreme example of this would be if the risks to a child from a carer were exaggerated in order to obtain some resource. The parent gets the service at the expense of being labelled – on the record – a potential abuser. There is a very real danger that, in hard-pressed children and family services where cases are prioritised on the basis of risk, families may indeed end up getting unnecessarily labelled as 'child protection cases' because of this dynamic.

So a system in which social workers and others compete for limited resources by pressing the case of their respective service users does have its dangers, particularly when it operates in a context – which actually exists in most statutory agencies – where only 'at risk' cases are regarded as high enough priority to be eligible for service. It is therefore important for social workers to think about the principles that should underlie rational resource distribution so as to be able to try, as far as possible, to prevent those principles from being eroded by the exigencies of day to day practice.

ACTIVITY 6.3

Before continuing you may like to sketch out the principles under which you think limited resources should be allocated in a given social work context.

Philosophy and resource allocation

A reduction in home-help hours ... and delays in admissions to residential homes ... represent the fruits of resource decisions which have given to some while placing increased burdens on others. Decisions of such critical importance in people's lives require sound philosophical underpinning. Pragmatism is not enough.

Bamford, 1993: 34

What should determine how time and other resources are allocated? The study of philosophy may seem a far cry from the messy, day-to-day realities we have been discussing, and yet, as Girling (1993) observes, in a discussion of resource allocation in the health care field, various philosophical assumptions do underlie the different ways that these decisions are made. He adds that clinicians and managers typically start from different philosophical bases. Clinicians, he argues, tend to take a more *deontological* approach: the approach based on inherent duties and rights associated in particular with the 18th century German philosopher Immanuel Kant. Managers, by contrast, tend to take a more *utilitarian* approach: an approach based on a calculation of the benefits that will accrue from each possible course of action, an approach associated with the 18th century Scottish philosopher, David Hume. (For a general discussion on the distinction between deontological and utilitarian approaches see Beckett and Maynard, 2005; Banks, 2006).

*... if the culture of management is informed by a theoretical tradition at all, then its closest affinity is with utilitarianism. [But] the clinical culture on the other hand is much more comfortable with ... deontological concerns. **This may incidentally account for the apparent fact that managers and clinicians sometimes seem to inhabit different ethical universes.***

Girling: 1993: 41–2 (my emphasis)

An extreme example of the utilitarian approach that has been tried in the health care field is the concept of Quality Adjusted Life Years – or QALYs – which attempt to provide an objective scale for decision making between different investment options, measuring returns in terms of the patients life expectancy, adjusted for quality of life. In other words, if a given treatment

Table 6.1:   Cost per 'QALY'

Intervention	Cost in £s per QALY
Hospital haemodialysis for kidney failure	£19,000
Heart transplant	£6,700
Hip replacement	£1,030
Cholesterol-lowering diet programme	£176

From: Ovretveit, 1998: 114

or surgical procedure conferred an additional year of healthy life, then it could be said to confer one QALY. It is conferred a year of life rated at 0.5 of full life quality, then it confers half a QALY.

Using this (in theory) 'objective' measure of the benefits conferred by different procedures, it is then possible to compare the benefits of different ways of deploying resources. Table 6.1 (above) shows the cost *per QALY* of different medical procedures. You should bear in mind that the actual figures are out of date (this table comes from Ovretveit, 1998) but this is not important for the present purposes.

On the basis of the figures in Table 6.1 the most efficient use of resources is the cholesterol-lowering diet programme as every pound invested in it will be much more productive in terms of health benefits to patients, measured in QALYs, than any of the other procedures listed. On the other hand you may well argue, taking a rather more deontological approach, that anyone who is in imminent danger of dying should be entitled to every possible effort being made to save them, regardless of cost, and that society as a whole has a duty to try and save life regardless of cost.

To most people, the latter approach probably appears less cold and calculating, and therefore more attractive, than an approach based entirely on utilitarian calculation. But it does have a distinct downside. Concentrating resources on acute services means that preventative services end up being underfunded with the result that many people end up needing acute services who might not otherwise have done so. If more people went on cholesterol-lowering diets, after all, less people would *need* heart transplants.

Exactly the same dilemma exists in social work and social care, concerning the allocation of resources between acute services and preventative services. What is more, we would suggest, the same philosophical gulf also exists in social work and social care between managers and front-line practitioners ('clinicians' in Girling's account). A manager who says no to a given request for funding may feel she is doing her best to deploy limited resources to the maximum possible effect, but to a practitioner the manager may seem like a heartless bureaucrat, denying a service user a right to a better life.

Bamford (1993: 39) argues that social care provision could only be provided in a genuinely empowering way if service users were given an unambiguous legal right to a given level of service provision:

> *If there is a genuine desire to establish citizenship rights for the clients of personal social services, the stranglehold of professional discretion in determining eligibility has to be broken. Equity has to be translated into entitlement – a clear, publicly stated and legally enforceable entitlement to a given volume of service.*
>
> Bamford, 1993: 39

But this is not the case at the moment. *The NHS and Community Care Act 1990* gave a right to an *assessment*, not a right to a given level of service. *The Children Act 1989* placed a duty on local authorities to assess the needs of children and their families and provide services, but it does not specify the *level* of service. We are therefore somewhat stuck with having to decide between competing claims.

Resources and intervention

Up to now I have been discussing the question of resource allocation and its relationship to assessment. But resource considerations are equally unavoidable when making a care plan and considering what type of intervention to make. In this area too it is impossible to separate out purely 'practice' decisions from resource decisions.

In a medical context for instance, it is obvious that, in a given case, the decision as to whether to perform, say, a heart transplant should be based not only on the condition of the patient but on consideration of the resources available: the type of equipment available, the training of staff, the amount of aftercare that can be provided – and so on. It would be absurd to say 'This man needs a heart transplant and therefore that is what he must have', and then to proceed without considering all these other questions, since the chances of a successful outcome would vary from quite good to zero depending on the human and material resources to hand. Exactly the same is true of many kinds of social work interventions,

though it isn't always quite as obvious. Nevertheless in social work you will often encounter those who demand an intervention regardless of whether the resources are available to do it properly. In fact a social work intervention carried out without ensuring that the necessary resources are available is as irresponsible and unethical as – if you will forgive a rather lurid analogy – a heart transplant carried out by an untrained nursing auxiliary with a kitchen knife!

I would suggest that all social work interventions are likely to do *some* harm so that (as with surgical interventions or military ones) they are only justified if there are reasonable grounds for believing that the benefits would outweigh the harm. *Realistic consideration of the resources available should properly be part of this calculation.*

To give an instance: placing a 11 year old child with an adoptive family is a high-risk intervention (the risk of breakdown for an adoptive placement for a child at this age may be as high as 50 per cent see PIU, 2000). Any decision about whether this is a suitable plan for a given child should take into account not only the child's needs and wishes, but also factors such as:

- Availability of suitable adoptive families.
- Availability of skilled long-term support available to adoptive families.
- Availability of skilled intensive input in support of the child.
- Commitment of agency to provide adequate funding to keep this services in place, if necessary until the child is 18.

If these things are not forthcoming, it might well be the case that this is simply not an appropriate plan for the child and that other arrangements might be preferable.

There are those who might argue that every child has the 'right' to a permanent family and that therefore, regardless of resource considerations, this should be the plan. My point here is that it is not appropriate, or ethical, to lay down fixed rules for practice unless a specific resource context is specified (a point which I discuss in detail in Beckett, 2007).

ACTIVITY 6.4

Can you think of instances of interventions which should not be attempted unless adequate resources were secured in advance?

Commentary

You will probably be able to think of other examples, but it seems to me that many psychotherapeutic interventions should not be attempted unless the person carrying them out has the necessary skills and training and funding is secured to allow them to bring the process to an appropriate conclusion. What is more they should not be carried out unless adequate support is available to the user of the service, and her carers, during the difficult period while the work is underway.

Time is a resource

While management of *financial* resources is, as we have seen, traditionally the province of social work managers, day-to-day time management is a task which all practitioners need to take on board. The daily business of juggling competing demands and deciding which to respond to, which to defer and which to decline to meet, may not seem to be the same kind of activity as (say) determining how to spend the financial budget, but it is in essence exactly the same task. Just as managers allocating funds will try to ensure that limited money is used to best possible effect, so the individual social worker, deciding how to use their own time, is trying to deploy a limited resource to best effect. All the same issues that I have been discussing about resource decisions in general occur here, as it were in microcosm. (How to respond to crises without squeezing out preventative work? Whether it is right to take a purely utilitarian view or whether there are some calls on social work time that have, on principle, some sort of absolute priority?) Indeed, even to describe this sort of decision making as resource management 'in microcosm' is perhaps misleading, as it implies that it is only a minor part of the overall task. In fact the staff budget is the largest item in any social work agency's budget, so that effective use of staff time should be the single most important management priority.

However one of the problems that flow from the traditional management-practitioner split is that managers can be surprisingly indifferent to how staff actually spend their time. A social worker is given a 'case' but it is not usual for a 'budget' of time to be agreed for the social worker to deal with the case in the same way that a budget of money would certainly need to be agreed. In fact as I have observed elsewhere,

simple arithmetic places very severe restraints on what a social worker can offer:

> If a social worker has 20 families on their caseload and works a 40-hour week, they have less than two hours per week per family to spend on all the visits, telephone calls, recording, travelling, completing forms and attending meetings that each family case requires. Actual contact time with family members would, of course, be far less than two hours: I understand that one local authority in my area calculated that contact time constituted only about one-eighth of an average social worker's week, in which case two hours per week per family would translate into one hour per month of actual contact with family members. This really is not very much time in which to achieve the hugely ambitious objectives which social workers set themselves and are set by others.
>
> Beckett, 2007: 277–8

That social work *time* is just as much a limited resource as money is commonly forgotten. If social workers want to spend their agency's money in some new way then it is normal to ask where the money is going to come from and (if the budget is fixed) where savings are going to be made in order to make it available. But for some reason this sort of thinking process is often cast aside when it comes to the allocation of time. Additional tasks are given to people who are already fully occupied, the unspoken assumption being that 'they will fit it in somehow'. This is poor practice and is the basis of my criticism of the Laming report above. I would suggest that there is no merit in demanding that, for example, social worker agencies should routinely interview every child in need referred to them, unless the person making the demand can identify where the time is going to come from and (assuming that additional staff time is not going to be made available) what tasks are going to be dropped in order to create time for this new one.

In particular it is worth noting that the principle, discussed above, of not undertaking an intervention unless adequate resources are available, should apply with equal force to questions about time as it does to questions about funding (for example: funds to buy in services from external providers). In many areas of social work, extremely ambitious pieces of social engineering are attempted, of which establishing a child in a new family is a good example: arguably it is the social work analogue of a surgical transplant. It is not realistic to expect such endeavours to work without a really substantial input of time on planning, negotiation and preparatory work with all parties.

My suggestion is that, just as one would normally want to negotiate a cash budget in advance before undertaking an ambitious new project, a 'time budget' should really be agreed between a social worker and her manager before she embarks on complex, demanding and ambitious pieces of work of this kind. There are many projects which are *simply not worth doing at all* unless a reasonable amount of time is made available for them.

ACTIVITY 6.5

Can you think of other examples in your own experience of complex pieces of work which should not be undertaken unless an appropriate amount of time is made available?

Commentary

You will have thought of other examples, but the following are a few suggestions:

- Helping a person with a learning disability to move from long-term institutional care to community living, a process which requires having to relearn long-established habits and expectations. (I recall for instance an encounter with a middle-aged mildly learning disabled man who looked back nostalgically to his days in an institution from which he had been discharged and effectively left to cope on his own: theoretically 'in the community' but in practice in very miserable isolation.)
- Changing the functioning of a family which has, for several generations, been viewed by professional agencies as abusive or neglectful. (Some middle class users of private therapists think nothing of attending weekly sessions for years on end in order to resolve what may be, on the scale of things, relatively minor psychological problems: yet social workers, juggling a therapeutic role with several other roles, set themselves the task of radically changing family functioning in a few sessions.)
- Working to change long-established patterns of behaviour such as drug addiction or sexually abusive behaviour.

Avoiding waste

If it is sensible for all levels of a social work agency to take some responsibility for the management of resources then it follows that front-line practitioners, as well as managers, should ensure that resources are not wasted by being used in ways that are predictably unproductive, or in ways whose likely benefits are minimal in relation to the costs. Wasted resources are resources that are not being used for the benefit of service users.

There are many ways in which resources – both in terms of social work time and in terms of money – are commonly wasted. For instance:

- An elaborate and costly assessment process is wasteful if the outcome is really a foregone conclusion, or if the recommendations flowing from it are not likely to be carried out, or if the possible options are very limited and a decision could be made between them on much more limited information. One might ask, for instance, whether the very substantial information-gathering exercise that is entailed in carrying out an assessment under the *Framework for the Assessment of Children in Need* (DoH, 2000) is always proportionate to the often quite limited interventions that flow from it?
- As we have just discussed, many interventions are wasteful if they are not properly followed through to ensure that any change achieved is durable. (For example: sending a service user with a long history of family relationship problems on a six session anger management course and then closing his case.) Unless a realistic 'time budget' is made available to see through a task, many tasks would be better not undertaken at all, so that the time and money could be used to more effect in other ways and service users would not be set up to fail.
- Completion of elaborate paperwork is wasteful if the paperwork is not actually going to be read or used.
- An interview with a service user may be largely a waste of time (and therefore of resources) if the social worker has not adequately prepared for it and is not clear what the purpose of the interview is.
- Many meetings are wasteful if they have no clear purpose or if there is no mechanism whereby decisions made in the meeting can be effectively translated into action. (An hour's meeting attended by eight salaried employees takes, after all, eight hours of staff time: the equivalent of a whole day's work.)

ACTIVITY 6.6

In your own experience of social work what have been the main forms of waste that your have identified?

Economy and efficiency

A later chapter will discuss the evaluation of social work practice. There is an increasing emphasis on asking questions about the efficacy and performance of public services, including social work. Actually measuring the performance of public services is a complex matter, but among the criteria by which they are judged are economy, efficiency and effectiveness. Of these three, the first two both relate to the use of resources. *Economy*, in these terms, is a measure of the cost of inputs used. An organisation which is doing well on this measure will be one which obtains inputs of a given quality specification at the lowest possible cost. Consider a social work agency which is in the business of purchasing domiciliary care for elderly service users from independent providers. The agency will score well on measures of economy if it works hard to negotiate the cheapest possible rate and will score better than agencies which pay more for domiciliary care of the same specification.

Efficiency is the cost to the organisation of producing a given output. If the same outcome for a service user can be achieved in several different ways, then the most efficient way is the one that costs the least, whether the cost is measured in cash, or in time. Clearly any responsible social work agency should try to obtain the maximum benefits for its service users from whatever limited resources available and it follows that a responsible social work agency should try to be efficient as possible. Pursuing efficiency is not just some bureaucratic notion: it is, or should be, an ethical requirement.

Having said this, though, we should also note that, as we discussed, it is often a false economy to try to do tasks in too little time, or with inadequate resources, because the input then achieves nothing at all, meaning that the expenditure is entirely wasted. Investing insufficient resources to successfully complete the task in hand may superficially look like saving resources but it is in fact *wasting* resources and is extremely inefficient.

Chapter summary

This chapter has tried to introduce some ideas about resource management into the discussion about social work practice, both in relation to assessment and to intervention.

It has been argued that rationing of resources is often a key part of the social work task and that rationing per se is an inevitable part of social work not only in the public sector but also in the voluntary sector.

There is a tendency for resource issues to be set aside in discussion about social work practice. A form of 'splitting' can occur within social work agencies, as in other public services, where resource matters are in the hands of managers and casework decisions are in the hands of practitioners and we raised the question as to whether this sort of split is healthy for social work practice. The alternatives have been considered, including the radical alternative of 'direct payments' or 'individual budgets' in which the service user is given a budget from which arrange and manage his or her own care.

I have considered the dynamics of systems in which social workers are effectively competing with each other for limited resources for their clients and identified the distinct risk of negatively labelling service users.

How choices about appropriate interventions are – or should be – influenced by the resources that are available to carry them out has been discussed together with the philosophical underpinnings of resource allocation decisions and I have considered the difference between utilitarian and deontological approaches.

Time is a resource and the importance of time management and waste in social work has been considered.

Finally I noted that, when evaluating social work agencies, the way that resources are used is an important measure. I suggested that efficiency – maximising the benefit to service users that is obtained from limited resources – is, or should be, an important aim for any social work agency, but pointed out also that many attempts to save resources can be counter-productive.

CHAPTER 7

Aiming for Consistency and Fairness

Learning objectives

- Recognise the role of social worker in making decisions about priorities on the basis of levels of need, and the role of thresholds in these decisions.
- Recognise the similar decisions that are made about not only the level, but the type of response that is appropriate to different levels of risk.
- Develop an understanding of the complex nature of risk, a term which encompasses the idea of probability as well as the idea of harm. Decisions made on the basis of evaluations of risk may have poor outcomes, even if competently made.
- Be able to define true and false positives and true and false negatives, and the hindsight fallacy.
- Consider the nature of bureaucracy, and whether bureaucratic processes may have some benefits in terms of achieving consistency and equity.

Introduction

One of the main tasks of a social worker carrying out assessments is to *discriminate*. Given that it is generally agreed that social work should strive to be *anti-discriminatory*, this sounds like an odd thing to say, but there is a difference between being discrimina*tory* and being discrimina*ting*. Indeed, though both words refer to making distinctions, they are in some ways opposites. Being discriminatory means making bad judgements on the basis of irrational prejudice. The adjective 'discriminating' is often used in a positive way, referring to an ability to make fine judgements based on skill and knowledge. It would be *discriminatory* to exclude people of a particular ethnic group from receiving a service. It would be *discriminating* in a useful sense, however, to recognise that, either because of culture, or because of physical characteristics, or because of their different experiences in this society, people from different ethnic backgrounds may have different needs.

From the outset, a social worker dealing with a new case has to ask herself, 'What kind of situation is this?' Clearly it is important not to label people, or to put people into pigeonholes – we all have our own unique biography and we can all change in ways that others would never be able to predict – but if a social worker is to be able to make use of her previous experience, she *has* to be able to tentatively make links and comparisons between one service user's case and another. To give an obvious example if we know that an elderly man has been diagnosed as suffering from Alzheimer's disease we should be careful not to think or act as if this label was the only important thing about him. But nevertheless it is useful information. It tells us that he is likely to suffer from poor short-term memory and may not be able to retain things that are said to him. It tells us that one of the things we need to look at is the extent of his difficulty with retaining and processing information and the impact this has on his everyday life.

More generally workers carrying out assessments have to make – or participate in – difficult decisions about the level of service users' needs in order to determine what kind of service they will receive. This happens in two ways. Firstly, as discussed in the previous two chapters, one of the functions of a social worker carrying out assessments is to assist with decisions about rationing: that is, decisions about how an agency can best and most fairly deploy its limited resources. This requires that service users' needs be categorised in terms of *eligibility*. (Is their level of need such as to make them eligible for a service and, if so, what level of service?) Secondly, in many contexts, it is necessary to categorise service users' circumstances in terms of *risk*. (Is this a high-risk or a low risk case?) This is required not only to determine eligibility – though in circumstances of limited resources it can indeed be the case that only high-risk cases are considered eligible for a service – but also to determine the *type* of response. In children and family social work, for instance, there is a distinction to be made between 'children in need' and 'children in need of protection' and the response to the two is different, the latter typically involving the social worker playing rather more of what I have called a 'control agent' role.

So there are thresholds of need and thresholds of risk. Assessing social workers may be assigned the task, in any given case, of determining which thresholds that case has crossed and which it has not. The remainder of this chapter will look at the issues this raises.

ACTIVITY 7.1

Before going on to look at thresholds of need, you might like to consider what kind of systems, in your experience, social work agencies use to decide whether or not someone referred to them is eligible for a service?

Commentary

As discussed in the last chapter, any agency will have to set some limits on what it takes on. Large statutory agencies, with a high volume of work referred to them, may have quite formal systems (like the one I am about to discuss). These may involve tools such as charts or checklists which are used to determine the level of need against some sort of numerical scale. But this is not necessarily the case. Eligibility for service may be determined in less formal ways. For example a team may meet and go through referrals and arrive at a decision by discussing how much work they should take on, and which cases should be given priority. Or a team manager may make this decision alone, without using any formal framework. In such situations the basis on which priority is determined may be implicit rather than explicit: and even those making the decision might be hard-pressed to define precisely the criteria they are using.

Thresholds of need

Quite specific guidance is given by the government to local authorities as to how to go about determining whether adult services users are eligible for social care services. In England the government offers guidance for determining eligibility for adult social care 'in a way that is fair, transparent and consistent, accounting for the needs of their local community as a whole as well as individuals' need for support' (DoH, 2010: 9). It sets out a framework for measuring eligibility which involves categorising cases into the following four bands:

Critical – when

- Life is, or will be, threatened.
- Significant health problems have developed or will develop.
- There is, or will be, little or no choice and control over vital aspects of the immediate environment.
- Serious abuse or neglect has occurred or will occur.
- There is, or will be, an inability to carry out vital personal care or domestic routines.
- Vital involvement in work, education or learning cannot or will not be sustained.
- Vital social support systems and relationships cannot or will not be sustained.
- Vital family and other social roles and responsibilities cannot or will not be undertaken.

Substantial – when

- There is, or will be, only partial choice and control over the immediate environment.
- Abuse or neglect has occurred or will occur.
- There is, or will be, an inability to carry out the majority of personal care or domestic routines.
- Involvement in many aspects of work, education or learning cannot or will not be sustained.
- The majority of social support systems and relationships cannot or will not be sustained.
- The majority of family and other social roles and responsibilities cannot or will not be undertaken.

Moderate – when

- There is, or will be, an inability to carry out several personal care or domestic routines.
- Involvement in several aspects of work, education or learning cannot or will not be sustained.
- Several social support systems and relationships cannot or will not be sustained.
- Several family and other social roles and responsibilities cannot or will not be undertaken.

Low – when

- There is, or will be, an inability to carry out one or two personal care or domestic routines.
- Involvement in one or two aspects of work, education or learning cannot or will not be sustained.
- One or two social support systems and relationships cannot or will not be sustained.

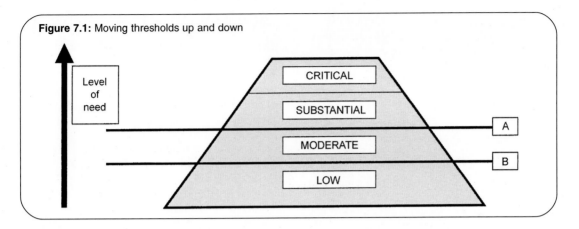

Figure 7.1: Moving thresholds up and down

• One or two family and other social roles and responsibilities cannot or will not be undertaken.

Department of Health, 2010: 21

The guidance does not, however, specify a particular level at which a service must be provided. The decision as to where this level should be set is acknowledged to be dependent on the level of resources available to the local authority concerned. But the guidance seeks to set down a way of categorising the level of need and prioritising cases.

> *In constructing and using their eligibility criteria, and also in determining eligibility for individuals, councils should prioritise needs that have immediate and longer-term critical consequences for independence ahead of needs with substantial consequences. Similarly, needs that have sub-stantial consequences should be placed before needs with moderate consequences, and so on.*
>
> (DoH, 2010: 21–2)

An eligibility threshold (or any other kind of threshold) requires a notional *scale*. The threshold of eligibility, then, is a line drawn *across* that scale. The government is choosing not to dictate the level at the which the threshold of eligibility is drawn, but is defining the scale to be used. In theory, as a result of this guidance, every local authority should assign service users with the same level of need to the same level in the scale (that is: to 'Critical', 'Substantial', 'Moderate' or 'Low'). But it still remains open to one local authority to decide that it can only meet 'Critical' needs, for instance, while another local authority might decide that it has the resources to meet 'Critical' and 'Substantial' needs. Suffolk County Council, for instance, states on its website that 'In Suffolk we can only provide services for needs

that fall within the Critical or Substantial bands. If however your needs fall within the Moderate and Low bands you will be offered information, advice and guidance as to where to obtain help.' (Suffolk CC, 2010). Fig. 7.1 illustrates this, showing the four levels of need defined by the government as four layers arranged in a pyramid (which is narrower at the top because a smaller number will have high care needs as compared to low care needs). The level at which Suffolk residents are eligible to social care is indicated by the line marked (A). An authority in which residents in the 'moderate' band were also eligible, would have the threshold marked as (B).

ACTIVITY 7.2

What advantages can you see to a standardised system such as the one I have just described as a way of determining which requests for services are met? And what difficulties can you see?

Commentary

You may have thought of others, but some of the advantages that strike me are:

• By making local authorities have an explicit 'scale' and an explicit threshold, this system promotes 'transparency'. Service users can see how it works, where they have been placed on the scale and how this relates to the eligibility criteria set by the local authority in question. (As noted earlier, many local authorities make their eligibility criteria for adult services available on the internet as well as on paper). If service users think they have been placed wrongly on the scale then they have the information they need to challenge the assessment. If service users think that the eligibility criteria are set too high then they have the information they need, as citizens, to lobby for them to change. The more informal systems which I mentioned in Activity 7.1 are less transparent and therefore harder to challenge.

- Arguably, the existence of an explicit scale and an explicit threshold makes the system less 'subjective'. Since all staff involved in determining eligibility must work to the same scales and thresholds, this should mean more consistency and therefore a fairer system. A more informal system, where criteria are not made explicit, is more open to being shaped by the prejudices of those who administer it and therefore may be more in danger of being *discriminatory*.

Disadvantages that strike me are:

- A fixed scale and a fixed threshold is rigid. It does not allow for subtleties and anomalies or for rare and unexpected situations. It limits the ability of staff to develop their own, perhaps more sophisticated ways of coming to decisions.
- Such systems are in fact much more 'subjective' than at first sight they appear. For instance, the categories within the governments four bands of risk include the following: *'there is, or will be, only partial choice and control over the immediate environment'* (one of the categories within 'substantial need'), and *'there is, or will be, an inability to carry out several personal care or domestic routines'* (one of the categories within 'moderate need'). One can imagine situations in which it would be a matter of opinion whether a person's disability placed them in the first or the second of these two categories – and yet (as we've seen) in some local authority areas this could make the difference to whether the service user gets a service or not. The system is far from immune to discriminatory prejudices creeping in and influencing the level of priority that a case is given.
- Although the 'scale' is (in theory) standardised across the country, the threshold is not. While this is the case, service users with the same level of need may or may not receive a service depending on the area where they live. When this occurs in respect of health care it is commonly described in the media as a 'postcode lottery' and is generally regarded as unfair.

Need and eligibility in children's services

The above scheme applies only to social care services for adults in the UK. The government has not laid down a comparable scheme for measuring eligibility in the case of services for children and families. But, as I discussed in the previous chapter, services to children in need and their families do also have to be rationed, and in practice a major function of social workers taking referrals and undertaking Initial Assessments (DoH, 2000: 31) is to gather information that can be used for determining which cases should be a priority when limited resources are allocated. The concept of 'eligibility' – of a specifically defined threshold above which a service user becomes eligible for a service – is not such a feature in childcare social work and is not, for instance, a topic covered *Framework for the Assessment of Children in Need and their Families* (DoH, 2000). The difference may reflect the different political context in which childcare services and services for adults operate. (There appears to be a certain coyness about acknowledging that services for children are also rationed!) However, since resources for children and families are no less finite than resources for adult care, essentially the same issues arise and you may like to consider whether services for children and families would benefit from a uniform national framework for assessing *level* of need such as exists for adults, or whether less formal (but also less transparent) methods are preferable.

Thresholds of risk

A person who is seriously at risk is, of course, also a person who is urgently in need of help. It is therefore not surprising that eligibility criteria such as we have been discussing categorise those at most risk as having the highest priority for services. However in statutory social work a decision about the level of risk does not just determine whether or not a service is offered but also the *kind* of intervention. An Approved Mental Health Professional (AMHP) making an assessment of a client under Section (2) of the *1983 Mental Health Act*, and under the *2007 Mental Health Act*, is not primarily trying to decide whether the service user should *receive* a service, since quite probably the service user will be eligible for a service whether or not the AMHP decides to make a Section (2) application. The question that the AMHP must address in this

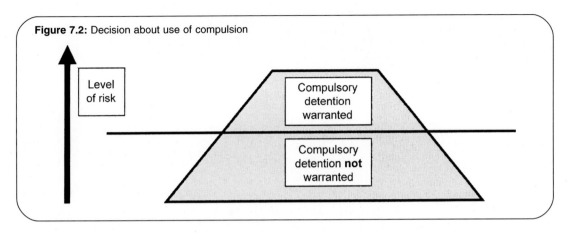

Figure 7.2: Decision about use of compulsion

Level of risk

Compulsory detention warranted

Compulsory detention **not** warranted

context is whether the service user should be offered – or continue to be offered – services on a voluntary basis, or whether the risk that the service user poses to herself or others is sufficiently grave to merit compulsory detention. The AMHP may not conceptualise it in this way, but you could say that we have a scale and a threshold again. This time, though, the scale is not level of need, but level of risk and the threshold is not a threshold of eligibility but the point at which the social worker feels that it is appropriate to move into 'control agent' mode (to return to the terminology of Chapter 4). This is illustrated by Fig. 7.2

As I mentioned earlier, in social work in the UK with children and families there is a crucial distinction between 'children in need' and 'children in need of protection', with local authorities having different duties and responsibilities in each case, defined respectively by Section (17) and Section (47) of the *1989 Children Act*. Here again is a risk threshold which does not necessarily determine eligibility for a service (though there have been times and areas where only child protection case have been regarded as high enough priority to receive services) but does determine the *type* of service. Specifically it determines whether or not the agency should move more into 'control agent' mode. This risk threshold could be represented in a diagram such as that in Fig. 7.2.

Actually in childcare social work, one could identify a number of *different* thresholds of this kind, including, for instance:

- The threshold of risk above which the names of children are made subject to a child protection plan (DfES, 2006: 133. This is of course a

multi-agency decision and not a decision made by social work agencies on their own).
- The threshold at which care proceedings are initiated (1989 Children Act Section 31).
- The threshold at which use of an Emergency Protection Order (1989 Children Act, Sections 44–6) to remove children immediately from home is considered to be warranted.

In each of these instances, guidance and legislation specifies that the test as to whether the threshold conditions are met should be based on the concept of 'significant harm', as discussed in the *Working Together* guidelines:

5.94 The conference should consider the following question when determining whether to register a child: Is the child at risk of significant harm?

The test should be that either:
- The child can be shown to have suffered ill-treatment or impairment of health or development as a result of physical, emotional, or sexual abuse or neglect, and professional judgement is that further ill-treatment or impairment are likely.

or

- Professional judgement, substantiated by the findings of enquiries in this individual case, or by research evidence, is that the child is likely to suffer ill-treatment or the impairment of health or development, as a result of physical emotional, or sexual abuse or neglect.

5.95 If the child is at continuing risk of significant harm, safeguarding the child will therefore require inter-agency help and intervention delivered through a formal child protection plan. It is also the role of the initial child protection conference to formulate the outline child protection plan, in as much detail as possible.

DoH, 2006: 128

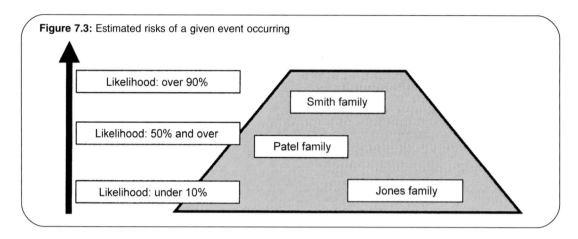

Figure 7.3: Estimated risks of a given event occurring

Likelihood: over 90%

Likelihood: 50% and over

Likelihood: under 10%

Smith family

Patel family

Jones family

'Significant harm' is not defined – and actually could not really be defined in such a precise way as to make it immune from different understandings and interpretations – but risk of significant harm is the basic criterion for registration, as it is for the making of orders under the 1989 Act.

Harm and risk

The quotation from *Working Together* just given included the phrase 'likely to suffer ill-treatment or the impairment of health or development'. This phrase encapsulates the two components that are contained within the idea of 'risk' (a topic which was discussed earlier in Chapter 3). If we are assessing the risk posed by a particular situation we are looking at:

- The harm that may result (from whatever circumstance is being discussed).
- The *likelihood* that this may occur.

Thus, although air crashes and train crashes do occur and can have fatal consequences, we do not describe air travel or train travel as high risk activities because the likelihood of a crash occurring is extremely low. It follows that when constructing a pyramid of risk as in Fig. 7.2 situations are arranged from cases at the bottom where the harmful event is very unlikely to occur, to cases at the top where the event is very likely – or even almost certain – to occur. Although in reality it is never possible to be anything like as precise as this, Fig. 7.3 illustrates this in a simplistic and idealised way for the sake of argument.

If we are carrying out a risk assessment in child protection (or in any other context), we are

seeking to come to a conclusion how likely a given set of harmful events are to occur in the absence of protective intervention. In child protection the set of harmful events we are trying to predict are the various kinds of 'significant harm' that a child may suffer. In an assessment under Section 2 of the *Mental Health Act*, the harmful events whose likelihood is being considered are the patient either harming herself or others. In theory our assessments of particular cases should allow us to be able to place them approximately in terms of such events occurring, as illustrated by the Smith, Patel and Jones families in Fig. 7.3.

ACTIVITY 7.3

- What difficulties exist in practice with trying to arrange situations accurately against a scale of risk such as that in Fig. 7.3?
- If these difficulties could be overcome and we could arrange cases against such a scale with confidence, what would remain the limitations of the scale as a decision-making tool?

Commentary

- You may have identified any one of a number of difficulties, of which some may have been:
  - Events such as 'significant harm' are not precisely defined.
  - Although there is certainly research information to draw on, there is no 'precise science' to tell us what will be the consequences of any given circumstances.
  - Human situations are extremely complex and it is never possible to know all the information.

– Every human situation is unique and therefore can only be compared in an approximate, tentative way with previous experience and research.

- Even if, just for the sake of argument, you could come up with a precise figure – such as 65 per cent – for the likelihood of a given event in a given situation this information has at least two limitations as a guide to action:
  – If an event has a 65 per cent likelihood of happening in a given situation, then it also has a 35 per cent likelihood of *not happening*. Conversely even if an event has a 99 per cent likelihood of *not happening* in a given situation, it still has a 1 per cent chance of happening. In fact there is no such thing as a zero risk situation. Accurate data about the likelihood of risk helps us to reduce the possibilities of harm happening, but it does not allow us to eliminate the possibility of harmful events. (I will explore this further shortly.)
  – Even if we have a very accurate scale, the question remains as to whereabouts on the scale to draw the threshold. Is a 5 per cent risk of significant harm sufficiently high to warrant (for instance) registration? Or should the line be drawn at 10, 20, or 30 per cent? The decision as to where to draw the threshold is a value judgement and therefore not a question which facts, however accurate, can answer. 'No amount of knowledge of what is the case can ever establish for us what we ought to do about it' (Downrie and Telfer, 1980: 22).

False negatives and false positives

The discussion so far may seem rather dry and theoretical, but we now come to a difficulty that creates very real problems for social work.

In the chart in Fig. 7.3, the situations placed at the top of the pyramid are those where the harmful event (whatever it may be!) is thought to have an over 90 per cent chance of happening. The situations placed at the bottom of the pyramid are those where this event is thought to have a less than 10 per cent chance of happening. If the risk calculation is correct it follows that, if there was no intervention, and if events were allowed to take their course, the harmful event would actually happen in more than 90 per cent of the cases at the top of the chart, but there would be small minority of cases where it would not happen. At the other end of the scale, the harmful event would also sometimes happen, but only in less than 10 per cent of cases. We could represent this by Fig. 7.4, in which the darkly shaded area represents those cases where the harmful event would actually happen if there was no intervention. Since by definition the event is more likely for high risk cases and less likely for low risk cases, the dark band gets progressively wider towards the top of the pyramid.

As I have already discussed, a risk threshold, like the eligibility thresholds that I looked at earlier, can be represented as a horizontal line drawn at a certain point on a vertical scale. The horizontal line across Fig. 7.4 represents a risk threshold. Depending on the type of harmful event that we are discussing, this could be the

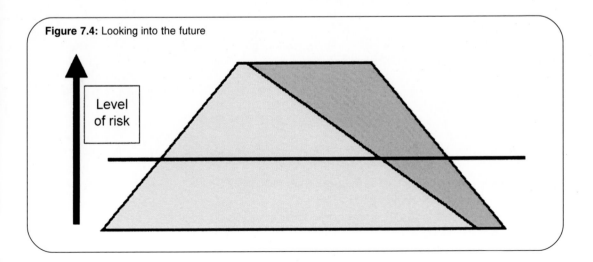

Figure 7.4: Looking into the future

Level of risk

threshold of risk at which a social workers feels that detention under the Mental Health is warranted, or the threshold of risk at which a child's name is placed on the child protection register.

What I want to draw to your attention about this diagram, however, is that, although most of the dark shading (representing cases where, if there was no protective intervention, the harmful event would actually occur) is above the threshold, there is also a substantial amount of light shading above the line. Similarly, while most of the light shading is below the threshold, there is also a small but significant amount of dark shading below the line. The dark shading below the line represents cases that are categorised as low risk but where a harmful event does actually occur. In other words they are cases where, with hindsight, we would wish that we had taken protective action even though, *on the information available* we may have been quite correct to describe them as low risk. The light shading above the line represents cases where protective action is indicated by whatever risk indicators we used to determine the level of risk, but where in fact, if protective action had not been taken, no harm would have occurred. What I am now discussing is the problem of false positives and false negatives: the false positives being represented by the light area above the threshold, the false negatives by the dark area below it. (See Table 7.1.).

Depending on the event in question, false negatives can be tragedies: a child left in the care of a parent in a situation deemed to be low risk but where the parent subsequently kills or abuses the child, a mentally ill person who an Approved Social Worker judges not to be 'sectionable' under the Mental Health Act but who goes on to (say) assault a member of the public and then commit suicide. Naturally such events are dreaded by social workers, as they are doubtless dreaded in any profession which has responsibilities for

managing risks. But we need to be clear that when such events occur, they are not necessarily mistakes and do not necessarily reflect incompetence on the part of the social worker. Any calculated risk sometimes goes the 'wrong' way. Just because such events occur does not necessarily mean that those who assigned these cases to a low risk category were wrong. (Just because it does, very occasionally, snow in June does not mean that we are wrong to predict that a given day in June will not be snowy!)

To believe that, when something like this happens it necessarily proves that a mistake has been made, is in itself a serious mistake. It is known as the *hindsight fallacy*:

> *If a decision involves risk, then even when one can demonstrate that one has chosen the unarguably optimal course of action, some proportion of the time the outcome will be suboptimal. It follows that a bad outcome in and of itself does not constitute evidence that the decision was mistaken. The hindsight fallacy is to assume that it does.*
> Macdonald and Macdonald, 1999: 22

This is not to say that actual mistakes cannot be made because of course they can. For example important pieces of evidence can be missed, or connections can fail to be made between pieces of evidence, resulting in cases being assigned to the wrong risk category. These are actual mistakes. But we should be careful to distinguish between risk indicators that should reasonably have been noticed in advance and those whose significance could not have reasonably been seen without the benefit of hindsight.

False *positives* may be no less tragic in their consequences than false negatives: a child taken away from parents with whom she would actually have grown up quite happily, a person forcibly detained under the Mental Health Act, who would actually have been alright if left in his own home . . . But since we cannot know what *would* have happened if we had not intervened,

Table 7.1:   True and false positives/true and false negatives

True positives	Situations identified as high risk where the harmful event actually occurs in the absence of protective intervention.
False positives	Situations identified as high risk where the harmful event actually would not occur even in the absence of protective intervention.
True negatives	Situations identified as low risk where no harmful event occurs.
False negatives	Situations identified as low risk, but where the harmful event does nevertheless occur.

false positives are relatively invisible as compared to false negatives. What *is* visible to all practitioners is that compulsory interventions in 'control agent' mode are distressing to all concerned and should therefore be kept to a minimum.

Where to draw the line?

In childcare social work, social workers have to deal with periodic exhortations to move thresholds in one direction or another, whether they be the threshold for initiating care proceedings or the threshold at which a child in need becomes a child in need of protection. Behind these movements of the threshold lies an awareness that both false positives and false negatives are undesirable. Unfortunately, however, there is a trade-off. If we move the risk threshold upwards we get more false negatives but *less* false positives. If we move it downwards on the other hand, we get less false positives, but more false negatives. You can see this in Fig. 7.5. If the threshold is set at level A, there are far fewer false positives than at level B. As a result setting the threshold at A would result in fewer invasive protective interventions and the service would probably be experienced as more 'user-friendly' with more 'partnership' working and less coercion. The government's 'Refocusing' initiative was an attempt to set the 'child protection' threshold at a higher level with precisely this sort of aim. But the downside of setting the threshold at level A is that you get more false negatives. You can see that, with the line at level B, by contrast you get far less false negatives, but only at the cost of more false positives.

What we need to be aware of is the fact that wherever the threshold is drawn there will be some pros and some cons – some people that benefit, some that suffer. In terms of, say, the threshold at which an Emergency Protection Order is applied for, a high threshold of intervention means fewer false positives, fewer needless intrusions into family life, but more instances where abuse carries on when it could have been stopped. A low threshold of intervention means fewer false negatives, less cases 'slipping through the net', but more intrusion into family life of a very distressing kind.

In the end, not only in Child Protection but in any field, there can be no objectively 'correct' place to draw the threshold, since any threshold is necessarily a compromise between competing benefits and disadvantages.

ACTIVITY 7.4

I have used the example of the threshold for the use of Emergency Protection Orders to demonstrate the pros and cons of setting thresholds higher or lower.

- What would be the pros and cons of setting the threshold higher or lower in respect of applications under the 1983 Mental Health Act (as modified by Mental Health Act 2007) to use compulsion to detain people in hospital?
- Going back to thresholds not of risk but of *need*, what would be the pros and cons of a local authority setting its eligibility threshold higher or lower up the scale of need?

Commentary

- A high threshold for Mental Health Act applications would mean that compulsory admission under a section of the Act became relatively rare. This is desirable from a civil liberties point of view, since it reduces the number of people whose liberties are restricted against their wishes. It would also perhaps contribute to a more user-friendly service. On the other hand a lower threshold would reduce the number of false negatives: which in this context would mean people who were not 'sectioned' but who did actually go on to harm themselves or others, or to suffer distress that could otherwise have been avoided.
- The same sort of dilemmas about setting thresholds apply to need and eligibility decisions as apply to risk. If the threshold of eligibility is set low, more people will become eligible for a service, but the available resources will be spread more thinly and less will be left for those who are in the most acute need. If the threshold is set high, by contrast, then those in

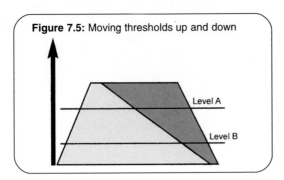

Figure 7.5: Moving thresholds up and down

Level A

Level B

the most acute need will benefit from better services but others will lose out.

Bureaucracy

The discussion in this chapter has revolved around the idea of looking at 'cases' – or situations – and placing them on a scale, whether that scale be one of 'need' or of 'risk'. But some might, with reason, object to thinking in this way. After all, what I have been called 'cases' or 'situations' in this chapter are always in fact actual human beings, or groups of human beings, struggling with some aspect of life. One of the dangers of too much preoccupation with scales and charts and eligibility criteria (or with diagrams and theoretical abstractions such as those I have offered in this chapter) is that we forget that social work agencies are not machines for processing 'cases', but collections of people whose job is to try and help other people to get their needs met.

Fears about the dehumanising consequences of too much preoccupation with procedures and systems often lie behind the complaints that are frequently made by social workers about the excessive 'bureaucracy' involved in the job. Indeed such fears lie behind the negative connotations that the word 'bureaucracy' itself possesses both within and outside of social work. These fears are surely legitimate. We have all at some times or another been at the receiving end of organisations that treat us as a 'case' or a 'number' and do not deal with us human beings.

The very idea of being able to measure a 'case' against some sort of 'scale', is perhaps in itself dehumanising. Arguably it presupposes the existence of some sort of body of 'objective' or 'scientific' expertise which is able, so to speak, to sit outside of human life and make measurements of it. Many writers about social work, specially those who are interested in 'postmodernist' ideas (for instance see Walker, 2001) would wish to challenge the validity of such a notion, which could be seen as imposing a particular kind of narrowly rational narrative on people in a way that leaves out 'local details and complexities, such as the diverse experience of people within a community' (Healy, 2005: 196).

These ideas represent important insights and important alternative ways of seeing the world. Nevertheless, there are many decisions in social work which require a yes or no answer. (Should this service user receive a slice of our agency's limited resources? Is the risk of harm posed by this situation so great as to merit the use of statutory powers to protect whoever is being placed at risk?) When answering such questions it simply is not practicable to respond to each new case as completely new and unique or to leave the decision to the service user. Equity and fairness *require* that we compare one case with another. Our responsibilities to protect the vulnerable *require* that we try and have a clear and consistent approach to assessing risk. For these kinds of tasks, I suggest, formal 'bureaucratic' structures actually have many advantages. Procedures, guidelines and clear lines of accountability do actually serve, among other purposes, the purpose of protecting service users against the whims, prejudices and arbitrary decisions of individuals. They provide some consistency and, potentially, also some clarity about what can be expected, as discussed in Activity 7.2. Bureaucracy, in short, is not 'all bad'. As Paul du Gay points out in a book entitled *In Praise of Bureaucracy* (2000):

> *The citizen who scoffs at the elaborate record keeping undertaken by government offices might well be equally annoyed should an official lose track of her affairs through relying on memory and telephone conversations. Similarly, the common complaint that government departments endlessly follow precedent might well lose its moral force if we find out that we have not received exactly the same treatment as our neighbour, friend or lover did in the same circumstances this time last year.*
>
> du Gay, 2000: 1

And he goes on to say that:

> *. . . while we may sometimes experience a sense of personal frustration in our dealings with state bureaux, we might learn to see such frustration as a largely inevitable by-product of the achievement of other objectives that we also value very highly: such as the desire to ensure fairness, justice and equality in the treatment of citizens – a crucial qualitative feature of modern government that we largely take for granted.*
>
> du Gay, 2000: 2

ACTIVITY 7.5

Think about the bureaucratic procedures and structures of a social work organisation you are familiar with. Consider:

1. What obstacles these procedures and structures place in the way of delivering a good service to the public?
2. What advantages these procedures and structures offer in terms of the service delivered to the public?

Commentary

Of course your answers will vary depending on the organisation you have in mind and on your own experience, but you may have come up with some of the following:

1. *Obstacles*:
- Scope for initiative and imagination is restricted by rules.
- Too much staff time spent on paperwork.
- Decisions are slow in being made due to having to be passed up the hierarchy.
- Service users are subjected to elaborate screening procedures and are passed between different members of staff.
- Service users are made to feel 'small' and disempowered by the organisation.
- Anomalies not anticipated by the procedures can create serious delays.

2. *Advantages*:
- Consistency of service.
- Fairness in terms of allocation of time and resources.
- Safeguards exist against dangerous or unprofessional practice by individuals.
- Speed: having set procedures for doing things saves workers form having to 'reinvent the wheel'.
- The organisation can be explicit about what it can and can't do – thus potentially empowering service users by providing them with the information they need to challenge the organisation's decisions.
- There is a clear line of accountability.

Chapter summary

This chapter has looked at a rather specialist subject: the setting of thresholds against notional scales of need and risk to determine eligibility for services and/or to determine the type of intervention. These are questions which touch on many aspects of social work as it is practised on a daily basis, especially in the statutory services.

I began by looking at frameworks to determine eligibility for services on the basis of different levels of need, considering in particular the government's current guidelines on assessing eligibility for adult care services. I noted that these systems tended to be much more formalised in the adult care field than in child care social work, though in both fields there is a similar need to ration services.

Having introduced the concept of a threshold as a notional level on a scale of need, I then moved on to look at thresholds related to risk, such as the point at which an application under Section (2) of the Mental Health Act is warranted, or the point at which a child's name should be placed on the child protection register.

The concept of risk was considered (discussed more fully in Chapter 3) and attention was drawn to the fact that risk has two components – harm and the probability that it will happen. Because risk is about probability not certainty, cases defined (by whatever measure) as high risk will include some cases where harm will not in fact happen and cases defined as low risk will include some cases where harm *will* in fact happen: these are false positives and false negatives. In human terms these translate into service users who receive a response that is not helpful and may cause harm, but it was pointed out that when this happens it does not *necessarily* mean that a mistake has been made. I drew attention to the so-called *hindsight fallacy*.

Wherever one chooses to draw the line on the scale of risk between acceptable and unacceptable risks, there will be false negatives above it and false positives below it, but the proportion of the two will vary. Deciding where to put thresholds, is a value-based decision, not one that the facts themselves can settle for us.

In conclusion, recognising that much of this chapter has addressed processes and systems that many would see as 'bureaucratic', I considered the nature of bureaucracy. It was observed that, while bureaucracy gets a bad press and can be rigid, oppressive and dehumanising, nevertheless bureaucratic systems can provide benefits too, including fairness, transparency and accountability.

Part Three:
Synthesising, Integrating and Developing Practice

CHAPTER 8

Empowerment and Socially Inclusive Practice

Learning objectives

- Illustrate the importance of anti-discriminatory practice for safeguarding children, young people and adults.
- Explain what changes can be made to contemporary practice to meet the needs of a diverse society.
- Describe the elements of socially inclusive practice and how to integrate them with legislation, agency guidelines and ethical practice.
- Understand the importance of empowering practice with socially excluded people.

Introduction

Assessment and intervention practice takes place in a context of personal or social needs mediated by factors such as eligibility criteria, legal obligation, priority and the quality and quantity of available resources in the short or long term. Social work is at the cutting edge of individuals', families and communities attempts to manage life challenges influenced by the effects of economic and social policy, welfare systems and their own internal psychological make-up. The concept of empowerment and socially inclusive practice in social work practice can therefore be seen as self-evident or problematic.

It is self-evident if we perceive people and their problems as the product of an inequitable economic system that disenfranchises the weak, vulnerable, disabled or poor from equal participation and access to the resources produced by society. The task of social work is in this context, to work towards liberating service users and empowering them to gain access to those resources. If we conceive empowerment as problematic however, we might think that it is our job to reduce expectations and accept the prevailing economic paradigm that automatically excludes sections of society from equal participation. Social work in this context becomes modest in aim and seeks to help people manage with whatever provision is offered to support them.

These two versions of how empowerment can be considered are reflected in the literature and

characterised as a radical or conservative way of conceiving the social work task (Howe, 1994; Payne, 1997; Dominelli, 1998). These simplistic dichotomies are limited in their usefulness for the modern practitioner. A more helpful device in the context of empowering practice is to think whether in practising social work you are (Trevithick, 2000):

- Doing things to service users.
- Doing things for service users.
- Doing things with service users.

Here is an example of how to ensure your practice is dis-empowering – it is a caricature of bad practice developed by Values into Action, the national campaign with people who have learning difficulties. Reflect for a moment or two and ask yourself whether any of this actually happens more, or less often in your assessment and intervention practice:

Exclude non professionals – This mustn't be done too obviously, so hold meetings at times and places which will be hopelessly inconvenient for friends and family. During working hours in a remote office with no bus service is best.
Intimidate advocates – If anyone with a personal interest in the discussion still manages to attend, ensure that they feel too uncomfortable to speak freely. Hold meetings on professional territory where there are lots of symbols of professional power, e.g. large desks, journals, and a good view of the staff car park.
Disempower the user – Don't risk the reputation of the service by excluding the user entirely (unless of course, they display challenging behaviours during the meetings, such as tearfulness or a tendency to disagree). Instead give them no time to prepare their own ideas about what kind of life they would like. Such thoughts are not helpful to sound practice.
Value all opinions – The widest range of viewpoints is recommended. Ideally participants should be total strangers with no shared value system.
Keep the meeting short – Thirty minutes is quite long enough to plan the life of any service

user. Ideally, ensure a prompt finish by either (a) planning the meeting just before a union meeting on threatened staff cuts; or (b) doing a batch of six assessments/reviews in one morning.

Stick to procedures – Use as many standard forms and checklists as possible, in different colours and using strange language. This has added benefit of giving people the feeling they are doing something really skilled and professional.

Be resource-driven – Whenever possible, ensure that needs are defined to match the resources available. Alternatively, identify a need for resources which are not available and under the control of another agency, so that everybody can just blame them.

Be objective – Always focus on needs, problems and deficiencies, and disregard any of the assets of the person or their community. Never, ever, dare to dream about people finding an escape from the service system to a life of freedom, dignity, and citizenship.

The term social inclusion has gained rapid acceptance within the social work lexicon at the beginning of the 21st century. It began to appear prominently in political discourse in the UK following the election of a Labour government in 1997 which regarded social exclusion as an impediment to its vision of a more open and equal society concerned with social justice as well as economic progress (Walker, 2003). The concept of social exclusion has its origins in France in the 1970s where the idea of citizenship and social cohesion highlighted the plight of *Les exclus* who were relegated to the margins of society (Barry and Hallett, 1998; Pierson, 2002). The social policy aim therefore is to advance a socially inclusive social and health care policy enabling any and every citizen to enjoy the opportunities offered by late capitalist Britain and the European Economic Community in an increasingly economically globalised world. This should fit with an empowering social work practice.

Each individual regardless of class, race, culture, age, religion, disability or gender should find the traditional barriers to their advancement being dismantled so that nobody is excluded from sharing in the wealth and resources being offered at a time of sustained economic expansion. These political aspirations fit with the value base of social work which embody anti-discriminatory practice, respect for persons,

and equal opportunities for every citizen. However just as the earlier stages of capitalism resulted in new approaches to the social management of the disruption, impoverishment, and alienation of the social casualties of economic progress, so too are the late stages of capitalism (Leonard, 1997).

Social workers are among those in the front line faced with the consequences of the failure of this latest social policy aspiration and the raised expectations of people in need. Evidence suggests that the process of exclusion continued in the 1970s as rising levels of poverty began to be quantified. In the process a new role has evolved for statutory social work not so much as a provider of services or even as a therapeutic intervention but rather as a front-line service focused on the management of exclusion and rationing of scarce resources (Jones, 1997). This has always been an uncomfortable position for social workers who subscribe to an empowering model of practice that seeks to challenge social injustice.

The evidence confirms that the gap between rich and poor is widening, there are more children living in poverty, the prison population is at its highest recorded level, and disabled people are more likely to live in poverty or be unemployed than non-disabled people. Children from working class families are less likely to receive a further or higher education and black families are more likely to live in poor housing. There are however differences within these broad examples of social exclusion that need to be taken into account when you are assessing strengths, resources, and gaps in social networks where you are trying to help. For example, inner city deprivation, migration patterns, and poorer health outcomes are factors also associated with class and are therefore likely to affect any family in disadvantaged social circumstances.

Community practice and social development

The idea of community social work is based on the premise that most people's problems are sorted out within and between their existing local network of friends, relatives and neighbours. Social work has a role in seeking to reinforce and support those networks or helping to facilitate their growth where they have declined, as a protective and preventive strategy. Community practice therefore is *par excellence* the optimum intervention strategy for promoting social inclusion. It does not as is sometimes assumed, exclude work with individuals. The spectrum of activity includes (Smale et al., 2000):

Direct intervention – work carried out with individuals, families and local networks to tackle problems that directly affect them.

Indirect intervention – work with community groups and other professionals and agencies to tackle problems affecting a range of people.

Change agent activity – this seeks to change ways that people relate to each other that are responsible for social problems whether at individual, family or neighbourhood levels by reallocating resources.

Service delivery activity – providing services that help to maintain people in their own homes, to reduce risks to vulnerable people, and provide relief to parent/carers.

Community practice is not just about transforming neighbourhoods whether on a small or large scale but it can also enable personal change and growth in individuals through social action and the fostering of co-operative activity. The reverse of course is also true. Individual work such as that described earlier in this book that focuses on the internal problems of children and families can also contribute to wider social transformation in neighbourhoods. Defining precisely what community social work is can be difficult, it can mean almost what anyone wants it to mean from visiting lonely housebound people to organising a protest march to the Town Hall to lobby for improvements to neighbourhood services (Thompson, 2002; Adams et al., 2002).

With such broad definitional parameters it is not surprising to conclude that there is a shortage of reliable empirical data about social work assessment and intervention activity in this area of practice (Macdonald, 1999). The available evidence does suggest however, that it is community-oriented, pro-active initiatives that are helping to support families and individuals in need. A modern, psycho-social model offers the appropriate holistic perspective for social workers to engage with other professionals in the community, to work in partnership with families, and employ the personal relationship skills the majority aspire to use.

You may feel that community practice lacks a focus for your aspiration to facilitate neighbourhood development and empowering experiences for socially excluded people.

Groupwork offers the optimum intervention in these circumstances whereby you together with other social workers or other staff, can engage in the extension of networks of carers, promotion of self-directed groups and the creation of new resources. Groupwork skills are distinctive but enshrine the core psycho-social base of social work practice and can incorporate elements of intervention skills we reviewed in Chapter 2.

Your decision to embark on a groupwork intervention as part of community practice should be on the basis that it is the best way of helping those people concerned, rather than because you want to try it or that it is cheaper than seeing people individually. Groups offer the opportunity to:

- Learn and test interpersonal skills.
- Provide a sense of belonging.
- Empower service users pressing for social change.
- Develop mutual support mechanisms.
- Exchange information and share experiences.

ACTIVITY 8.1

Consider the role of your agency in empowerment and socially inclusive practice. Do you recognise practices consistent with that role? List three changes to your practice that you can make and that aspire to empower service users.

Cultural competence

The concept of cultural competence has begun to emerge in the social science literature as a way of highlighting specific elements of a socially inclusive practice and these are developed more fully in Chapter 9. Drawing together the elements of practice that can contribute towards a model of culturally competent care means it is possible to define cultural competence as a set of knowledge-based and interpersonal skills that allow individuals to understand, appreciate and work with individuals of cultures, from other than their own. Five components have been identified (Kim, 1995) comprising culturally competent care:

1. Awareness and acceptance of cultural differences.
2. Capacity for cultural self-awareness.
3. Understanding the dynamics of difference.
4. Developing basic knowledge about the child's culture.
5. Adapting practice skills to fit the cultural context of the child and family.

These are consistent with other work which critique the historical development of cross-cultural services and offer a model of service organisation and development designed to meet the needs of black and ethnic minority families (Moffic and Kinzie, 1996; Bhugra, 1999; Bhugra and Bahl, 1999). Ethnocentric and particularly eurocentric explanations of emotional and psycho-social development are not inclusive enough to understand the development of diverse ethnic minority groups. Failure to understand the cultural background of service users can lead to unhelpful assessments, non-compliance, poor use of services, and alienation of the individual or family from the welfare system.

There is growing interest in the development of multidisciplinary and interprofessional working in order to maximise the effectiveness of interventions to meet the diverse needs of multi-cultural societies and service users (Magrab et al., 1997; Oberheumer, 1998; Tucker et al., 1999). The characteristics of such work apply in a framework familiar to social workers. It begins with assessment then proceeds through decision-making, planning, monitoring, evaluation, and finally to closure. It is argued that this common framework offers the optimum model for encouraging reflective practice to be at the core of contemporary social work (Taylor and White, 2000; Walker, 2002). Reflective practice offers the opportunity to shift beyond functional analysis to making active links between the value base, policy-making process, and the variety of interventions conducted.

Combining reflective practice with culturally competent practice, social workers have the opportunity to make a major contribution towards responding to the social policy aspiration of inclusion and anti-oppressive practice. In so doing you can facilitate closer co-operation between professionals coming into contact with vulnerable service users on a shared agenda of challenging institutional and personal discrimination (Eber et al., 1996; van den Berg and Grealish, 1996; Sutton, 2000). One of the defining features of social work practice is the ability to work closely with other professionals and communities, often in a co-ordinating role or as a client advocate. This role in the context of work with a variety of problems and contexts is crucial at various points of the intervention process to ensure culturally competent practice.

Social workers using an anti-discriminatory, empowerment model of psycho-social practice are ideally placed to work with other professionals in multi-disciplinary contexts to enable the team to maintain a focus on culturally competent practice. For example, the increased demand for help from parents and children themselves suffering the effects of mental health problems has prompted policy initiatives to invest in and reconfigure child and adolescent mental health service provision (Walker, 2003). The aim is to make them more accessible and acceptable to all cultures by improving multi-agency working (House of Commons, 1997; Davis et al., 1997; Mental Health Foundation, 1999). However, in order to be effective all staff need to address the different belief systems and explanatory thinking behind psychological symptoms. Your social work skills and values are required to articulate these concepts in such teams. Combined with respectful consideration of indigenous healing practices within diverse populations this can optimise helping strategies.

Socially excluded groups

Disabled people

Recent research into the experiences of disabled people has highlighted the difficulties in implementing policy designed to ensure that the right to an assessment actually delivers more appropriate social work Intervention. This discovered that the type of team with which disabled people made contact, was crucial to their experience of getting a proper assessment (Davis et al., 1997).

Standardised approaches to assessment based on a procedural model were set out in practice guidelines and decisions about access to assessment were influenced by risk-based service criteria linked to budget limits. However, social workers in specialist teams were more likely to open up access to assessment in collaborative ways and shift away from service-led agendas to identify and use community-based networks and resources.

Disabled people find social services contact confusing, fragmented, and often irrelevant to their concerns. Access to assessment produces feelings of uncertainty, marginalisation, and exclusion. Disabled people are fully aware of resource constraints but want creativity and flexibility from social workers to think of alternatives and priorities.

What disabled people want:

- Partnership practice is highly rated and face to face contact preferred.
- Advice and information to enable options to be considered.
- Equal participation in the planning of services.
- Assessment should be informed by equal opportunities policies.
- Service charges to be explicit to enable informed choices to be made.
- Assessment practice should build on the strategies already used by disabled people and their carers to manage their lives.

Black and ethnic minority families

Inspection of social work services for black children and their families in Britain shows that despite years of rhetoric of anti-racist and anti-oppressive social work practice, assessments and care planning are still generally inadequate (SSI, 2000). The guidance suggests:

- Ensuring that services and staffing are monitored by ethnicity to ensure they are provided appropriately and equally.
- Involving ethnic minorities in planning and reviewing services.
- Training in anti-racist and anti-discriminatory practice.
- Investigating and monitoring complaints of racial discrimination or harassment.
- Explicit policies are in place for working with black families.

Social workers skills in facilitating service user empowerment are indicated in any vision of the future shape of service provision (Walker, 2001c). A psycho-social practice framework employing community social work and groupwork skills are also required to enable black families and young people to support each other and raise collective awareness of shared issues. Investigation of indigenous healing practices and beliefs provide a rich source of information to utilise in the helping process. Advocacy skills in which young people are encouraged to be supported and represented by advocates of their choice with a children's rights perspective, would help contribute to influencing current service provision (Ramon, 1999). A traditional psycho-social practice, that links the internal and external world of the client, augmented with culturally competent skills, can help meet the needs of socially excluded children and families.

Continual reflection and evaluation of practice is required to maintain an anti-racist socially inclusive practice. Recognising racial harassment as a child protection issue and as an indicator for subsequent potential mental health problems is evidence for example, of how you can translate policy generalisation into specific practice change. Social workers who make sure they take full account of a child's religion, racial, cultural and linguistic background in the decision making process are demonstrating the link between social policy and socially inclusive practice. Ensuring for example, that black children in residential care have access to advocates and positive role models can assist in challenging institutionally racist practice.

Anti-racist and anti-oppressive social work practice will help develop strategies to overcome value judgements about the superiority of white British family culture and norms. Exploring the impact of white power and privileges in social work relationships with black people and drawing connections between racism and the social control elements of social work practice, is another example. Rejecting stereotypes of black and ethnic minority family structures and relationships will enable you to assess the rich cultural, linguistic and spiritual diversity of family life and permit the building of assessment and intervention practice that is not based on a deficit model judged against an anglocentric norm.

ACTIVITY 8.2

What could you do personally to translate policy guidance into effective practice with black and ethnic minority families?

Commentary

Continual reflection and evaluation of your practice will enable you to maintain an anti-racist practice. Recognising racial harassment as a child protection issue is crucial and making sure you take full account of a child's religion, racial, cultural and linguistic background in the decision-making process. Developing strategies to overcome value judgements about the superiority of white British family culture and norms requires continual checking of your assumptions about family life. You need to explore the impact of white power and privileges in your relationships with black people and draw connections between racism and the social control elements of social work practice. Rejecting stereotypes of black and ethnic minority family structures and relationships will enable you to assess the rich diversity of families and permit the building of an assessment not based on a deficit model judged against an anglocentric norm. The more powerlessness is reinforced by services which deny felt experience and choice, and practitioners expect partnership without addressing the impact of powerlessness, the less users will be empowered (Braye and Preston-Shoot, 1995).

Disabled children and their families

There are a growing number of disabled children and young people living in the community who are socially excluded and need high levels of support. Partly this is because more of these children are surviving infancy, and partly because there is no longer the assumption that disabled children should be cared for in hospitals or other institutions. Lone parents with disabled children, families from ethnic minorities, and families caring for the most severely disabled children have the highest levels of unmet need, and live in the poorest conditions. A social model of disability rather than an impairment-specific model, can be useful in recognising the environmental barriers to disabled children that prevent them participating equally in society. This model emphasises the need to identify the way in which structures and institutions further disable people with disabilities so that these disabling structures can be challenged (Sharkey, 2000).

Disabled children with a severe disability want to know how to deal with the social and psychological challenges they face – including dealing with other family members, coping with their own negative feelings, and planning for the future. Families require relief and request a range of support including home-based sitting services, residential or family-based respite care, or long-term care from social services departments (Beresford et al., 1996). Needs change over time. For instance a family with an autistic child may want a graded range of services. In the early years they want information and support with their child's development. When the child is a bit older they need respite care. But when the children reach early teens research shows that about 60 per cent of families want their child to be accommodated by the local authority (Oldman and Beresford, 1998).

Lone parents with disabled children, families from ethnic minorities, and families caring for the most severely disabled children have the highest levels of unmet need, and live in the poorest conditions. The mental health needs of disabled children are often masked by a narrow focus on their disability through a medical, rather than social model of disability. Behaviour causing concern can often be ascribed to the physical or intellectual disability rather than a separate psychological need. Thoughtful assessment in these circumstances is crucial.

Under part 3 of the *Disability Discrimination Act 1995* social services and other service providers must not discriminate against disabled children by refusing to provide any service which is provided to other children, by providing a lower standard of service or offering a service on less favourable terms. From 2004 service providers will have to take reasonable measures to remove, alter, or provide reasonable means of avoiding physical features that make it impossible or unreasonably difficult for disabled children to use the services including when they are undertaking or contributing to assessments. This means access to services needs to be considered from the disabled child's perspective. A socially inclusive practice would link with local disabled children's networks and involve parent/carers and children in the planning and delivery of necessary changes.

The needs of deaf children like other disabled children are often overlooked or simply poorly understood. The medical model of disability ensures that the disability itself is the focus of attention rather than the disabling environment and attitudes of society. Very little research has been undertaken with this particularly socially excluded group to try to understand their emotional and psychological needs and the impact on them of their disability. Deaf culture needs to be taken into account if a socially inclusive practice is to be employed by social workers. Its principle characteristics are:

- Sharing a common language (BSL) for communication purposes.
- Social interaction choices.
- Identity issues.
- Historic understanding of discrimination.

Deaf BSL users view their deafness as a cultural identity, they are proud of their language and feel they belong to a linguistic minority group. They do not want their deafness to be cured and are more concerned about improved access to services, information and democracy. The Disability Rights Commission was established to act as a watchdog for implementation of the *Disability Discrimination Act 1995*. The commission would be a powerful ally to social workers seeking to ensure that the specific needs of deaf children and young people are not hindered by the lack of specific and appropriate services.

The low uptake of respite services by Asian parents with a disabled child are still perceived by some as evidence of the closed-network of familial relationships within Asian culture, rather than evidence of the inaccessibility of existing service provision. Sometimes this is a matter of proper translating services being unavailable but it can also represent a lack of effort from social workers and other social care professionals to understand the families they aspire to help. For example, some Asian families are reluctant to have daughters cared for by male carers, or they simply have little knowledge of the health and welfare system in Britain (Shah, 1992). Even when good translators are available they do not always manage to convey the subtleties of meaning related to feelings and cultural differences. Trying to distinguish the mental health needs of children and young people with a physical or learning disability is difficult enough for many professionals let alone for Black families already disadvantaged and discriminated against.

ACTIVITY 8.3

In what ways do you think that guidance does not achieve its aims in relation to helping you meet the needs of disabled children and their families?

Commentary

The *Carers and Disabled Children Act 2000* entitles all carers, including parent carers, to be assessed in their own right. But assessments and eligibility criteria seem to be less of a problem than a shortage of services to meet assessed needs. And a lack of flexibility within social services provision often means families having to adjust to fit whatever services are available – rather than services fitting their needs. *The Children Act 1989* mirrors many of the provisions in the *UN Convention on the Rights of the Child* ostensibly promoting social inclusion. However local authorities have continued to locate the issue of exclusion within the disabled child rather than in the external social and environmental factors contributing to exclusion. This results in social services departments attempting to meet their obligations by locating care outside the disabled child's home, away from their families, and in ways that remove them from their communities (Morris, 1998).

Young offenders

According to recent figures there were 11,500 young people aged 15 to 20 in jail in England and Wales in 2000, of those 90 per cent had a diagnosable mental health disorder, and many had substance abuse problems as well as personality disorders (Lyon et al., 2000). Young offenders are among the most socially excluded groups in society and the evidence suggests that imprisonment simply makes matters worse not better. Within two years of release, 75 per cent will have been reconvicted and 47 per cent will be back in jail (SEU, 2002). If some of these young people become homeless or end up in insecure accommodation, they are between eight and 11 times more likely to develop mental health problems (Stephens, 2002).

Young offenders are three times as likely to have a mental health problem as other young people. Yet these problems are often neglected because there are no proper methods for screening and assessing mental health problems within the youth justice system (Farrington, 1995; Goodman and Scott, 1997; Royal College of Psychiatrists, 2002; Mental Health Foundation, 2002). Your assessment and intervention practice can make a huge difference to this vulnerable group of young people by:

- Challenging multi-agency decision-making meetings to consider alternatives to custodial sentences.
- Articulating the psychological and mental health needs of young offenders.
- Offering supportive interventions and diversionary activities to at risk young people.
- Combining and networking with like-minded staff from other agencies to offer groupwork or individual counselling to disaffected youth.

The evidence shows that more than 25 per cent of young men and 41 per cent of young women under 21 in prison had received treatment for mental health problems in the year before they were jailed (Lader et al., 1997). Once in the prison system, a lack of purposeful activity, long hours in cells, and a climate of brutality and bullying can reinforce negative attitudes and magnify underlying mental health problems. Prison is no place for young people. The risk of suicide is all too evident with frequent reports of suicide in young offenders institutions. Even the most progressive regimes are inadequate to the task of meeting these already damaged individuals' needs for stability, certainty, care, and proper support to tackle their offending behaviour within a context of restorative justice and personal responsibility, backed up by therapeutic input.

Looked after children

Nearly 60,000 children were being looked after by local authorities for the year ending 2001. About 60 per cent of these children had been abused or neglected with a further 10 per cent coming from 'dysfunctional families' (DoH, 2001). Abuse of this nature can lead to self-harming behaviour, severe behavioural problems and depression. 38,400 of these children were in foster placements and 6,400 were in children's homes, yet foster carers and residential staff are among the least qualified and supported people left to manage sometimes extreme behaviour.

A recent research study emphasised the importance of a preventive approach with children in the public care system who are more likely to be excluded from school following emotional and behavioural difficulties (Fletcher-Campbell, 2001). Teacher training that fails to adequately prepare newly-qualified staff to respond to the mental health needs of pupils is considered to be a factor in the increased use of school exclusions (OFSTED, 1996). Social workers using a preventive approach could be helpful to teaching staff and organise collaborative work aimed at preventing difficult behaviour escalating. Unless the mental health needs of these children and young people are addressed as part of a strategy that effectively nurtures children's inclusion in school the risk of deterioration is high. The risk factors for looked after children are probably the most extreme of any socially excluded group, they include (Richardson and Joughin, 2000):

- developmental delay
- school failure
- communication difficulty
- low self esteem
- parent/carer conflict
- family breakdown
- rejection
- abuse
- parental mental illness
- alcohol/drug abuse
- poverty
- homelessness
- loss

Families with HIV/Aids

The stress experienced by children and families infected with or affected by HIV is magnified by societal attitudes and prejudice about HIV/Aids, and is a risk factor for the development of a range of problems. These are some of the psycho-social stressors that can contribute towards the social exclusion of these vulnerable families (Boyd-Franklin et al., 1995):

- **Stigma and fear of contagion** – this can produce alienation and rejection by peers of children with HIV/AIDS. Parents can lose employment or become homeless as a result of perceived risks.
- **Shame, guilt and anger** – the stigma can produce intense feelings of shame guilt and anger which are difficult to manage within the family system. Professionals may also blame drug abusing parents for causing their child's illness further reinforcing feelings of despair.
- **Secrecy and social isolation** – families often live in secrecy with their diagnosis and the associated stigma of homosexuality, drug abuse or prostitution. The consequent social isolation and rejection from extended family support systems can trigger depression, suicidal thoughts, and poor compliance with medical care.

Denial and fleeing medical facilities are not uncommon responses to a positive diagnosis particularly among adults with alcohol or other substance abuse habits. The emotional shock following a period of denial may be characterised by intense feelings of hysteria and anger followed by depressive symptoms, withdrawal and feelings of shame and guilt. Unless these feelings are managed and contained in a helping relationship they will affect the emotional temperature in the household and pose a further risk to the emotional and psychological health of children in the family. Social workers need to bear in mind that a simple referral about a child with behavioural difficulties could involve a child in the centre of an emotional whirlwind where stigma prevents the underlying cause being revealed.

Working with HIV infected children requires similar skills to working with any child or adolescent with added emphasis on issues of trust, time, loss, secrecy and bereavement. Understanding the child's conception of the illness is a crucial task. This can build on what the child or young person already understands about chronic illness causality in general. The key is in adapting knowledge and information to the developmental level the child is at in order for effective communication to take place. An important and difficult issue is the decision about whether and when to disclose the diagnosis to the child. Conflicts between family members and professionals can take place over this most sensitive issue, and affect the emotional state of the child. These principles are generally followed (Pollock and Boland, 1990):

- The truth is generally less threatening to a child than fear of the unknown.
- Information needs to be presented at a level that is developmentally appropriate for the child.
- Disclosure is a process not an event.

Refugees and asylum seekers

Refugees and asylum seeking people are among the most disadvantaged ethnic minority group for whom culturally competent practice is essential. Some are unaccompanied, and many affected by extreme circumstances might include those witnessing murder of parents or kin, dislocation from school and community, and severing of important friendships. Lack of extended family support, loss of home, and prolonged insecurity add to their sense of vulnerability. These experiences can trigger symptoms of post traumatic stress syndrome and a variety of mental health problems (Dwivedi, 2002).

Parents coping strategies and overall resilience can be diminished in these trying circumstances disrupting the self-regulatory patterns of comfort and family support usually available at times of stress. Your social work involvement needs to take a broad holistic and psycho-social approach to intervention and not overlook the need for careful assessment of mental health problems developing in adults and children, whilst responding to practical demands. If these are not tackled promptly these people may go on to develop serious and persistent difficulties which are harder, and more costly to resolve, in the long term.

The number of applications for asylum from unaccompanied under 18s almost trebled between 1997 and 2001 from 1,105 to 3,469. DoH figures indicate that there were 6,750 unaccompanied asylum-seeking children supported by local authorities in 2001. Further evidence shows that many of these young people were accommodated and receiving a worse service than other children in need (Audit Commission, 2000). Very little research has been done to ascertain the needs of this group of children. However there is some evidence of the symptoms of post traumatic stress syndrome being present before they then experience the racist xenophobic abuse of individuals and institutions incapable of demonstrating humanitarian concern for their plight. This combination can shatter the most psychologically robust personality. It has been estimated that serious mental health disorders may be present in 40–50 per cent of young refugees (Hodes, 1998).

Roma, Gypsy and Traveller children may be included in recent groups of asylum and refugee seeking families escaping ethnic 'cleansing' from the Balkan region of Central and Eastern Europe (Walker, 2003). These children and families have a long history of persecution and flight from discrimination. Roma, Gypsy and Traveller families who have for many years made their home in Britain are probably one of the most socially excluded groups of people living in Britain. Unemployment among Roma/Gypsies is in the region of 70 per cent, while increasing numbers of children are failing to complete even a basic education (Save the Children, 2001). These factors-particularly the lack of proper education, are risk factors for the development of psycho-social problems. The overall context of social exclusion means an absence of contact with preventive services or the positive interaction with peers necessary for developmental attainment.

Elements of socially inclusive practice

Social workers have to assess needs, evaluate risks and allocate resources in a way that is equitable as far as possible for a wide range of service users in various situations. Challenging oppression in relation to key issues such as poverty and social marginalisation that underpin interactions in social welfare requires a holistic approach to social change that tackles oppression at the personal, institutional and cultural levels (Dominelli, 2002). An empowering social work practice can contribute to the defence of marginalised people. A review of the elements that constitute a socially inclusive practice lists four core intervention skills necessary to build on an authentic social work practice that reflects your humanitarian values (Smale et al., 2000):

- social entrepreneurship
- reflection
- challenging
- reframing

Social entrepreneurship is the ability to initiate, lead and carry through problem-solving strategies in collaboration with other people in all kinds of social networks. Reflection is the worker's ability to pattern or make sense of information, in whatever form, including the impact of her/his own behaviour and that of the organisation on others. Challenging refers to the ability of staff to confront people effectively with their responsibilities, their problem-perpetuating/creating behaviours and their conflicting interests. Reframing is the worker's ability to help redefine circumstances in ways which lead towards problem resolution.

Social workers must counteract oppression, mobilise users' rights and promote choice, yet we have to act within organisational and legal structures which users experience as oppressive (Braye and Preston-Shoot, 1997). Finding your way through this dilemma and reaching compromises, or discovering the potential for creative thinking and practice are the challenges and opportunities open to social workers committed to a socially inclusive practice. This means treating people as wholes, and as being in interaction with their environment, of respecting their understanding and interpretation of their experience, and seeing clients at the centre of what workers are doing (Payne, 1997). The unique psycho-social perspective of social work offers a vast reservoir of knowledge and skills to bring to bear on the multiple problems of socially excluded people.

Anti-racist practice

Anti-racist and anti-oppressive practice are repeatedly referred to in the social work literature

and they have a long historical lineage as part of the social justice basis of modern practice. The concepts are backed up in codes of conduct, ethical guidance and occupational standards requiring services to meet the needs of diverse cultures and combat discrimination. They are part and parcel of what attracts many of us into social work in the first place. Translating good intentions is however harder than it might at first appear.

For example in the case of child care practice there is still a tendency for social workers to proceed with assessment on the basis that the mother is the main responsible carer with the father taking a minor role. Women are perceived therefore as responsible for any problems with their children and for their protection. You may feel that this reflects the reality especially in cases of single parenthood, or domestic violence where fathers are absent or a threat. Anti-oppressive practice requires in these situations acknowledgement of the mother's predicament and multiple dilemmas. It requires an informed practice using feminist theory to evaluate the situation and seek every small opportunity to support the mother and engage the father.

A history of childhood mental health problems is strongly indicated in the risk factors for developing adult mental health problems. It is imperative therefore that the needs of all black and ethnic minority children vulnerable to mental health problems are addressed early and competently in order to prevent later problems. Your anti-racist work in multi-disciplinary ways as part of inter-agency groups co-ordinating efforts to support the child and family through temporary or moderate difficulties could be critical. As specialist social workers you can support other staff in statutory or voluntary resources by offering risk assessment and interpretation of behaviour through the spectrum of child development theories adapted to take account of cultural diversity.

One of the central aims of anti-racist and anti-oppressive practice is to exclude the risk of misinterpretation or underplaying significant emotional and behavioural characteristics in black families. An understanding of the reluctance and resistance of black parents to consider a mental health explanation for their child's behaviour or emotional state is important when considering how to engage parents or carers from diverse cultural backgrounds in the process of support. It is equally important to make efforts to understand cultural explanations and belief systems around disturbed behaviour as part of risk assessment work. Respecting rather than challenging difference should be the starting point for finding ways of moving forward in partnership and co-operation. The dilemma in aspiring to practice in anti-oppressive ways is in balancing this respect with knowledge and evidence of the consequences of untreated emerging mental health problems.

The characteristics of non-western societies such as collectivism, community and physical explanations for emotional problems, are in contrast to western concepts of individualism and psychological explanations (Bochner, 1994). The western model of mental illness ignores the religious or spiritual aspects of the culture in which it is based. However, Eastern, African and Native American cultures tend to integrate them (Fernando, 2002). Spirituality and Religion do not feature often in the social work literature, yet they can be critical components of a person's well being, offering a source of strength and hope in trying circumstances. You need to address this dimension as part of the constellation of factors affecting black families, avoiding stereotyping, and bearing in mind the positive and sometimes negative impact spiritual or religious beliefs might have on their mental health.

Basing your practice on anti-oppressive principles is not a soft option, signing up to political correctness, or about being nice to black people. It is about how you define yourself as a social worker and your relationship to service users. A recent powerful contribution to the literature on this issue makes the point that you cannot bolt-on a bit of anti-oppressive practice, it has to be part and parcel of all your everyday practice as a contribution to tackling poverty, social justice, and the structural causes of inequality (Dominelli, 2002). This means articulating an anti-racist agenda in every possible context and challenging attempts to deny or avoid the issue.

This goes against theories of social work practice that advocate maintenance, therapeutically narrow, or a care management role for practitioners. Wherever you position yourself you will probably find you can occupy different roles at different times in your work regardless of your explicit intentions. This is because if you are client-centred then you will engage with them in partnership to help meet their needs to maintain them in their current circumstances, provide therapeutic input or offer care management if that is what they want. Doing this while actively embracing anti-racist principles is what will make the difference.

Disability equality and social exclusion

Disability equality has established itself within the literature on social work practice and more broadly within theoretical debates about social inclusion. It is important therefore to consider some of the concepts attached to disability equality and how they can be translated into sound practice principles. A definition of disability that both encompasses the widest constituency of disabled people and the variety of disabilities they have, as well as the deepest understanding of the social construction of disability is a social model approach. This acknowledges that the lives of people with particular impairment labels or characteristics have the same value as the lives of people without that label. Although impairment may cause some disabled people pain and discomfort, what really disables is a socio-cultural system that does not recognise their right to genuinely equal treatment throughout the life course (Wolbring, 2001).

Within disability discourse there are complex arguments about the use of language and the meaning of terms such as social model that are instructive for you to acknowledge. Disabled critics of the social model suggest that the social model's conceptulaisation of disability as a structural/material process makes possible the objectification of their oppression. This can reinforce definitions of disability related to normalcy and impairment, thereby individualising the experience of disability and undermining the structural aspects of discrimination (Corker, 1999).

Disability is a global issue. More than half a billion disabled people live in the world today – approximately one in ten of the population. This number is set to rise over the next 25 years (International Disability Foundation, 1998). Many more young disabled people are surviving into adulthood and old age, and more and more older people are living with impairments acquired later in life. At the same time, disabled people are empowering themselves to claim greater participation, integration, independence and equality.

Disabled people therefore aim not only to claim greater control over their individual lives, but also achieve greater influence over the social structures within which such lives are lived. It is impossible to disentangle the lived experience of disability from the context of disabling societies. Most disabled people encounter both disabling barriers and barriers to scarce resources. Access to resources is biased against disabled women, children, and older people (Priestly, 2001).

Over the past 25 years disability has moved from the margins to the mainstream of the human rights agenda. This is a result of pressure from disabled people themselves organising locally, nationally, and Internationally to influence the policy and practice of those seeking to deliver services and support. In 1975 the United Nations General Assembly made its first Declaration on the Rights of Disabled Persons. In 1981 the UN proclaimed the International Year of Disabled Persons and embarked upon a World Programme of Action. In 1985, the Universal Declaration of Human Rights was specifically extended to include disabled people. In 1992, the first International Day of Disabled Persons was inaugurated. In 1993 the UN introduced: *Rules on the Equalisation of Opportunities for Disabled People* (UN, 1993) that addressed participation in eight specific areas of life:

- accessibility
- education
- employment
- income maintenance and social security
- family life and personal integrity
- culture
- recreation and sports
- religion

Social model definitions of disability became mainstream recognising that society creates a handicap when it fails to accommodate the diversity of all its members. The United Nations acknowledged that: 'People with disabilities often encounter attitudinal and environmental barriers that prevent their full, equal and active participation in society' (UN, 1994). Current government initiatives on standards in social care and health care such as SCIE and NICE, the NHS Plan, and clinical governance, are encouraging service providers to develop and promote best training and practice.

The practical expression of these aims is found, for example, in the White Paper *Valuing People* which focuses on learning disability services but reflects all the issues in disability training. The emphasis throughout legislation and policy

guidance is on the development of the health and social care workforce. This includes setting this within the context of the governments strategy of lifelong learning and training, a systems-wide approach, and partnership practice with disabled people.

Legislation and policy

The Chronically Sick and Disabled Persons Act 1970 was the first major piece of legislation attempting to strengthen the powers of local authorities in finding out and meeting the needs of disabled people. The Education Acts of 1944, 1976, and 1981 attempted to address the needs of disabled children for equal access to education. Over the past 20 years a number of attempts to introduce legislation in Parliament aimed at preventing discrimination and promoting the civil rights of disabled people, have been thwarted (Barnes, 1991).

The most recent and significant legislative change to impact the disability agenda is the *Human Rights Act 1998*. This incorporates in to English Law all the conventions of the European Convention on Human Rights. Under the Act all public authorities have responsibilities to abide by basic rights and freedoms of the individual. Frontline staff working with disabled people should be trained on the implications of the Act for their standards of care.

Article 14 of the Act prohibits discrimination against disabled people in their enjoyment of the European Convention on Human Rights. This provides wide scope for disabled people to bring action under the Human Rights Act. More specific rights are provided under Article 2 which guarantees the right to life and will have a direct impact on the service disabled people can expect in the health system. Article 3 protects disabled people against inhuman or degrading treatment. This article affects social services community care provision.

Article 5 provides for the right to liberty. It is especially relevant to people with mental health difficulties who may be compulsorily detained and to other disabled people institutional or community care. Article 6 provides rights of due process in criminal and civil law. It imposes standards in the determination of social security disputes and complaints in the health service. Article 8 protects the right to private and family life and Article 12 the right to marry and found a family. These rights have widespread implications. For example, rights to fertility treatment; the sterilisation of young women with learning disabilities; the rights of severely disabled people to live independently; and rights of adoption are among the issues likely to arise.

The *Disability Discrimination Act* 1995 has been implemented incrementally since being placed on the statute book. Health and Social Care agencies as employers and as organisations providing services to the public have to make sure they are not discriminating against staff or service users. The particular elements of the law brought into force recently make it clear that service providers should now:

- Amend policies, procedures and practices which make it impossible or unreasonably difficult for disabled people to use their services.
- Provide extra help and services to help disabled people get access to their services.
- Remove or alter physical barriers that prevent disabled people gaining access, or provide the service in an alternative way where reasonable.

According to a recent Social Services Inspectorate report (DoH, 2001) progress on Joint Investment Plans for welfare to work for disabled people is generally patchy. Eligibility criteria leading to an assessment for services generally make little reference to employment. Existing employment schemes tend to focus on people with learning disabilities or mental health problems, with little attention given to physically disabled people or those with sensory impairments. The report states that what disabled people need is:

- Effective co-ordination between agencies.
- Recognition of their value and needs as a whole person.
- Expert information and advice.
- Physical access to services.
- Guidance in making informed choices.
- Local training and employment reflecting people's diversity.
- Continuing support once in employment.

Independent living has become more of an option for disabled people as a result of the *NHS Community Care Act* 1990 and the subsequent introduction of direct payments in 1996. Social care practice has focused on independent living, generally defined as a disabled person living alone with support. Yet this may not be the same for young disabled people and is a complex issue

for young black disabled people. A significant research project (Bignall and Butt, 2000) discovered that for young people the most important feature of independence was not living alone, but being able to make decisions, develop skills and do things themselves. For young black disabled people living apart from their families loneliness and pervasive racism were major issues. A number of existing disability groups either do not cater for young people or for black disabled people.

ACTIVITY 8.4

With a colleague at work discuss the ways in which your agency conceptualises disability, then measure this against the notion of a social model of disability. Consider placing this issue on the agenda of your next team meeting.

Globalisation and emancipatory practice

The term globalisation has begun to feature in the social work literature reflecting profound concerns about the shifts in the economic and social patterns of relationships between the richer industrialised countries and the poorer developing countries. It involves closer international economic integration prompted by the needs of capitalism, but also has demographic, social, cultural and psychological dimensions (Midgley, 2001). Consistent with the link between the social context of social work practice, it is therefore important to consider the global context in terms of the challenges for building empowering socially inclusive practice.

Critics of globalisation argue that its impact is to maintain unequal power relationships between the richer and poorer countries so that patterns of wealth and consumer consumption in Europe and North America can be sustained. This involves the exploitation of labour and other resources in poorer countries thereby preventing them achieving a diverse and equitable economic and social structure within which health and social welfare programmes can develop. In Britain the consequences of globalisation are being noticed in the way traditional social care systems are taking on the characteristics of business ethics and commercialism (Dominelli, 1999; Mishra, 1999). One of the side effects of this process is the standardisation and conformity required for consumer consumption patterns in order to maximise profit. The consequence is the steady and inexorable erosion of traditional markers of indigenous cultural identity combined with the elevation of global branding.

This critique of the latest phase of capitalist development echoes earlier concerns about the impact on economic growth and subsequent erosion of traditional government policies of full employment and social welfare (Corrigan and Leonard, 1978; Bailey and Brake, 1980). A failure to fully develop social welfare services, or to have them subjected to the gyrations of speculative global financial markets, invariably corrodes the quality and the depth of services designed to reach children and families in personal and culturally appropriate ways. This means that services are pared to the minimum, oriented towards crisis intervention and designed in the narrowest terms to conform with inflexible eligibility criteria that limits access. These features are inconsistent with empowering practice that aims to spread accessibility, improve acceptability and enrich social worker's creative potential to respond to a diverse society.

Dilemmas in trends towards cultural competence have been highlighted by reference to the practice of forced/arranged marriages and dowry, genital mutilation of children, and harsh physical punishments condoned by some societies (Midgley, 2001). These practices can be used to counter the argument for respecting ethnic and cultural diversity and support the notion of universal social work values as the basis for competent practice. Ethnic rivalries and the pride in national identity on which they are based also sit uneasily with culturally competent aspirations of international collaboration and mutual understanding.

However, rather than seek answers to these difficult issues in an introspective way, this emphasises the need for social workers and their professional representatives to reach out to the international social work community with service users, to continue to debate, discuss and strive for ways to discover solutions. We need to understand the impact such practices and the beliefs on which they are based are having on the mental health and emotional development of those families experiencing them.

Cultural competence has been defined as developing skills in assessing the cultural climate of an organisation and being able to practice in a strategic manner within it. It has also been broadened to include *any* context in which social workers practice in order to permit effective direct work at many levels (Baldwin, 2000; Fook,

2002). Whether at the strategic organisational level or the direct interpersonal level social workers can actively resist those pressures to conformity and routinised practice that in often discreet and inconspicuous ways, can undermine efforts to practise in empowering ways. The requirements of social justice demand vigilance and creativity in order to contribute towards an emancipatory practice that can liberate both social workers and service users from prescribed practice orthodoxies. Such practice is the antithesis of stereotyped, one-dimensional thinking and is characterised by (Leonard, 1994):

- A commitment to standing alongside oppressed and impoverished populations.
- The importance of dialogic relations between workers and service users.
- Orientation towards the transformation of processes and structures that perpetuate domination and exploitation.

These characteristics are in harmony with socially inclusive practice. They do not imply that social workers should reject statutory practice for the voluntary sector, child care for community work, or psychodyamic theories for advocacy. These simplistic oppositional devices do not help social workers manage the complexities and dilemmas in seeking different practice orientations (Healy, 2002). The possibilities for creative practice within organisational constraints are there. They may be limited and subjected to pressures of time but in the personal relationship with service users, the rewards are unquantifiable for both worker and client. Even introducing a small change in practice can have a much larger disproportionate and beneficial impact.

The evidence from other European countries supports the need for social work to pay more attention to the social policy issue of social exclusion and how to build a practice that reflects that concern in practical ways. Emerging democracies in Eastern Europe are learning to take the best of traditional social work and combine it with community practices that address social development issues (Connely and Stubbs, 1997). The rise of ethnic nationalisms and increasing oppression of ethnic minorities, the dismantling of structures allowing gender equality, and the increasing inequalities generated by unemployment and poverty, are all illustrating the need for social work to emphasise a socially inclusive practice. The argument for a pan European paradigm of social work based on social innovation is articulated by those who envisage social work being a more explicit part of social change and that in order to help our clients we have to engage with the social and political reality (Zavirsek, 1995).

Chapter summary

In this chapter we have reviewed the concept of empowerment and socially inclusive practice. The task of social work is in this context to work towards liberating service users and empowering them to gain access to those resources required to enable equal participation in society. The evidence confirms that the gap between rich and poor is widening, there are more children living in poverty, the prison population is at its highest recorded level, and disabled people are more likely to live in poverty or be unemployed than non-disabled people.

Children from working class families are less likely to receive a further or higher education and black families are more likely to live in poor housing. There is growing interest in the development of multidisciplinary and interprofessional working in order to maximise the effectiveness of interventions to meet the diverse needs of multi-cultural societies and service users.

The needs and problems faced by particular groups of excluded children and families have been identified. An empowering social work practice can contribute to the defence of such marginalised people. A review of the elements that constitute a socially inclusive practice lists four core intervention skills necessary to build on an authentic social work practice that reflects your humanitarian values – Social entrepreneurship, Reflection, Challenging, and Reframing. Anti-racist and anti-oppressive principles have been articulated in the context of the disability equality agenda.

Social disadvantage, unemployment, bad housing and impoverished surroundings are among the characteristics of socially excluded families and indicate risk factors for child abuse. However, poverty does not cause child abuse.

There is increasing evidence for the need to refine and develop our methods and models of assessment and intervention so that they are more relevant and accessible to children and young people from a much wider range of backgrounds, cultures and ethnic communities. A traditional psycho-social practice, that links the internal and external world of the client, augmented with culturally competent skills, can help meet the needs of socially excluded children and families.

Challenging oppression in relation to key issues such as poverty and social marginalisation that underpin interactions in social welfare requires a holistic approach to social change that tackles oppression at the personal, institutional and cultural levels.

CHAPTER 9

Cultural, Spiritual and Religious Dimensions

Learning objectives

- Describe what is meant by culturally competent practice in the context of assessment and intervention.
- Understand the importance of religious belief to many individuals and communities and how this influences them.
- Develop an awareness of the distinction between spirituality and religion.
- Incorporate a respectful, person-centred perspective in using assessment and intervention tools with people from diverse ethnic communities.

Introduction

The concept of cultural competence has begun to emerge in the social science literature as a way of highlighting specific elements of a socially inclusive practice that can improve practice in terms of assessment, intervention and evaluation (O'Hagan, 2001). Drawing together the elements of practice that can contribute towards a model of culturally competent care means it is possible to define cultural competence as a set of knowledge-based and interpersonal skills that allow individuals to understand, appreciate and work with individuals of cultures, from other than their own. Five components have been identified (Kim, 1995) comprising culturally competent care:

1. Awareness and acceptance of cultural differences.
2. Capacity for cultural self-awareness.
3. Understanding the dynamics of difference.
4. Developing basic knowledge about the child's culture.
5. Adapting practice skills to fit the cultural context of the child and family.

These are consistent with other work which critique the historical development of cross-cultural services and offer a model of service organisation and development designed to meet the needs of black and ethnic minority families (Moffic and Kinzie, 1996; Bhugra, 1999; Bhugra and Bahl, 1999). Ethnocentric and particularly Eurocentric explanations of emotional and psychosocial development are not inclusive enough to understand the development of diverse ethnic minority groups. Failure to understand the cultural background of service users can lead to unhelpful child protection assessments, non-compliance, poor use of services, and alienation of the individual or family from the welfare system.

Cultural competence can initially be understood in the context of a desire to improve our practice in order to meet the needs of the growing multi-cultural and ethnically diverse society developing around us. It assumes that historical and orthodox assumptions about human growth and behaviour have served their purpose in meeting the needs of troubled or vulnerable people in particular circumstances and at particular points in time. Now in the early stages of the 21st century changes we are required to address and respond to a modern generation of families who cannot be easily fitted into existing theoretical paradigms and require safeguarding. There is increasing evidence for the need to refine and develop our methods and models of assessment and intervention so that they are more relevant and accessible to people from a much wider range of backgrounds than was the case in the not too distant past (Madge, 2001).

This is not to say that people in the majority ethnic communities do not require improved methods of help and support. They are being socialised and exposed to a quite different society than former generations. The pace of life, enhanced stressors, individualism, and consumerism are blamed for producing heightened states of arousal and stimulation. Evidence has begun to emerge of genetic changes, the development of new illnesses and of course a range of new risk factors to their mental health – especially the availability of cheap psychoactive drugs, depression in old age and greater access to alcohol. The internet is a source of fascination but also danger as paedophiles use it as a vehicle for grooming vulnerable children. Depictions of family life, for example in children's literature has changed dramatically in the past 40 years from misleading idyllic paternalistic havens of safety and security to the grim reality of poverty, child abuse, divorce, mentally ill parents and personal and institutional racism (Tucker and Gamble, 2001).

Ethnicity requires some clarification as another term that can be used in a variety of contexts but without much thought as to its meaning. Its use alongside the term culture causes confusion especially when the two become almost synonymous. This is because there is no easy definition, but we at least need to know the complexities of the use of the term ethnicity because it perhaps reflects something deeper and more ambivalent about the way we internally manage difference and other-ness. Part of the problem lies in mixing up birthplace with ethnic identity. A white person born in Africa and a black person born in Britain can be defined by their ethnic grouping and place of birth. Further confusion has historically prevailed due to the way the official census data have been collated. In the UK since 1951 the methods of data collection have altered from just recording the country of birth, to the birthplace of parents, to 1981 when there was no question on ethnicity. In 1991 a question on ethnicity offered a range of categories and in 2001 there were further changes to account for citizens with dual or mixed heritage.

The term 'race' is now generally accepted to be redundant as a meaningful scientific category however *the idea of race* as a general descriptor of assumed national, cultural or physical difference persists in society (Amin, 1997). The concept is embraced at the policy level with legislation such as the *Race Relations Act* in the UK and institutions such as the Commission for Racial Equality. Legislation such as the *1989 Children Act*, the *2004 Children Act* and *2004 Children's National Service Framework* which contextualise work with children and young people, expects practitioners to take account of a child's religious persuasion, racial origin, and cultural and linguistic background, without adequate guidance as to what is meant by 'race' or 'culture'. The issue becomes more complex when we consider census data that show the increase in numbers of children from dual and mixed heritage backgrounds and consider the particularly complex set of problems they can encounter (Walker 2005).

Applying theory to practice

In the context of integrated practice, multidisciplinary and interprofessional working there is an opportunity to maximise the effectiveness of interventions to meet the diverse needs of multi-cultural societies and service users (Magrab et al., 1997; Oberheumer, 1998; Tucker et al., 1999). The characteristics of such work apply in a framework familiar to all professionals. It begins as we discussed in Chapters 1 and 2, with assessment then proceeds through decision-making, planning, monitoring, evaluation, and finally to closure. It is argued that this common framework offers the optimum model for encouraging reflective practice to be at the core of contemporary practice (Taylor and White, 2000; Walker, 2002). Reflective practice offers the opportunity to shift beyond functional analysis to making active links between the value base, policy-making process, and the variety of interventions conducted.

Combining reflective practice with culturally competent practice means that you have the opportunity to make a major contribution towards responding to the social policy aspiration of inclusion and anti-oppressive practice. In so doing you can facilitate closer co-operation between professionals engaged in supporting people on a shared agenda of challenging institutional and personal discrimination (Eber et al., 1996; van den Berg and Grealish, 1996; Sutton, 2000). One of the defining features of contemporary practice is the ability to work closely with other professionals and communities, sometimes in a co-ordinating role or as a client advocate. This role is crucial at various points of the assessment and intervention process to ensure culturally competent practice.

ACTIVITY 9.1

Review work undertaken over the past few months and reflect on how often, if at all, culture, religion or spirituality was mentioned in meetings with clients or colleagues.

Citizenship, nationality and race

Issues of citizenship, nationality, race and immigration provide the overarching context within legislation and public policy which sets the scene for racist and oppressive practice to go unchecked and the cultural needs of black people to be overlooked. In the United Kingdom, the

British Nationality Act 1948 provided legal rights to immigration which have served as a focal point for a continuing racialised debate about the numbers of black immigrants and refugee/asylum seekers and the perceived social problems subsequently caused (Solomos, 1989). The *Race Relations (Amendment) Act (2000)* came into force in 2001 extending the scope of the *Race Relations Act (1976)* to counter racism. The new Act strengthens the law in two ways that are significant to practice:

- It extends protection against racial discrimination by all public authorities, making the legislative remit wider by covering any service provided to the public.
- It places a new, enforceable positive duty on public authorities to not just avoid racial discrimination, but to actively promote better race relations in the community.

The *Nationality, Immigration and Asylum Act* (2002) is the fourth piece of primary legislation attempting to reform the asylum system in 10 years. Previous measures related to dispersal and support measures and were widely regarded as harmful to children because they resulted in sub-standard accommodation, isolation, discrimination and poverty (Dennis and Smith, 2002; JCWI, 2002). The new law proposes establishing accommodation centres housing huge numbers of people in rural areas. Protection of children in such places is difficult due to the high turnover of residents, while these children and young people are impeded from opportunities to integrate and feel part of society.

In addition, the new law denies asylum-seeking children the right to be educated in mainstream local schools. Such segregation contravenes the *Human Rights Act (1998)* and the UN Convention on the Rights of the Child (1989) because this is not in the best interests of the child and will very likely harm their development and mental health. Children, who have suffered extreme trauma, abuse, anxiety and hardship, need to feel safe, included and part of their community with their peers in order to begin to thrive and rebuild their fragile sense of self.

What is culture?

Culture is a word that appears in everyday discourse – so much so that as with much common parlance it ceases to require any great effort at understanding what it means. We all seem to know what we are talking about when we mention culture. Yet the variety of definitions and interpretations of the word allow it an elasticity that is more a hindrance to clarity than a help. The increasing need to improve our therapeutic work with children and young people requires us to examine their changing cultural environment for evidence of how we might harness new ways of understanding them and their troubles. At a general level culture is associated with high art, refinement, superior taste etc. or there is popular culture which is associated with the masses, low taste, tabloid media, and TV soap operas.

We can also acknowledge that there is a 'therapy culture' – that is, something associated with western methods of responding to individual human psychological difficulties. Depending on the context it can be used as a term of criticism implying that the problems of society are caused by the culture of therapy which posits people as victims and weak-willed (Masson, 1988; Furedi, 2003). Or it can be used in a benign sense illustrative of how advanced societies are becoming in attending to the stresses and pressures of modern life. What is certain is that those of us seeking to help troubled people need to develop our understanding of how cultural influences affect, maintain and ultimately provide solutions to, the psychological difficulties of people.

Culture in the anthropological sense has come to mean the way of life followed by a people. This concept developed as the history of western expansionism and colonialism encountered manifestations of difference around the world. These encounters prompted a reaction at several levels of consciousness. Politically there was a need to justify the appropriation of native land and resources, economically the imperial explorers required raw materials to service industrialisation, but *psychologically* there was a fear of difference that had to be rationalised. Hence the early attempts at racial categorisation and efforts to construct order from diversity and chaos in human lifeways.

Culture can also be defined in opposition to nature – the product and achievement of human beings representing a rising above of our natural instincts. In this sense human nature is typically understood as the opposite of culture. Culture can also mean the difference between humans and animals – the capacity to use language and complex communication to symbolise that which is not present (Jenkins, 2002).

Thus the bearers of a culture are understood to be a collectivity of individuals such as a society or community. However the cultural patterns that shape the behaviour of people in groups should not be confused with the structure of institutions or social systems, even though there is a link between them. We can think of culture in one sense as the organisation of experience shared by members of a community including their standards for perceiving, predicting, judging and acting. This means that culture includes all socially standardised ways of seeing and thinking about the world; of understanding relationships among people, things and events; of establishing preferences and purposes; of carrying out actions and pursuing goals (Valentine, 1976; Haralambos, 1988; Jenkins, 2002). As the history of the past three centuries demonstrates the impact of western imperialism has reproduced its economic and political structures worldwide resulting in the development of industrial societies in former agrarian countries that have disrupted and disfigured cultural patterns.

Professional cultures

Critics suggest that reorganising services as a means to improving inter-agency co-operation, will not succeed because professional groups tend to create their own cultural boundaries irrespective of organisational structure (Reder and Duncan, 2003). Also there is strong evidence that it is the organisational *climate* rather than the structure that is a major predictor of improved outcomes in children's services (Glisson and Hemmelgarn, 1998). Practitioners have to assess needs, evaluate risks and allocate resources in a way that is equitable as far as possible for all citizens. Challenging oppression in relation to key issues such as poverty and social marginalisation that underpin interactions in social welfare requires a holistic approach to social change that tackles oppression at the personal, institutional and cultural levels (Dominelli, 2002). An empowering practice can contribute to the defence of marginalised people and better safeguard and support them.

Anti-racist and anti-oppressive practice are repeatedly referred to in the professional literature in health, education and social work and they have a long historical lineage as part of the social justice basis of modern practice. The concepts are backed up in codes of conduct, ethical guidance and occupational standards

requiring services to meet the needs of diverse cultures and combat discrimination. They are part and parcel of what attracts many into vocational work in the first place. Translating good intentions is however harder than it might at first appear.

For example in the case of child care practice there is still a tendency for staff to proceed with assessment on the basis that the mother is the main responsible carer with the father taking a minor role. Women are perceived therefore as responsible for any problems with their children and for their protection. You may feel that this reflects the reality especially in cases of single parenthood, or domestic violence where fathers are absent or a threat. Anti-oppressive practice requires in these situations acknowledgement of the mother's predicament and multiple dilemmas for example when women decline to press charges against abusive partners fearing retribution. It requires an informed practice using feminist theory to appreciate the patriarchal power structures in society, evaluate the situation, and seek every small opportunity to support the mother and engage the father.

The characteristics of non-western societies such as collectivism, community and physical explanations for emotional problems are in harmony with a socially inclusive perspective but are in contrast to western concepts of individualism and psychological explanations (Bochner, 1994). The western model of mental illness ignores the religious or spiritual aspects of the culture in which it is based. However, Eastern, African and Native American cultures tend to integrate them (Fernando, 2002). The significance of adult mental health problems as a risk factor in child protection is well established and has led to criticisms of the lack of integrated practice between adult mental health and child protection services.

Spirituality and religion do not feature often in the social work literature, yet they can be critical components of a person's well being, offering a source of strength and hope in trying circumstances. You need to address this dimension as part of the constellation of factors affecting families where this features, avoiding stereotyping, and bearing in mind the positive and sometimes negative impact spiritual or religious beliefs might have on a person's safety. Black and other ethnic minority families where strong religious beliefs are held require particular sensitivity where their faith and cultural practices do not correspond to eurocentric models. Basing your practice on anti-oppressive principles is not a soft option, signing up to political correctness, or about being nice to black people. It is about how you define yourself as a worker and your relationship to other people.

A recent powerful contribution to the literature on this issue makes the point that you cannot bolt-on a bit of anti-oppressive practice, it has to be part and parcel of all your everyday practice as a contribution to tackling poverty, social justice, and the structural causes of inequality (Dominelli, 2002). This means articulating an anti-racist, socially inclusive agenda in every possible context and challenging attempts to deny or avoid the issue. Equally it especially does not imply that when working with a black family you should not challenge parents/carers who deny access or avoid contact where concerns have been raised about child safety.

Care, control and partnership

This tension between care and control and the ambiguity from which it arises is apparent in government guidance in that whereas partnership practice figures prominently elsewhere, it is not emphasised in the elements on risk with their greater emphasis on protection and control. This points to the apparent conflict between an emphasis on working in partnership with service users – which is fundamental to modern practice – and the statutory requirement to protect vulnerable people (Jack and Walker, 2000).

Whilst the values underpinning partnership practice and the evidence of its efficacy are fairly unequivocal, this is not the case with the requirement to protect and control where there is much greater ambiguity about both the cultural values on which it is based and the practice methods which it involves. The problem of the social and cultural relativism of concepts of dangerousness and significant harm create uncertainty for practitioners. Similar problems exist in relation to the values underpinning practice in relation to control and protection.

Thus both the underpinning values and methods associated with practice in relation to control and protection are fraught with uncertainty and seem far removed from the aspirations of partnership. It is important to acknowledge these tensions and recognise that a defining characteristic of good assessment practice is the need to balance these competing

demands within different forms of practice. These try to maintain your commitment to the value base of professionalism whilst fulfilling your duty to both care and control.

Partnership practice with young people

For children and young people participation needs to be appropriate to its social and developmental context and to take account of the issues involved, the objectives sought and the complex cultural context of the young people concerned. Making partnership working meaningful in a culturally competent way is challenging but ultimately very beneficial. For example, different kinds of participation might be appropriate for different parts of a safeguarding project, care proceedings, alcohol and drug awareness or at different stages in a child protection investigation. The following barriers and solutions to the participation of children and young people in social care service development and strategic planning in general were identified in recent research (McNeish and Newman, 2002):

Barriers

Attitudes – many children think nothing happens as a result of their involvement and they less willing to get involved.
Time – proper consultation and involvement take time.
Methods – children find formality, complexity and bureaucracy off putting.
Forums – are the least favourite methods, although local authorities commonly use these.
Lack of information – many children don't hear about chances to get involved; there is often little feedback about what has happened as a result.

Solutions

Support mechanisms – adults need to support children in decision-making, thinking carefully about how and when to intervene. Staff need support to change their way of working, to be given time to involve children and to increase their skills in talking and listening to children.
Methods children like – variety is needed; so is fun. Groups are popular; children tend to like talking rather than writing and to talk in groups rather than one to one.

Little is currently known about why young people choose not to be involved or why they get excluded. There is a research gap about issues to be addressed when trying to involve excluded children and young people in participation. It is recommended that the notion of being 'hard to reach' is examined, as there is a danger in seeing this as something to do with the young people rather than a reflection on the agency's ability to communicate with a diverse group. It appears that the voices of younger children, disabled children (particularly those with communication or learning difficulties) and children and young people from black and ethnic minority backgrounds (who may have English as a second language) or from families living in poverty can remain unheard. This reinforces the importance of developing children's services staff skills in direct work with children.

There is a lack of research, monitoring and evaluation on the impact and outcomes of the participation of children and young people on change and improvement in services. There is some knowledge about participation techniques but little or no examination of the relationship between the process and the achievement of tangible change. It is reported that children and young people can gain personally from positive experiences of participation. Feeding back the results of their participation to children and young people is vital as it is related to engagement and commitment. It is recommended that some knowledge-based standards could be developed (with children and young people) around evaluating participation impact, tracking change and feeding back to participants.

It is also worth noting that there is much that is helpful to learn about children's participation from participation developments with adult service users. Children's participation would be supported by developing an explicitly participatory approach to practice with training developed to enable this to happen, including imaginative approaches to training involving the viewpoints and involvement of children and young people. Partnership practice whilst apparently being at odds with some of the requirements of child protection work is in fact one of the methods through which this balance can be sought – if not always attained. The next activity is intended to clarify this.

ACTIVITY 9.2

Write a paragraph describing how you think working in partnership with service users can help to integrate

the requirements of both care and control. In doing this you might find it helpful to briefly re-read the section on the social construction of risk in Chapter 3.

Commentary

In the section on social construction we discussed the social and cultural factors involved in the definition and perception of dangerousness. Working in partnership involves a genuine commitment to the attempt to understand the world from the client's perspective and communicating this effectively without necessarily condoning any particular behavioural expression of their perception of the world. Partnership however also involves mutuality – there is an expectation that the client will be willing to make a similar attempt to understand the perceptions and behaviours of others. Obviously the worker has the professional responsibility to enable clients to work on problems in this way when initially the nature of their problems may inhibit the flexibility which this entails. This will involve entering the social and cultural context of the client – rather than attempting to promote change by imposing an alien cultural context.

In such ways partnership practice can work with the social and cultural relativity which, as we have seen, is a characteristic of assessment practice. What may be seen as the problem of ambiguity and uncertainty which in some circumstances leads to draconian attempts to control, can in this way be turned into a positive strength in the attempt to care and enable. In this case, knowledge of cultural diversity, the skills of interpretation and negotiation in building partnership, and the values of individualisation and respect for uniqueness and diversity which are the foundation of such partnership practice. It is important to acknowledge that the commitment to partnership should not be misinterpreted as an invitation to relinquish boundaries in professional relationships. Loss of boundaries can place vulnerable clients and workers at risk.

Understanding spirituality and religion

Religion and spirituality are dimensions of mental health and emotional well-being which must be actively considered in order to practice in a useful way. The principles underpinning the psycho-social helping relationship offer a complementary model to build on the capacity for healing that is associated with religious and spiritual experience. They also fit with the concept of personal growth and social justice enshrined in a modern, progressive social work practice. The subject of religion and spirituality has not featured strongly in much of the classic social work literature until quite recently (Nash and Stewart, 2002; Moss, 2005). Perhaps it touches on too many sensitive issues for some social workers or contradicts their personal constructs about society, the causes of problems and the solutions. However it is a subject of great importance to many people whether they are atheists, agnostics, believers, evangelists or fundamentalists. As part of their lived experience we need to engage in this area and investigate ways in which we can use it to help with a variety of problems.

It is suggested that religion and spirituality can be equated together or seen as quite distinct concepts. Spirituality, it is argued, refers to one's basic nature and the process of finding meaning and purpose whereas religion involves a set of organised, institutionalised beliefs and social functions as a means of spiritual expression and experience (Carroll, 1998).

Religion and spirituality have traditionally been separated in their application to an understanding of the human condition in education and training contexts and by qualified social workers (Walker, 2005). It is as if our desperate need for recognition and importance has to be privileged over all other influences-particularly those that impinge on the realm of the unconscious and psychological. Some go further and suggest that religions typically act to increase anxiety rather than reduce it, or they are an instrument of oppression and control over women and the poor (Sinha, 1998; Guerin, 1998).

The complexities and subtleties of different cultural manifestations of relationship dynamics are lost on those relying on religious media stereotypes and deliberately obscured by those seeking to exploit them. The central features of spirituality have been described as (Martsolf and Mickley, 1998):

- **Meaning** – the significance of life and deriving purpose in existence.
- **Transcendence** – experience of a dimension beyond the self that opens the mind.
- **Value** – standards and beliefs such as value

truth, beauty, worth often discussed as ultimate values.
- **Connecting** – relationships with others, God or a higher power and the environment
- **Becoming** – a life that requires reflection and experience including a sense of who one is and how one knows.

These spiritual needs can be understood in psychological terms as well. The conventional literature available to social workers can be used to explain these ideas in many ways using evidence from orthodox science and theories that have stood the test of time and served professionals well. Yet there is a lingering doubt perhaps that on deeper reflection the concepts of faith, purpose and the search for meaning are inadequately quantified in the language of scientific certainty that asserts they are just thought processes or embroidered survival needs. Even in this age of evidence-based practice we know that to ignore our intuitions and gut feelings risks denying us and the people we aspire to help a most valuable tool.

It cannot be coincidental that the further the human race moves towards scientific and rational certainty aided by the bewildering power of computers and technology able to explore and manipulate the biological foundations of life using genetic research, that people seem more determined than ever to seek answers to fundamental questions about existence whether from organised religions or alternative forms of spirituality (Walker, 2005). Jung believed that therapists needed to recognise the relevance of spirituality and religious practice to the needs and workings of the human psyche. He suggested that a psychological problem was *in essence* the suffering of a soul which had not discovered its meaning – that the cause of such suffering was spiritual stagnation or psychic sterility:

Religions are psychotherapeutic systems in the truest sense of the word, and on the grandest scale. They express the whole range of the psychic problem in mighty images; they are the avowal and recognition of the soul, and at the same time the revelation of the soul's nature.

Jung, 1978

Jung's concept of archetypes suggests that unconscious components of the psyche are revealed through dreams and fantasies at critical points of internal conflict. This transcendent process mediates between oppositional archetypes in order to produce a reconciling symbol. This experience enables children and young people to achieve gradual individuation and the revelation of the self. Some of the central experiences of individuation such as the hero's journey, the metaphor of death and rebirth or the image of the divine child are paradigms of religious experience (Nash and Stewart, 2002). They migrate into myths, fairy stories and legends as we shall see later and are therefore accessible for work with troubled children and adolescents.

ACTIVITY 9.3

Take some time to reflect on your own personal belief systems, religion and/or spirituality.

Think about how these beliefs or non-beliefs have shaped and informed your social work practice.

Note the advantages as well as the advantages.

Commentary

A sense of religion or spirituality has the capacity to inhibit or enhance culturally competent therapeutic work with people. You may feel that an over-reliance on beliefs of this nature are symptomatic of a denial defence and a fatalistic outlook in your clients (Walker, 2005). On the other hand you may believe that having faith in something outside of themselves permits a person to experience a sense of purpose and greater good that can enhance a therapeutic intervention. As a social worker you may also have religious beliefs or a sense of spirituality that helps you in your assessment and intervention work. It might also hinder your work if you encounter an atheistic belief system in a person or a religious affiliation that contradicts your own. The evidence although yet to be fully developed, does suggest that spirituality has a protective function against developing psychological problems. Children and young people who possess such a sense of spirituality are considered more resilient in the face of traumas including sexual abuse and less prone to mental health and adjustment problems in adolescence (Valentine and Feinauer, 1993; Resnik et al., 1993).

Religion and belief

The relevance to modern social work practice of religion and spirituality cannot be underestimated as they form a part of the covert or overt belief systems of people that will to a larger or lesser extent impact on your assessment and intervention. This is not to say that only those who have a religious faith or a belief in spirituality will be affected. The impact of *not believing* or of having firm ideas about the absence of spiritual feelings can be just as important. What is relevant is the existence of the ideas of religion, Gods, and spirituality in society and how individuals and families orientate to them – or not. Most cultures can trace back into deep history evidence of their ancestral heritage and the ways early civilisations sought to explain the world around them. These tend to involve the intervention of a supreme being or power with the capacity to control the natural elements vital for the survival of the species.

We can understand how without the tools to predict the climate and manipulate food production methods, primitive people thousands of years ago felt vulnerable and frightened by natural phenomena. Seeking explanations for unpredictable events – good or bad was perfectly natural. These ancient understandings echo throughout history. They form part of the fabric of World heritage. They have evolved, changed, or in some cases stayed more or less the same (Walker, 2005). Settlers in developed countries embrace unorthodox and ancient customs while some native cultures in developing regions absorb modern theological concepts and spiritual practices. There are pockets of Christianity in strict Islamic states and places where minority religious beliefs are persecuted. Thus for many people these frightening experiences will already have become part of their psychological lives.

The age of enlightenment and the scientific paradigm provided an alternative set of explanations for why things happened as they did. This started a perennial tension between rationalism and religious divinity symbolised in the creationist versus evolutionist debate about the origins of humanity. The polarisation of these two ideas should intrigue the inquisitive practitioner – the need to find extreme opposites to charge an argument or debate might mask deeper ambivalence that is too uncomfortable to bear. In the same way that certain religions seek to claim a single truth or denounce others as *heretical* should serve as useful material for engaging with people:

- What meaning does this have for the person's temperament or problem-solving skills?
- What are the advantages and disadvantages for holding such profound beliefs?

The certainty of a person's belief could be measured by the depth of their mixed feelings and/or their absolute terror of the other point of view. Here again we encounter the concept of the other – the opposite which is not part of us and must be avoided, rejected or overwhelmed. In earlier centuries countries went to war and mass murders took place with official sanction on the strength of one's religious beliefs. The history of modern societies has been shaped as much by the religious struggles of previous stages of development as by the economic and political forces motivating people to embark upon social change or revolution.

To try to better understand these processes, psycho-social practice would look for the interactive nature between religious development and political and economic movements – how one influences the other and vice versa. Social workers might formulate an explanation based on the primitive insecurities driving those individuals leading these mass movements and ideologies. They offer us a therapeutic understanding of these powerfully important contexts within which individuals evolve their own psychic road map and sense of well-being.

Today, the world is said to be constructed into geo-political blocks based on economic power and geographical position. But there are the equivalent and much more complex *theo-political* blocks which have the capacity to invoke strong feelings and mass change in whole nations or significant sections of them. The contemporary range of known religions and sects in the UK is enormous. This offers evidence of the incredibly rich tapestry of religious material available to incorporate within our comprehension of the enormous culturally diverse world our clients inhabit. It also demonstrates the potential for inter-faith rivalries and offers a fertile seed bed for those charismatic figures seeking to influence people towards a religious and spiritual certainty that claims priority over all others. As with any strong belief, when it turns into obsession it has the potential for great destructiveness.

Culture and spirituality

The decline of organised religious expression in the western world has been documented in recent years and to some extent is blamed on the increasing prevalence of emotional and behavioural problems in children and young people who are a generation supposedly without

moral guidance or social values according to reactionary pundits. But what is less well documented is the evidence that experiences of the sacred or spiritual remain widespread especially among children (Cobb and Robshaw, 1998). Evidence suggests a strong underlying belief system in young people in the concept of spirituality – even by those avowed atheists. Spirituality goes beyond the narrow definition of religion and offers a different and arguably *more difficult* paradigm within which to understand the troubles of children and young people. There are identifying characteristics that can help us in our work but with such diverse meanings and interpretations it becomes harder to be certain about what spirituality is, how it can be defined and whether there are universally accepted categories (Swinton, 2003).

If the client from whatever culture, has a belief system that accepts and takes account of a spiritual dimension then rather than *pathologising* this, a social worker needs to reflect on how this meaning may be affecting the problem concerned. It could be part of the problem or it could be maintaining the problem or it could be stopping matters getting worse or it could offer a way out of the problem. Resisting the impulse to make untested and unfounded assumptions may be hard but bearing uncertainty and keeping open all possibilities will be more helpful in the long run. Spirituality therefore can be seen as an intra, inter and transpersonal experience that is shaped and directed by the experiences of individuals and of the communities within which they live out their lives (Swinton, 2003).

An example to illustrate this is provided by the development of the Family Group Conference approach to child welfare in New Zealand which is based on a cultural-religious indigenous concept among Maori people emphasising the relationship between celestial and terrestrial knowledge. The origin of the Family Group Conference was, according to Maori belief, a rebellious initiative by the children of Ranginui the great Sky Father, and Papatuanuku, the matriarch Earth Mother. Protected in a darkened cocoon by their parents the children desired freedom to explore the outer limits of the universe. The family conference that was convened included close and distant relatives and grandparents who were all regarded as part of a single spiritual and economic unity (Fulcher, 1999). Thus each Maori child's cultural identity is explicitly connected to their genealogy or *whakapapa*. The Family Group Conference is now being incorporated into mainstream child protection and adult mental health services in the United Kingdom where extended family members are invited to participate in care planning.

There are studies of folklore contained in holy books such as the Qur'an, Torah and Bible where proverbs, parables and surah are used to convey powerful religious truths (Dundes, 2003). There is increasing evidence of the power of faith as an important variable in the prognosis for a variety of medical conditions and alternative or complementary medicine is increasingly being incorporated in public health provision. Sales of homeopathic or herbal medicines is a huge business and at the very least are testimony to people's appetite for solutions that are unconventional and perhaps more mystical than orthodox scientific cures.

Psychology, religion and spirituality

The therapeutic value of western individualistic concepts is incomplete in attempting to alleviate suffering and alienation for collectivist and land-base cultural groups. Beatch and Stewart (2002) in their work with Aboriginal communities in the Canadian Arctic show how significant problems related to depression, addiction, and family violence are linked with cultural loss through colonisation, environmental destruction and assimilation by western influences. Aboriginal healing includes strengthening cultural belonging, identity and community-based self-determination. Indigenous outlooks indicate a preference for ecological systems, holistic processes, belonging at the community level and reliance on traditional beliefs and values. A culturally competent approach embracing this context requires practitioners using counselling and psychotherapeutic skills to adapt and synthesise their work with prevailing indigenous ideas in order to maximise effectiveness.

Multiple caregiving of young children in Australian aboriginal culture has attracted concerns based on western notions of attachment theory and the need for secure attachment relationships with primary carers. However this concept is inappropriate when we consider that research has demonstrated that Aboriginal children can sustain and thrive with multiple attachment figures that are wholly consistent with societal norms (Yeo, 2003). Indeed, there are sometimes lengthy absences from parents related to important sacred initiations or religious ceremonies necessary for the child or young person's spiritual development. These findings resonate with research in the UK and elsewhere studying the developmental progress of black children raised in single parent households with multiple attachment figures (Daycare Trust, 2000).

In South American countries the influence of the Catholic church and family planning combined with poverty, a history of military dictatorships and a culture of *machismo* has produced a culture of extreme social inequality where children can easily drift into prostitution, child labour or become homeless. In these conditions authoritarian family structures create a climate where domestic violence thrives (Ravazzola, 1997). Here liberation theology translates Christian concepts into activity that challenges the prevailing order offering hope of better circumstances and prospects through revolutionary struggle. People can thus link religion with empowerment and liberation from inequitable and socially unjust conditions.

ACTIVITY 9.4

Review the material above and consider whether it is possible to draw together the knowledge, theories and ideas from diverse communities and define some common characteristics.

Commentary

People may well wonder about religion and spirituality either directly or indirectly. They may encounter friends, family members or others for whom such beliefs are an intrinsic part of their lives. In our work as social workers these people may well enter into the conversations and reflections ventilated by children. This could trigger an interesting exploration by the child or adolescent about the meaning of life or a search for the answer to the question what is religion? Your own perspective and theoretical orientation will guide you in considering how to respond:

- Do you take this literally or metaphorically?
- Do you enable the client to speculate, describe their hidden fears about such matters or suggest an interpretation that seeks to address underlying dilemmas or conflicts around the issue?

The following list attempts to bring forward a definition or to describe the common characteristics of religions around the world (Whiting, 1991):

- They look for the something else or somebody beyond the world of senses and scientific measurement. This something or somebody controls all.
- They have great figures, men of vision who seem to perceive the something else more than other people.
- They all express themselves in the written word trying to encapsulate what they believe in.
- Each religion gives to its own people advice on how to behave and what to do to draw close to the something else or somebody.
- Religions are often practised by people coming together in common worship at special places.
- Religions often bring people together at special times for particular celebrations.
- All religions hold special funeral ceremonies and grapple with the problem of whether there is life after death.

Children involved in war as victims or forced combatants are deprived of the enjoyment of spiritual rights. Research demonstrates the severe and enduring mental health problems experienced by refugee and asylum seekers from areas of conflict (Hodes, 2000). Social workers can utilise spiritual beliefs in helping children recover from dehumanising and traumatising atrocities by enabling the expression of terror and fearfulness through re-connecting them with their prevailing religious constructs that may have been abandoned. Some of these children will perhaps have a strong sense of guilt inherited from a religious belief system that blamed humanity for the death of Jesus. The death of parents, siblings or close relatives will probably have resonated with these inherent guilt feelings compounding them into a persecutory frame of mind. Social workers would need to be careful with evoking a religious construct that could inadvertently exaggerate already troubling feelings.

The link between spirituality and psycho-social practice is emphasised if we enlist an understanding of spirituality that suggests it is the outward expression of the inner workings of the human spirit. In other words it is a personal and social process that refers to the ideas, concepts, attitudes and behaviours that derive from a person's or a community's interpretation of their experiences of the spirit. It is intrapersonal in that it refers to the quest for inner connectivity and it is interpersonal in that it relates to the relationships between people and within communities. And it is transpersonal in so far as it reaches beyond self and others into the transcendent realms of experience that move beyond that which is available at a mundane level (Swinton, 2003).

Therapy and cultural belief

Therapeutic work with people will amongst other things address the belief system of the individual and/or their family. Belief in this sense usually means exploring the client's beliefs about their problem as the start of establishing a helping relationship. The client may believe that their problem/s are the result of divine intervention – a punishment for a sin or misdemeanour of some kind. Among some cultures there is a potent belief system that spirits can possess people and make them unwell or be invoked to help them with a problem. In the case of a child or young person who is causing concern among teachers, social workers or health professionals there may be a simple diagnosis or assessment of the cause of the problem but this may not fit with the family's beliefs about the cause.

However belief also relates to religion and spirituality. If you unable or unwilling to explore this aspect of belief then you may be missing a vital component of the individual or family's overall belief system about how the world works and how problems arise and more importantly what is likely to be effective treatment (Walker, 2005). The key is to open communication and seek a greater depth to your understanding of the way the family works as part of progressive assessment practice.

The importance of spirituality is illustrated when we appreciate for example that spirituality is the cornerstone of the Aboriginal identity. Australian aboriginal spiritual tradition places the origin of each aboriginal clan in its own land. These clans hold deep spiritual links with their lands which were formed in Dreamtime. The ancestral creative beings that travelled across the continent at the beginning of time established land boundaries between different Aboriginal clans and the sacred sites. Ritual obligations and religious ceremonies are carried out at these sites in order to reinforce the bond Aboriginal people feel to their lands. If they move from the land or it is taken from them they lose their cultural identity and self-esteem (Yeo, 2003). For example psychological problems have been linked with the Australian government policy of forced removal of people from Aboriginal lands (Human Rights Commission, 1997).

A powerful argument is advanced by several authors who recommend incorporating a more explicit acknowledgement of the role that religion and spirituality can play in our work. A recent study found that the cost of not taking religious and cultural beliefs into account resulted directly in lack of attendance at specialist CAMH services. Insisting on holding certain support sessions on set days and times meant that some Muslim children could not benefit from appointments because they were expected to attend Mosque after school (Jayarajan, 2001).

ACTIVITY 9.5

Consider how often religion and spirituality are mentioned in relation to your clients in general.

Are these aspects or non-aspects of their lives taken into account when undertaking assessment and reviewing strengths and resources?

How active are you in mentioning these topics when engaging in work with people?

Commentary

In order to respond to this dilemma and enable social workers to harness positive aspects of religion and spirituality in their work a theory of multicultural therapy has been advanced that offers a multidimensional paradigm to guide practice (Sue et al., 1996; Raval, 1996). The authors suggest that:

- It is necessary to have a meta-theory of counselling and psychotherapy to allow different theoretical models to be applied and integrated where possible.
- Both counsellor and client identities are formed and embedded in multiple levels of life experiences and contexts therefore treatment should take greater account of the child or young person's experience in relation to their context.
- The cultural identity development of the counsellor and client and the wider power differentials associated with this, play an important role in the therapeutic relationship.
- Multi-cultural counselling and therapy effectiveness is enhanced when the counsellor

uses modalities and defines goals consistent with the life experiences and cultural values of the client.
- The theory stresses the importance of multiple helping roles developed by many cultural groups and societies. Apart from the one to one encounter aimed at remediation in the individual, those roles often involve larger social units, system intervention and prevention.

Multi-cultural counselling and therapy helps the person develop a greater awareness about themselves in relation to their different contexts. This results in practice that is contextual in orientation and which is able to respectfully draw on traditional methods of healing with a spiritual or religious dimension from many cultures. Paul Tillich (1963) alluded to this when he described something called *theonomy* meaning the *pursuit of culture under the impact of spiritual presence* – a liberal humanism with an underlying spiritual depth.

It is perhaps a paradox that the decline of organised religion in white western societies combined with the consequences of previous imperialist expansion throughout the World has produced a growing culturally diverse population among who are large numbers of devout religious communities with highly developed spiritual belief systems that organise social behaviour. Modern, progressive social work practice aspires to understand and support groups of people to help them make sense of their beliefs or lack of them in terms of vulnerability or resilience.

Chapter summary

Knowledge of cultural diversity, the skills of interpretation and negotiation in building partnership, and the values of individualisation and respect for uniqueness and diversity are the foundation of culturally competent practice. The relevance of religion and spirituality cannot be underestimated as they form a part of the covert or overt belief systems of adults, families, communities and children and young people that will to a larger or lesser extent impact on your work.

Most cultures can trace deep evidence of their ancestral heritage and the ways early civilisations sought to explain the world around them. These tend to involve the intervention of a supreme being or power, with the capacity to control the natural elements vital for the survival of the species.

The history of modern societies has been shaped as much by the religious struggles of previous stages of development as by the economic and political forces motivating people to embark upon social change or revolution. A psycho-social model offer us an inter-personal and intra-psychic therapeutic understanding of these powerfully important contexts within which individual people evolve their emotional well-being.

The western model of psychological illness tends to ignore the religious or spiritual aspects of the culture in which it is based. However, eastern, African and Native American cultures tend to integrate them. Spirituality and religion can be critical components of a person's psychological well being offering a source of strength, and hope in trying circumstances. This dimension is part of the constellation of factors affecting all communities, bearing in mind the positive and sometimes negative impact spiritual or religious beliefs might have on their mental health.

Four core qualities of spiritual experience have been identified – awareness, mystery, value, and meaningfulness/insight. They are often assumed to be consistent with positive life-affirming experiences. Many religions contain concepts of hell and punishment which could trigger profound feelings of despair that are experienced as completely physically and psychologically overwhelming.

Children are especially creative in providing a potent context for reflection – it may be a church, mosque, synagogue, temple or even a tree, or gang den. Using this concept therapeutically opens up another avenue for practitioners who seek to explore and heal the inner world of children and young people.

CHAPTER 10

Integrating Methods, Skills and Values

Learning objectives

- Integrate knowledge, skills and values in analysing information and weighing its significance and priority.
- Demonstrate how an assessment leads to a set of concrete objectives for intervention.
- Work in partnership to negotiate and plan responses to assessed needs, risks, responsibilities, strengths and resources.
- Effectively generate and manage resources in practice to creatively enable and support clients working with personal and structural change.

Introduction

We have reviewed the contemporary evidence for assessment and intervention practice, and in preceding chapters examined some of the dilemmas arising from the aims and aspirations expected within national occupational standards and other practice guidance. It is now important to consider ways of integrating the knowledge, skills and values required to analyse information and weigh their significance and priority. We also need to pay attention to considering how to demonstrate how an assessment leads to a set of concrete objectives for intervention. Working in partnership to negotiate and plan responses to assessed needs, risks, responsibilities, strengths and resources should form a significant part of the process of integration. These are some of the ways you can effectively generate and manage resources in practice and how to enable and support clients working with change:

Integration

Integrating knowledge, skills and values in analysing information and being able to weigh its significance and priority as a basis for effective planning is a demanding task. O'Sullivan (1999) suggests that sound planning will happen provided the following elements in the decision-making process are delineated:

- **Being critically aware of and taking into account the decision-making contexts** – Knowledge of legal requirements and agency procedures are the critical ingredients of planning what is possible and permissible. Statutory duty has to be balanced against your endeavour to take a holistic perspective of the situation. Involving the client to the highest feasible level. There can be four levels – being told; being consulted, being a partner, and being in control. A key skill is to fit the level of involvement to the nature of the particular planning situation.
- **Consulting with all stakeholders** – There could be numerous stakeholders involved in your work with a particular service user. Some will have more systematic contact but only general knowledge about the client, but they could be as valuable as someone with limited contact but who has specialised knowledge. A range of perceptions can either enhance the clarity in a situation and confirm your hypothesis, or produce a disparate and confusing picture which hinders rather than helps. Being clear in your thinking and aware of your emotions. A heightened element of self awareness is always useful. Over-reacting to a situation on the basis of tiredness, stress, the day of the week or simply false information need to be guarded against. Equally under-reacting to a risky situation because of feelings of pity, empathy, or over-optimism can contribute to an escalation of risk factors.
- **Producing a well-reasoned frame of the decision situation that is consistent with the available information** – Through framing processes you can shape the information into a picture of the situation, planning goals and a set of options. Listing key factors and considering the weight to give to each requires knowledge, experience, and the capacity for short and long term predictions of the consequences of various interventions. Basing your course of action on a systematic appraisal of the options. The plan could be based on the principle that a statutory duty overrides the traumatic impact of the subsequent intervention. Or which option is likely to provide the best outcome in the context of risk assessment and available supportive resources.

Strategies for integration

Learning arises as a result of the four-stage process of concrete experience; reflective observation; abstract conceptualisation; and active experimentation according to Thompson (2000). You can use this model to describe and facilitate the application of your knowledge and theory to practice. Guard against the false belief in theory-less practice. The skill is not whether – but how to use your theory to best effect. Being explicit about your knowledge base and resisting complacency about the values, ideas, and assumptions underpinning your practice will help.

Common sense is often invoked to justify conclusions. However this is another way of repeating dominant cultural values, and trying to avoid a more refined explanation for the thinking behind your judgement. Better to spend a little time on developing a critical perspective. Research-minded practice can help integrate theory and practice. It involves recognising the parallel between research activity and social work practice. A participative approach embodies this concept by blending creativity and rigour, and encouraging participants to share decisions, goal-setting, and the most desirable process to be followed.

The critical incident technique is a way of analysing a situation where strong emotions were raised in your practice and which interfered with your ability to function effectively then or could in future. It involves reflecting on the incident and asking three questions:

1. What happened;
2. How would you account for this;
3. What other conceptual frameworks could help understand this incident?

Developing a group approach for narrowing the gap between theory and practice can be very effective. It provides opportunities for mutual support within a team setting where critical exploration of ideas takes place in a safe environment. This approach promotes a sense of ownership and shared responsibility which can be empowering and facilitate continuous professional development.

Intuition versus analysis

Planning intervention in social work and the decision-making process includes thinking and feeling about the situation being addressed. But there is debate about whether intuitive or analytical thought is more suited to social work decisions. A contrast between these two distinct forms of thinking is drawn in the social work literature with the tendency to favour intuitive rather than analytical thinking, rejecting the latter as a technical, calculative approach not in harmony with social work values. As with many polarised debates the desire to simplify in order to heighten differences can obscure the valuable resources within each approach. It needs to be acknowledged that analysis is not inevitably technical, that intuition can be unreliable, but both can offer equally useful ways of thinking.

Intuition

Intuition has been variously described as the absence of analysis, the pinnacle of expertise, or the unconscious processing of data. This means that the basis for the consequent judgement is not made explicit at the time. It can be thought of as deciding in a relatively holistic way, without separating the decision situation into its various elements. This enables it to be a quick way of deciding by making use of limited information by sensing patterns and filling in gaps. To be reliable and accurate intuition needs to be based on expertise developed over time, but it has a fundamental drawback which stems from its implicit nature. This is that the reasons behind intuitive decisions are not readily available for comment and scrutiny, which is necessary for partnership practice.

Analysis

Analysis can be defined as a step by step, conscious, logically defensible process. There is deliberation over the different elements in a situation in a systematic and organised way. It can be thought of as using selected information in a precise way, whereas intuition uses all of the perceived information in an imprecise way. The strength of analysis is that it encourages openness about reasoning and so potentially holds your work open to scrutiny. The disadvantage in this approach is that it can induce misplaced faith in the ability to make predictions particularly in the increasing social work field of risk assessment.

Synthesis

Seeing intuition and analysis as opposites can obscure the potential compatibility and complementarity of the approaches. Some social work planning decisions will require breaking down into their component parts and given careful consideration. But because this involves issues of uncertainty and values, intuition needs to be used within analysis in the making of judgements about the significance of information. Combining the explicitness of analysis with the skilled judgements of professional intuition offers you the advantages of each approach. When facilitating client decision making or making decisions in partnership, some degree of analysis will be helpful as it involves being explicit about the basis of choice.

Ethics and values

There are several sources of guidance for you in trying to juggle the variety of competing demands on your time and on the ethical dilemmas that contemporary social work practice present you with. Trying to do this while seeking to integrate and synthesise all the different elements of practice is challenging. Clients, your agency management and professional principles all clamour for attention in your assessment and planning practice. There is a professional code (BASW, 2002) in which the expectations for professional practice are described and defined. There are your duties as prescribed in your job contract and are based in part on legislative and practice guidance. And there are the rights of service users that are being defined in the context of government health and social care policies informed by statutes such as the *Human Rights Act 1998*.

In all of these sources the ethics and values of social work practice are being indirectly put under the microscope and require careful examination if you are to achieve good practice standards and competencies. The ethics and values inherent in social work practice will help you navigate the sometimes turbulent waters where clients, your employer, the professional code and your personal position are all in conflict. Your duties as an employee and your obligations to service users will sometimes come into conflict causing angst and mixed feelings. It is important that you arrive at a position in which you can feel relatively at ease with your stance on a certain issue or with your practice decisions.

Assessment practice presents many situations where such conflicts can arise. For example over eligibility criteria for a particular service which

you might regard as too restrictive and leaves clients vulnerable. Or in the case of needs assessment many social workers feel uneasy about conducting a full and comprehensive assessment of a person's situation that highlights many needs that cannot be met by their employing agency. The concept of identifying unmet need causes a great deal of difficulty in practice compared to the apparently innocuous administrative requirement to detail those unmet needs. Social workers are rightly sceptical about the claim that identification of such unmet need translates into effective data for future resource allocation.

The following summary of the different levels of duty inherent in your social work role can assist in positioning yourself in situations of ethical conflict (Banks, 1995):

- **Duties to users** – where you respect user's rights to make decisions, their rights to confidentiality, and to safeguard and promote the welfare of children. Guidance includes the professional code of ethics, agency policies, codes of practice the law, public opinion and charters for user's rights.
- **Duties to the profession** – where you uphold the good name of social work by maintaining ethical and effective practice. Guidance here includes the professional code of ethics and guidance.
- **Duties to the agency** – where you follow the prescribed rules and procedures safeguarding the reputation of the agency. Guidance includes your job description, contract and agency policies and procedures.
- **Duties to society** – where you help maintain social order consistent with the responsibilities of social services departments or probation services as laid down in statute. Guidance includes the law, government guidance, and public opinion.

Is there a hierarchy of ethical practice in the context of these duties? The professional code of ethics is often quoted as the dominant source of guidance for your practice when you are faced with professional conflicts. In cases where agency policies contravene the professional code you may feel entitled to change or challenge those policies by refusing to comply with them. There can be no easy prescription or detailed guidance to cover every nuance within each unique situation you face. Each individual has to arrive at their own conclusion which will be decided by your own personal ethical code. Only you can make the decision to risk disciplinary proceedings from an employer or challenge practices inconsistent with your values by invoking grievance procedures backed by your trades union or BASW representative.

Probably the worst position is to feel disempowered, undervalued and forced into practices with which you fundamentally disagree yet carry on in a spirit of resentful collusion. This can corrode your sense of worth and undermine the humanitarian principles that brought you into social work practice. It results in low morale, routinised practice, poor staff retention and recruitment that affects service quality and impacts on your relationship with service users. It is of course this relationship which is at the heart of professional practice and is the one aspect of service that clients consistently report valuing highly. In the wider context of increasingly managerialist styles of supervision in social work agencies where the needs of the bureaucracy seem to come before clients, it is little surprise that many social workers find their position untenable.

You may find a variety of answers to help you deal personally with these conflicts and impossible dilemmas. At times and in certain circumstances your position might change or as your career develops you may find your views changing on certain issues that were previously certain. It is likely that you might recognise the following strategies as options for dealing with these ethical challenges (Banks, 1995):

- **Defensive practice** – where you carry out to the letter agency duties and procedures. You perceive yourself as an official of the employing agency and find yourself referring clients to your managers or elected councillors when they complain about the level of service. You are aware that you have separated out your duties to your agency and your personal values, with the latter being subsumed to the agency rules.
- **Reflective practice** – where you recognise more actively the ethical dilemmas in practice and their roots in social inequalities. You are perhaps more confident about your own values, how to put them into practice and integrate them. This enables you to reflect, learn from practice and take risks. It also makes you more likely to challenge agency procedures and advocate on behalf of service users.

Social work skills

Separating out the distinctive skills of assessment and intervention is difficult and as we have seen already there are a plethora of methods, models and a variety of distinctions in their underpinning practice philosophies. The following summary is intended as a guide to help illuminate your way through the available material and provide a framework for integration within which your own personal values and ethical social work identity can flourish (Trevithick, 2000):

- **Information gathering** – one of the major criticisms of contemporary assessment practice is the vast amount of time spent on assessment and in particular information gathering. There could almost be an inverse relationship between the quantity of information gathered and the quality of the assessment. More in this case seems to be less. It is however understandable as a symptom of defensive practice and the needs of the bureaucracy rather than what might be in the best interests of the client. It is also tempting to think that a vital piece of information needs to be found in order to provide a significant clue that can aid analysis. It is probably better to learn to judge what information is relevant in particular situations – but without descending into robotic routinised practice.
- **Communication** – the bedrock of social work practice often taken for granted within the compassionate, caring instincts of your desire to help. Communication is a two-way process, it is as much about listening and observing as it is about talking. It includes non-verbal gesture, posture, tone of voice and the interactive nature of the assessment process. Recording and writing skills are part and parcel of everyday practice and these are almost an art in themselves. It is crucial to think about the impact your case notes might have on another worker or a service user who requests access to information held about them. Inspections frequently highlight the poor quality of case note recordings so it is important to spend time improving your skills in this area.
- **Analysis** – involves identifying the key elements of a situation and recognising significant patterns and interrelationships (Thompson and Thompson, 2002). The trouble is two workers might recognise different

patterns in the same piece of work, or the pattern may be a result of the way assessment is carried out rather than inherent within the information. Systems theory could help you here because of its attention to circular reflexive patters in family's, groups and institutions. Analysis calls for a process of weighing the significance of the elements of an assessment and forming a judgement based on valid evidence to support it.

- **Planning** – can take place in a variety of contexts such as formal meetings, case conferences, supervision etc. it also occurs within the helping relationship with your clients. It may not be expressed as such overtly but during the assessment process the service user will be indicating what they hope to achieve or where the want to be at some point in the future with your assistance. Whereas in formal professional meetings the overt function is to draw up a plan there may be a covert agenda about relationships, responsibilities and resources. The skill is in recognising these subtle interactions and placing their significance in your own strategic aims. Having a degree of imagination will help, so will having the capacity to stand back and see the bigger picture and being able to articulate your views in an authoritative way.

- **Partnership** – the fundamental skill in all social work practice but essential to assessment and intervention. Not an equal partnership because this is not possible given the power differential and ultimate statutory responsibility underpinning your role, but a partnership in the sense that your client's views are taken seriously, recorded and properly acknowledged. Partnership includes having the capacity to engage with some people who are so overwhelmed or distressed by their circumstances that their aggressive, violent behaviour or feelings make it extremely hard work. Recognising that much of what is aimed at you is not personal and is a product of neglect, fear or abuse can help you maintain a professional stance. Also, taking on board the service user's perception can be done without deceiving them into thinking they can dictate terms.

ACTIVITY 10.1

Spend ten minutes thinking about the constraints on planning intervention in social work. Discuss your findings with a colleague or supervisor and consider the strategies you might use for managing.

Commentary

Your findings might include the excessive demands placed on you combined with diminished resources and increased expectation for accountability and efficiency. You have less time to think with more complex situations to deal with. There is pressure to narrow the scope of the assessment and work in the short term to purchase or commission services from sources with variable quality. You might feel constrained to think narrowly, to resort to routinised practice yet the diversity of modern life challenges simplified eligibility and pro-forma guidelines. There may be a feeling of being expected to know everything and therefore to specialise in a particular area or client group. However this obscures the generic knowledge base in social work that transcends client group specialisms and minimises broader concepts of social welfare, practice methodology, human growth and development, anti-racist, and anti-oppressive practice.

Your strategies for managing might include reflection and self awareness techniques to develop stress management skills. Supervision and consultation are central to this. Thinking big and acting small. This means keeping in mind the broader picture of the social and economic context of people's lives and the personal consequences which you may be able to help with. Without being pessimistic or underestimating service users capacity you may find having small attainable goals which can be sustained and built on more useful than expecting dramatic shifts in people's situations.

The practice context

An illustration of the potential for integrating methods, skills and values can be found in the practice context example of child and family social work. Here we can detect a potential distinction between the specialised area of family therapy intervention with the more diffuse and broadly defined practice of family support. Family support can be defined as self-help or volunteer help with little statutory involvement, or it can mean a continuum of advice, support, and specialist help geared to provide early preventive intervention. The intervention can be directed at individual parents, couples, the child, the whole family, or in groups. It can consist of individual counselling, psychotherapy, groupwork, advice and information, or the provision of practical help. Within the mix of interventions are the hallmarks of the family therapy paradigm that assumes problems are interpersonal.

The status and perception of preventive family support work can be usefully conceptualised using a three-stage model identifying different levels of intervention (Hardiker, 1995).

1. The primary level offers universally available services that can strengthen family functioning provided by a mix of state welfare providers and parent education services often organised by voluntary organisations.
2. The secondary level provides services targeted on families in early difficulties such as relationship counselling for couples, informal family centres, and home visiting schemes by voluntary agencies to help families with young children.
3. At the third, or tertiary level, work with families can include those who are suffering severe difficulties and on the threshold of care proceedings characterised by intensive work either by the statutory or voluntary sector to prevent family breakdown.

Services geared towards the needs of specific age groups of children or young people, or adults can determine the type of help offered and whether it is perceived as family or individual support (Walker, 2001b). At each level you could be involved as family therapists and family support workers, becoming involved with the same families.

Services geared towards the needs of specific age groups of children or young people, or adults can determine the type of help offered and whether it is perceived as family or individual support. This becomes particularly important in the area of child and adolescent mental health for example, where the initial assessment of the presenting problem could be formulated on an individual or family basis. Social workers trained in family therapy are particularly alert to the potential for scapegoating individual children within family systems functioning in negative and punitive ways. Family Therapy has evolved into definitions as simple as offering a view of problems as inter-personal rather than individual (Dallos and Draper, 2000). Or, as comprehensive as Gorell-Barnes (1998) who describes the activities as:

- Encompassing a philosophy of relational events.
- Methods of description between people and their social context.
- A relational approach to work with families.
- A variety of therapeutic methods.

Some of the literature on family support describes ways of helping families (Sutton, 1999; Hill, 1999; Pinkerton et al., 2000). They provide the following common characteristics:

- Using listening skills.
- Getting alongside families.
- Emphasising collaboration.
- Developing cultural awareness.
- Gathering information.
- Recognising positives in the situation.

An examination of these terms quickly shows similarities with skills considered important for family therapy accreditation, even though different vocabulary is employed. How far support or therapy directly address the social context, or succeed in doing so is a moot point. The debate about the fit between family therapy practice and its application in social policy contexts has generated thoughtful contributions (Reimers and Treacher, 1995; Sveaass and Reichelt, 2001). The most recent focus on the socio-political discourse generated around refugees and asylum seekers, and how these meta-contexts invariably intrude on the therapeutic encounter.

Families from areas of conflict will encounter family therapy or family support services, particularly when the effects of trauma manifest in child behaviour problems. Without an active engagement with the social policy context that portrays these families as objects of pity or welfare scroungers, therapists and support staff can limit their helping potential. It could be argued that family support services by their very nature, would be orientated more towards this social policy context, and are created to specifically address issues raised within it.

But they may be missing important 'therapeutic' opportunities that are masked by too narrow a focus on human rights, legal, or welfare benefit tasks. On the other hand, family therapists employing an inflexible therapeutic model, and concentrating on the inter-familial beliefs, behaviour and patterns of communication, might be missing an important 'social' dimension to the family's experience and neglecting to find culturally competent ways of engaging them. The use of interpreters adds yet another complication. The important point is that your practice is not being too tightly prescribed as you move between various roles in your contact with families. You can therefore integrate the most useful parts of a family therapy intervention and combine it with broad family support measures. Your practice is more whole and families benefit from multi-skilled practitioners.

Social workers have the opportunity to employ communication and relationship skills in direct family support work which they traditionally find rewarding and which service users find more acceptable than intrusive, investigative risk assessment. Your role in multi-agency assessment and planning becomes significant in this context where several perceptions can be expressed, based on diverse evidence and different levels of professional anxiety. Managing these processes with individuals or groups in planning meetings, case conferences, or case reviews, requires advanced negotiation and decision-making skills which are the hallmarks of integrated practice.

The renaissance of family support in Britain is currently perceived as an alternative to child protection, rather than part of a connected architecture of resources to be activated as different needs emerge. Therefore the policy to develop indirect voluntary provision of family support services in Britain can be better seen as a symptom of, rather than solution to, retrenchment in family support offered by professional social workers. The literature on social work in Europe acknowledges the dilemmas in seeking a common professional social work identity, and family support practice which can simultaneously value autonomy in each member country (Shardlow and Payne, 1998; Adams et al., 2002). This illustrates at a meta-level the complexities in trying to integrate all the elements making up modern social work practice.

Participatory practice

One of the key characteristics of contemporary social work services is the partnership approach to work with service users mentioned in Chapter 3. This is enshrined in practice guidance and codes of ethics. It involves a process of negotiation with families about the venue for work, and the choice of practice methods particularly during the assessment process. It is important to make distinctions about the different levels of partnership possible in your intervention as you begin to integrate your practice. The assessing social worker rarely meets with an individual on a truly voluntary basis therefore the experience is characterised by unequal power relations with decisions requiring professional judgement. However it is crucial to differentiate between making a judgement and being judgmental. The former requires facing up to the challenge of responsibility in order to be helpful, while the latter involves prejudice, blaming, and a closed mind.

Participatory practice has become embedded along with empowerment in social work practice to the extent that there is little debate about whether this is always an appropriate strategy and whether service users have said they desire this approach. Participation is normally thought of as a process where the key stakeholders in a service co-operate in defining how the service should be designed and delivered. This can happen in an individual or an organisational context. Parents may negotiate with a service for the best course of action to take in the interests of their child. Or people who use services may represent other service users' opinions in an organisational forum.

Research by Barnardo's concluded that of the parents who used their services none came with the intention of becoming a partner (Daines et al., 1990). Staff interviewed saw participatory practice as a strategy to empower users and build services around their views. Users on the other hand, saw participation embodied in the friendliness, accessibility and helpfulness of staff. Other research highlights the challenges in working in partnership with absent parents of children in long-term care. In these situations social workers have to contribute to planning on the basis of several conflicting issues and make a judgement about the viability of a partnership approach and how far to risk further harm on the child:

- The importance of promoting contact with parents, relatives, community and culture.
- The failings of the care system to enable children to reach their potential and fully meet their needs.
- The importance of birth families and the value of different attachments in helping children form their identity.

- In conflict-laden situations parents have often been passively hindered by inadequate resources, inaccurate information, or changes of social worker.
- The potentially destructive effects of persistent abandonment, rejection or neglect from a parent failing to maintain arranged contact.

One means of working in partnership is by conferring rights such as the approach adopted by the disability movement and which is often linked to discussions about citizenship. This is further defined as participation and has been summarised by Mullender and Ward (1991):

- All people have skills, understanding and ability.
- People have rights to be heard, to participate, to choose, to define problems and action.
- People's problems are complex and social oppression is a contributory factor.
- People acting collectively are powerful.
- Methods of work must be non-elitist and non-oppressive.

In this form of practice you have to assess needs, evaluate risks and allocate resources in a way that is equitable as possible for a wide range of people in various situations. Here are some common pitfalls experienced in attempting to achieve a balanced assessment as a basis for planning your intervention (Thompson, 1995; Milner and O'Byrne, 1998):

- **Selective attention** – research shows that while striving for objectivity we commonly weigh some evidence from assessments more heavily than others. It is easy to develop a mental check list of factors considered important or relevant thereby excluding other potentially valuable information. First impressions tend to stick and these are invariably negative when clients are in crisis or not coping. This makes it hard to perceive strengths and can lead to an attempt to compensate by being unrealistically optimistic about a service users ability to change.
- **Stereotyping** – this can lead to compartmentalising people into ready-made classification rather than working hard to see the uniqueness in a person. The skill is being able to generalise to some extent about client groups and use broad parameters to ensure equitable service, but to avoid crude stereotyping which denies individuality. Superficial adherence to social work values and

anti-discriminatory practice will not equip you to resist stereotyping. Research has shown that social workers for example describe challenges to their decisions as 'manipulative' (Davis and Ellis, 1995).
- **Attributional bias** – research shows that we attribute successes to our own efforts and our failures to events outside ourselves. However we judge other people oppositely. This is called attributional bias. It is an attempt to make sense of situations so that we can exert some control over and influence events. But this can lead to victim-blaming and in social work intervention results in a tendency to locate the problem within the individual rather than their social circumstances. This concept also helps explain the notion of learned helplessness with people who are depressed and who behave passively towards social workers.
- **Sensory distortions** – the most obvious sensory distortion in personal perception is the effect of physical appearance on judgements. Attractive people are usually ascribed positive personality traits whereas someone smelling of stale urine is not likely to be assessed as having strength of character. Clients in stressful or crisis situations with raised voices or disorganised thinking are going to affect your perception of their personality-however much you intellectually understand the context of their behaviour.

ACTIVITY 10.2

Think about yourself and events that have made an impact on you in your past. Consider situations where you felt vulnerable, desperate or in need. Think about how those present or concerned about you may have perceived you and the situation you were in. What sort of judgements were they making about you? Did they see someone with strengths or just weaknesses?

Commentary

In recalling your personal past you may now be able to see how others were influenced by your behaviour and feelings to the extent where they were restricting their assessment and drawing stereotypical conclusions. At the time, or now in retrospect you may feel a sense of injustice at how limited this perception of you was, and how it reinforced your sense of failure or vulnerability, if it persisted. Timing is as always crucial. It may be inappropriate to start identifying strengths in someone too early in your work in case it is interpreted by them as a signal of your impatience or punitive beliefs about pulling themselves together.

On the other hand dwelling on deficits may further push the client into a state of helplessness and despair. A good guide as always is your own feelings – these will be connected to how the service user is feeling, so by practising the habit of interrogating your own feelings you will begin to sense how the client is. For example you might feel angry with the client during a piece of work with them so instead of making yourself feel guilty about this another way of dealing with the feeling of anger is to see it as a transference from the client. By openly acknowledging this with them and offering an interpretation of their anger you may open up an avenue of exploration that can help them at a deeper level.

This technique is sometimes misconstrued as amateur psychoanalysis or mystification, but actually it is based on simple humanitarian concepts and the real feelings generated during the helping process. It is also more liberating for service users to gain some insight into themselves as a step towards recovery and self-determination rather than allowing your embarrassment or timidity to prevent them from moving on in their lives.

Multi-disciplinary and inter-agency working

Partnership practice is not restricted to how you work with service users but also how you follow best practice guidance in relationships with other agencies. Government and professional expectations are for more integrated and therefore effective joint working across professional boundaries in Community Care, Children and Families, and Mental Health contexts. Research shows there are still barriers to effective working which have a negative impact on clients and hinder integrated practice. These include:

- Financial constraints.
- Differing organisational and managerial structures.
- Different priorities.

Joint working can be improved and is influenced by intentional approaches as well as informal evolutionary factors. The intentional approach may formalise joint working arrangements but these can neglect the more personal and creative aspects of partnership. Embedding such approaches can take a long time, constrain opportunities into restrictive prescriptions, and result in relatively unresponsive mechanisms. An evolving approach, on the other hand, allows for informal networking but can become over-reliant on key personalities and historical associations. Charismatic individuals may be highly effective in the short term but prove impossible to replace and leave a void behind them, when they leave. A combination of formal and informal strategies can optimise the conditions for effective joint working by:

- Joint planning meetings.
- Creation of joint posts.
- Development of joint strategy.
- Individual initiatives.
- Shared goals and vision.
- Track record of joint working.

Inter-professional or multi-disciplinary care are contemporary terms often used synonymously to mean joint working between staff from different professional backgrounds. Staff may work in the same team location or operate from separate uni-professional teams. Within the same agency they may represent different disciplines or client groups. In whatever configuration joint working has always been recommended as the best way of delivering coherent and effective care in health and social work practice. Every social or health care textbook features injunctions for closer working between agencies, better communication, and clear lines of accountability.

Absence of these elements of practice is usually highlighted in all-too frequent inquiries into deaths involving child abuse, mental health, or social care situations. Government practice guidance emphasises these ideas in slick managerialist terms and appeals to systems-level co-ordination, enhanced procedures, and strategic planning. Translating these ideas into practice skills is more difficult than rhetorical slogans.

There have been attempts to identify some key and common skill and knowledge elements that inform work with children and young people for example Tucker et al., 1999. The conclusions are that different workers from different professional contexts can share a common perception of what needs to be understood about a child or young person's life in order to intervene effectively. These can be transferred to all client groups:

- The social and environmental context.
- Gender, class, ethnicity, disability.

- Articulating a human rights perspective.
- Recognising the individual characteristics of all people.
- Developing reflective practice.

These are recognisable as consistent with social work practice knowledge and skills, however they are operationalised in different legal and organisational contexts which is where problems arise in trying to foster better inter-agency working. Staff in whatever agency context are hampered and hindered to some extent by the constraints of budgets, resource limits and service specifications. One way of mitigating these factors is to promote more joint education and training opportunities and to foster moves towards shared professional qualifications.

Social workers are often reminded of their pivotal role in multi-disciplinary working and the core skills of social work practice are cited as a major asset in helping achieve better inter-professional work (Parsloe, 1999; Smale et al., 2001; Adams et al., 2002). The care manager role has perhaps institutionalised this concept where social workers are employed to organise and monitor care plans using a variety of other agency staff, often in multi-disciplinary settings. In other situations you may be directly or indirectly involved in work in which your contribution, *however small*, could make a big difference to a successful outcome. In the context of child and family work for example, the social work role is pivotal in the following circumstances:

- As child and family workers involved in assessment.
- As convenors of inter-agency planning meetings.
- At case conferences involving child protection concerns.
- In long-term care planning and reviews.
- In the formal care management role.
- As contributors to multi-disciplinary intervention.
- In young offender teams.
- As referrers to specialist and community resources.

In whatever context of practice you need to examine the complex web of agencies and staff available to contribute to the needs of your clients. This offers an opportunity to reflect on the potential for success, spot potential areas of professional disagreement or confusion, and

clarify the social work contribution. The unique professional profile of social work embodying psycho-social principles, and a social model of human growth and development, find expression in the values enshrined in the latest social work code of ethics. Together with national occupational standards they offer a powerful intellectual *corpus* to bring to inter-professional and multi-disciplinary work (BASW, 2002).

The challenges in working together

The range of staff involved in the delivery of health and social care services is broad and the potential for disagreement, confusion or poor communication is high (Koprowska, 2005). The benefits of working together cannot be overstated but this should not happen at the expense of proper professional debate that sometimes can be difficult. However, before considering the diversity of professional and voluntary backgrounds engaged in this work, it is worth remembering that parents/carers provide over 90 per cent of the care of their children. They are the people who will be in most contact with the child or young person at the centre of concern. Therefore they must be seen as partners with whom an appropriate alliance is formed, even in the face of profound disagreements about the way forward.

There is growing interest in the further development of inter-professional and multi disciplinary working in order to maximise the effectiveness of interventions to meet the diverse needs of multi-cultural societies and service users (Magrab et al., 1997; Oberheumer, 1998; Tucker et al., 1999). The evidence suggests there are cost-benefit advantages if duplication of tasks can be avoided, relationships between staff are improved and there is more opportunity to maintain the client at the centre of attention rather than the needs of the various organisations.

Other professionals do not experience the same level of supervision or the same type of supervision that permits reflective practice and the opportunity for stress management and exploration of strategies for coping with difference. The tradition in social work of such supervision is constantly under pressure by managerialist prescriptions for brief, task-centred working practices, risk assessment and prioritisation of caseloads. However, supervision that enables a worker to understand and learn from the interactive processes experienced during work is a valuable tool to encourage you to reflect on practice that can be emotionally draining.

Some social workers may find the experience unsettling while others will draw immense comfort from it. Both will benefit and have their practice enhanced as a result. In multi-disciplinary and inter-professional contexts a culture of such enlightened supervision for all staff can create a rich climate for professional growth and improved quality of service to service users. The evidence suggests there is an appetite to incorporate this social work model of supervision into the new multi-disciplinary teams that are becoming more common in health and social care (Debell and Walker, 2002).

Social workers bring a distinctive contribution to inter-professional and multi-disciplinary work. Effective multi-disciplinary team working or inter agency working requires the notion of power to be addressed and shared more equally between staff. It also requires power to be shared by more participative practices with service users and the community being served. Your skills in advocacy and empowerment are therefore crucial in making this happen. We also bring a concept of oppression and how discriminatory social contexts can blight the lives of children and families. This wider social and political perspective can raise awareness among other staff and inform and enrich the intervention practice of other professionals (Middleton, 1997).

ACTIVITY 10.3

The case study below gives an example where partnership appears fraught with difficulties and may appear unachievable. You have just been allocated this case. Think about how you would try to work in partnership with the family, taking into account the concerns of other professionals.

Father (Michael) age 45, unemployed.
Mother (Susan) age 32, left family 6 months ago, whereabouts unknown.
Daughter (Anne) age 11, at special school for children with learning difficulties.
Son (Adam) age 6, attends primary school.
Twins (Steve and Linda) age 38 months, Steve is brain damaged and Linda has a hole in her heart. Both have developmental delays.

The case was transferred from another local authority and has been dealt with on a duty basis. The father, Michael, has been uncooperative with many agencies concerned about his children. He has been rude, hostile and racially abusive. Hospital appointments for the twins have been missed and your concerns have been increasing over time. Adam and Anne bed wet and both have missed a lot of schooling. Michael feels there is nothing much wrong with them and focuses his attention mostly on the twins. He feels that professionals are exaggerating and he is determined to care for his family on his own.

The following questions might help in your planning:

- What are your feelings about working with members of this particular family?
- What are your anxieties about this case?
- How would you handle Michael's anger?
- How would you propose to share your concerns about the children with Michael?
- What strategies would you hope to develop to work in partnership with the family?

Commentary

Reflecting on your feelings may produce elements of fear, disapproval, and frustration. Or perhaps you might be aware of a certain admiration for Michael's tenacity and self-sufficiency. You may feel protective towards the children and angry that Michael is not putting their needs first. As a black worker you may want to discuss whether you should be allocated this case given his racist language, on the other hand you may feel quite challenged to work with him.

Your main anxieties may come from Michael's lack of co-operation and from concerns about the children's needs being neglected. The long-term consequences of this on their development, together with the impact on Michael of soldiering on heighten your concerns. Michael's anger could be explored to tease out the cause and help him manage it more usefully. Is it due to his wife's exit? Being perceived as an inadequate parent? Professional interference? His feelings of helplessness and his own needs being eclipsed?

Being open and honest with Michael about your concerns for the children is important but tricky. If you are less open you are likely to be disempowering Michael by not sharing the same information about the reasons for your involvement. So the issue is *how* you share your concerns and whether you achieve this in a supportive manner, avoiding being patronising or accusatory.

You might find joint working with a colleague helpful in managing Michael's anger and protecting your own safety.

Arranging a multi-agency case conference might be useful for planning and using resources and offers a chance to share concerns and measure the level against other perspectives. You might find it useful to explore the family's wider network as a possible source of support. Thought also needs to be given to the significance for the children of Susan and her absence. You might think about the use of a contract with Michael. This could set out the purposes of involvement and what is possible or not in terms of support, help and resources. It could give Michael space to outline his concerns, need and goals.

As part of the planning work, it might be helpful to list the needs of each child in the family, any concerns, and identify areas of agreement and disagreement between yourself and Michael. You may decide that Michael cannot be worked with and that legal intervention is the only way to secure the children's welfare. If this is the case, it is important that such a judgement is soundly based on evidence from other professionals, research, and only comes after all possibilities for engagement have been explored.

Imagine you have a supervision session arranged with your team leader. Supervision is part of a consultation and thinking process. Explore with your team leader, peer group, tutor or a colleague, some of the issues that have arisen when considering how to work in partnership with service users described above or in practice. This might include managing your own feelings, dilemmas and conflicts. You can also consider the challenges in trying to work in an anti-discriminatory way in partnership with other professionals and colleagues.

Supervision is a good opportunity to explore issues and feelings that you are uncertain or unconfident about. It gives you space and time to think and work through issues raised. You may find the questions below useful in helping you identify areas for further exploration, self-development and awareness:

- What particular dilemmas does partnership present for me?
- What are the advantages and disadvantages of working in partnership with clients?
- Do I find it easy or difficult to be open and honest with service users about my concerns?

- What strategies do I need to develop to handle difficult feelings?

Advocacy

Advocacy is associated with a rights-based approach to planning intervention and arises from a recognition that social work has not always empowered service users. It is at its simplest about speaking up for or acting on behalf of another person. The aim of advocacy is to make sure the client's voice is heard; to make sure the person gets the services they need; and to make sure the client knows their rights so they can work towards getting what they are entitled to. It should be part of your integrated practice knowledge and skills.

Key principles

- The service user's voice and views are paramount.
- Good advocacy leaves the person more able to do it themselves.
- Advocacy should help people to make informed choices.
- Ensuring the user feels in control of the process and trusts the advocate.
- Advising, assisting and supporting – not pressurising or persuading.

It is important to make the distinction between the role of care manager and advocate. The social worker as care manager may be intervening for the needs of the service user in negotiations about services to be provided, but they have also to make judgements about what they think is needed in the client's best interests. Direct Payments are an example where budgets can be controlled by service users to select provision, but a social worker still assesses need and makes a judgement about the ability of a person to manage that budget. An advocate on the other hand can maintain their focus on representing the views of the client.

There are three main types of advocacy:

1. **Citizen advocacy** – works on a one to one basis where usually volunteers act on behalf of those who require services. The citizen advocate primarily performs an instrumental role which can focus on welfare benefits problems or negotiating a care plan. There is also an expressive role which involves meeting emotional needs, befriending and providing support.

2. **Self advocacy** – involves training and group support to help people learn skills and gain emotional strength to advocate for themselves. It is also about personal and political needs focusing on participation in all areas of service planning and delivery. The aim is not just to improve services but to improve the status of service users. Self advocacy has the important function of facilitating collective action as well as making it easier for individuals to be assertive.

3. **Group advocacy** – brings people together with similar interests, so that they can operate as a group to represent their shared interests. Similar to self advocacy, the aim is to influence service delivery decisions and to reframe how certain problems or groups of clients are perceived by professionals. Group advocacy may be part of campaigning organisations operating in the voluntary sector. People with learning difficulties and mental health problems have been in the forefront of group advocacy as they have responded to depersonalised and institutional services failing to meet their needs.

A practical example of advocacy work is in enabling service users to access Direct Payments with which they can engage in self-care planning. Using a social model theory you could concentrate on identifying the way in which structures and institutions further disable people with disabilities, and then set about challenging the disabling structures. Your accountability to your agency and legal responsibilities will however create a tension in trying to authentically fulfil the requirements for effective advocacy practice enshrined in these points (Bateman, 2000):

- Always act in the client's best interest.
- Always act in accordance with the client's wishes and instructions.
- Keep the client properly informed.
- Carry out instructions with diligence and competence.
- Act impartially and offer frank independent advice.
- Maintain rules of confidentiality.

The skill is in making provision for the person's abilities and circumstances to begin to change as they are released from a disempowered position, rather than continuing to assess them in the here and now. This developmental perspective requires a certain amount of judgement and assumptions about the impact such a liberating intervention could have. It also assumes a degree of support to enable the transition from disempowered to empowered with a tapering of input and the inevitable feelings of dependency.

ACTIVITY 10.4

Think about some recent practice you have been involved in and reflect back on whether there were elements of advocacy in your work, or if not how you might evaluate whether your approach encompasses principles of advocacy.

Commentary

The following questions might be useful in helping decide whether and how you might incorporate an advocacy approach in your social work practice. How do service users have a say in these areas, what is the evidence their contribution is valued, and what helps or hinders advocacy? Look at the following and decide how far and how much service users are involved in these activities:

- Collecting and sharing information.
- Meeting the training needs of staff and service users.
- Policy-making and planning.
- Implementing policy and running the service.

Providing service users with resources to enable them to meet and discuss policy and practice issues is evidence of a genuine effort to engage and facilitate empowering strategies. Training in committee skills is required to help demystify official ways of working unfamiliar to those on the outside of the power system. It is very important to support and sustain people who may falter, feel nervous and appear ready to withdraw at the earliest obstacle to their participation. Try to resist assuming this proves they are not capable, instead build confidence and have a strategy in place to deal with anxieties about competence.

The smallest detail can make a big difference. For example remember to invite a user group to send a representative rather than submit to the temptation to select someone of your choice with whom you feel comfortable. It is probable better to invite more than one person because an individual can easily feel outnumbered in a meeting full of professionals. Two people can support each other and give each other confidence in speaking. It is also important to pay them to attend, and offensive to expect them to attend regularly as the only unpaid people in a roomful of salaried professionals.

Integrated practice

The volume of material to consider when seeking to assess, plan and intervene in social work can often feel overwhelming. The number of central government legislative and practice guidelines, research reports, agency priorities and procedures is awesome. Together with books like this crammed full of information-some of it contradictory, can present you with too many choices. It might make the task of putting it all together seem impossible. However there are some basis principles that can be useful as a quick reference point and a broad guide within which you can add particular concepts or specialist areas of practice theory and knowledge. One of these is the foundational qualities of effective helping, which have been identified as (Lishman, 1998):

- genuineness
- warmth
- acceptance
- encouragement and approval
- empathy
- responsiveness and sensitivity

Another is to cultivate a professional perspective that locates your practice in an organisational context. This can help make sense of the contradictions and impossible dilemmas that seem to present themselves to you frequently. The contemporary organisational context of social work practice is commented upon as producing a mechanistic, soulless practice that is driven by the demands not of service users but of the bureaucracies we work in and the political process in late capitalist societies. This results in an undermining of your expertise and judgement and a prioritisation of mechanistic practices in assessment work leading to form-filling routinised practices. These are not welcomed by clients or social workers as they disempower people, constrain choices and leave precious room for creative practice.

Political ideologies of the government dictate to a large extent the parameters of professional practice. These dictate the way that decisions are made about resource allocation and funding of health and social care programmes. Your skills in understanding this context to your practice can enable you to find ways of using it to the advantage of your clients. Seeking allies in specific practice interest groups or trades union activity or professional associations can help reduce any isolation you feel and help share strategies for overcoming bureaucratic obstacles to sound ethical practice. Part of the process of understanding the organisational context is to appreciate that resources are finite and boundaries to your practice have to be drawn. The key is whether you can feel satisfied that this is done with your co-operation and contribution consistent with service user participation or whether it is an imposed, artificial limit based on inequitable socially unjust imperatives.

Service user involvement

Integrating your commitment to service user empowerment and participatory practice in a meaningful way rather than a vaguely expressed desire to do something means challenging and reflecting on the way you practice on a daily basis. The difficulty is to ensure that service user involvement becomes a practical and routine activity that is absorbed into the very fabric of your social work practice. One way of helping you navigate through this potentially difficult task is the approach recommended below which uses the four concepts of inclusion, diversity, impact and location (Beresford and Croft, 1992):

1. **Inclusion** – Participatory ways of working are favoured by service users and groups representing them. This does not mean reducing the role of other stakeholders but adding another element to the process of service improvement. You need to be aware that there are two versions of user involvement. One is the managerialist or consumerist approach that focuses on the service system and obtains service users input to inform provision. The second is a more egalitarian approach that puts service users lives at the centre of the process of involvement. In other words improving service users lives is what matters most.
2. **Diversity** – Initiatives for user involvement must challenge rather than mirror prevailing social exclusions and discrimination. They should ensure that people are involved on an equal basis, which means offering particular support to those most marginalised and excluded, or who have difficulty

communicating in writing or verbally. This means making sure that proper access and enough support is available to enable everybody to contribute.

3. **Impact** – Enabling service user involvement in the design, delivery and monitoring of services is of little help unless there is a demonstrable difference to the lives of service users. The most effective basis for effective service user involvement is the provision of adequate and secure resources for independent user controlled organisations. More democratic and empowering approaches to participation are required that change the balance of power so that service users are directly involved in the decision-making process.

4. **Location** – Service user organisations have begun to prioritise areas where they feel they can make the most difference. These include professional practice where service users are involved in discussion and negotiation that influences practice development. Training is another area where service users can be involved directly with students on pre and post qualifying courses, the design of curricula, and assessment of student practice. Involvement in policy development can be another way whereby service users views can be collated and integrated into policy formulation. Finally, service users have much to offer in terms of research, evaluation and monitoring of service provision. But this means challenging the prevailing orthodoxy in research methodologies and the hierarchy of knowledge and the evidence base so that users views are afforded equal status.

Recording and record keeping

Recording and record keeping are probably the least addressed task faced by social workers in whatever practice context yet they consistently appear in critical comments from joint inspections and public enquiries into deaths of clients. They can be perceived as routine mundane tasks and afforded little priority in the busy schedule of most practitioners. Yet they are a potentially rich source of information not just for the sake of recording facts but for their analytical and interpretative value.

Training manuals and staff development opportunities will emphasise the importance of accuracy in case recording and you will be advised to distinguish facts from opinion. Access to files for service users in the *Data Protection Act 1984* and the *Access to Personal Files Act 1990* provide a powerful incentive to make sure that what you commit to official records can be justified by evidence and open to scrutiny. In the spirit of partnership practice you should be routinely offering clients opportunities to witness what you have written about them and enabling their perceptions, comments and disagreements to be recorded equally.

However the conclusion is still that recording is a bureaucratic exercise designed to meet service specifications or agency requirements. Ostensibly they are expected to be clear, precise and understandable to a range of people including other agency staff, managers, and service users. In practice case notes can be either so brief and perfunctory or so long and meandering to be both lacking in utility and satisfying no-one. Depending on your practice context you might be encouraged to more or less record client contact and decisions or record process interviews for therapeutic evaluation of the casework relationship. The optimum is to incorporate both so that service user records can be accessed by others in order to maintain continuity, measure your intervention progress and evaluate the effectiveness of your work.

The value in this activity is that clients can feel a real sense of empowerment if you facilitate access in terms of their rights to examine files kept on them, rather than conveying a sense of reluctance and unimportance. Records can be an incredibly important documentation of a young person's life story that will at some stage in their life prove invaluable as they look back to make sense of circumstances and events. Great care should therefore be taken to ensure that material is accurate and contains positive as well as negative information (Macdonald, 1999).

Chapter summary

In this chapter we have considered how to plan intervention on the basis of the assessment you have conducted and how to integrate knowledge, skills and values. We also paid attention to considering how to demonstrate how an assessment leads to a set of concrete objectives for intervention. Working in partnership to negotiate and plan responses to assessed needs, risks, responsibilities, strengths and resources should form a significant part of the process of integration.

Planning intervention in social work and the decision-making process includes thinking and feeling about the situation being addressed. But there is debate about whether intuitive or analytical thought is more suited to social work decisions. A contrast between these two distinct forms of thinking is drawn in the social work literature with the tendency to favour intuitive rather than analytical thinking, rejecting the latter as a technical, calculative approach not in harmony with social work values.

We argued that one of the key characteristics of contemporary social work services is the partnership approach to work with service users. This is enshrined in practice guidance and codes of ethics. It involves a process of negotiation with families about the venue for work, and the choice of practice methods particularly during the assessment process. It is important to make distinctions about the different levels of partnership possible in your intervention as you begin to integrate your practice.

Inter-professional or multi-disciplinary care are contemporary terms often used synonymously to mean joint working between staff from different professional backgrounds. Staff may work in the same team location or operate from separate uni-professional teams. Within the same agency they may represent different disciplines or client groups. In whatever configuration joint working has always been recommended as the best way of delivering coherent and effective care in health and social work practice.

We acknowledged that integrating your commitment to service user empowerment and participatory practice in a meaningful way rather than a vaguely expressed desire to do something, means challenging and reflecting on the way you practice on a daily basis. The difficulty is to ensure that service user involvement becomes a practical and routine activity that is absorbed into the very fabric of your social work practice. We have examined the skills and resources necessary for effective decision-making in the context of inter-agency working, considered the role of advocacy as an empowering approach, and concluded with a discussion of the process of change and the implications for each stakeholder in the change process.

CHAPTER 11

Evaluation and Evidence-based Practice

Learning objectives

- Define what is meant by evidence and explain why practice should be evidence based.
- Describe the relationship between evidence and evaluation and what dilemmas this poses for you.
- Identify methods of practice evaluation and involve clients in evaluation that is meaningful to them.
- Explain how evaluation can contribute to the effective planning and management of resources.

Introduction

The importance of evaluation and the evidence base that informs our practice cannot be overstated. It has now been given extra weight in the context of health and social care service delivery with the creation of two independent organisations charged with producing high quality evidence relevant to social work practice. The National Institute for Health and Clinical Excellence (NICE) provides guidance, sets quality standards and manages a national database to improve people's health and prevent and treat ill health, and the Social Care Institute for Excellence (SCIE) is expected to identify and spread knowledge about good practice to the large and diverse social care workforce and support the delivery of transformed, personalised social care services.

Both aspire to drive the government's agenda for modernisation of local government and health and welfare services leading to better efficiency and effectiveness. In practical terms you will be expected to draw upon research evidence in order to inform the decision-making process during assessment and intervention, for example, seeking to understand more about the effects of long term residential care on young people in favour of placing a child in foster care or for adoption. Or it may be the need to argue for the removal of a child from an abusing parent on the basis of evidence of the risks and consequences of abuse. More than ever before you are going to have to base your judgements on the best available evidence combined with sound theoretical principles.

Considering the idea of evaluating social work can take us into several different areas of exploration. One is the methodological arena where debate and discussion centre around what form the evaluation should take – typically revolving around arguments about the merits of quantitative and qualitative evaluative methods. Social workers are caricatured as obsessed with the qualitative methodologies preferring to hear the voice of the service user and regarding statistical quantitative research as unfeeling and mechanistic. You may indeed have an aversion to mathematical techniques and the research employing what appear to be obscure methodologies for presenting significant data. However you will find that both complement each other and power is added to the weight of your arguments that are based on such mixed research. Hard facts about gaps in service provision or the needs of certain clients can be brought to life with personal testimony and verbatim comments derived from qualitative research with real people.

Another area of interest might be to define what we mean by evaluation, and discuss whether this is an appropriate use of our time. Different methods of evaluation require different evidence and therefore produce different results-even though they are examining the same thing. There can be a sense that research is done by academics who have the time, resources and motivation whereas practitioners have no time for such activity but depend on the results to help inform practice. This feeds the artificial divide between research and practice and fosters resentment and frustration in equal measures for all concerned. Nevertheless attempts to bridge this gap and present research in meaningful and accessible ways to busy social workers continue so that influence can be achieved at various levels from the ground level of practice to the strategic policy level.

We might consider the question of the usefulness of evaluation-what is it for and how will it be used? Here there are a raft of issues connected to the use of resources and in the public sector the inevitable constraints on resources that are employed in the service of social work clients. As a busy practitioner you might wonder what the point of evaluation is if it does not lead to more resources or enable the conclusions of the evaluation to be put into effect. You might cynically feel that evaluation is invariably going to lead to disruption in working practices and further disempower you and the service users to whom you personally feel accountable. Are measures used by evaluators practical or relevant to your social work practice for instance?

Many are based on audit and clinical outcome measurement designed for clinical controlled environments, rather than the messy, sometimes chaotic and uncertain environment of our clients. It is also useful to consider what we mean by social work when seeking to evaluate it. This might seem a redundant question if we consider the variety of tasks, processes and factors involved in work with a family, group or single client that all go into the casework file. We might wonder whether it is possible or even feasible to consider measuring and quantifying something as ephemeral as social work. Isolating the myriad of factors influencing a family from beginning of work to case closure and seeking to identify those that can be proven to have made the most effective impact is a challenge. Much research activity is focused on the outcomes of particular interventions. Two ways of categorising outcomes can be considered (Cheetham et al., 1992):

- **Service-based outcomes** – outcomes of a particular service to identify the nature, extent, and quality of what is provided.
- **Client-based outcomes** – outcomes for service users to identify the effects of a particular provision on its recipients.

In attempting to match resources and services to service users expectations and perceived needs, social workers are faced with increasing and more complex demands to improve efficiency and effectiveness. Central to all this is the concept of quality assurance which demands a commitment to the pursuit of a high standard of services. Policy statements setting out performance indicators in all areas of social work practice stress the essential role of monitoring and evaluation. You need to know what these terms mean, how they are used, and how you can engage positively with them.

Types of evaluation

It is a useful start to think about evaluation and distinguishing between subjective and objective approaches. Subjective evaluation concentrates on gauging how clients have experienced what you and your agency have offered them. Objective evaluation involves identifying particular objectives in the work and then deciding whether or not these have been achieved.

ACTIVITY 11.1

Imagine that your agency has been criticised for the way it evaluates its services. Your job is to devise a more explicit way of doing this. You are about to make a brief presentation of your initial thoughts on how evaluation might be improved. Think about how you might use subjective and objective evaluation in your work.

Commentary

Subjective evaluation could be carried out either through discussion or through some form of questionnaire, either in the company of a social worker or not. Or you might also wish to think about how, in devising a questionnaire, you could focus on partnership and empowerment by:

- Asking specific questions on degree of involvement, for example whether the client felt they were properly listened to.
- Working together with the service user to make sure the questionnaire reflected their agenda.
- Looking at whether the outcome of intervention was satisfactory, and if not how it could be done differently.
- Tackling issues of power and discrimination such as asking particular questions related to the service users needs as a black person, lesbian or gay, woman or someone with a disability.

With objective evaluation your objectives will depend on your particular work setting. The important point is that they are clearly measurable such as:

- Removal from the child protection register, or return home.
- A young person finding accommodation or a job.
- Finding an adoptive family.

- Maintaining an older person in their own home.
- Improving a child's school attendance.
- Helping a person avoid readmission to psychiatric hospital.

Central to the ideas of efficiency and effectiveness within evaluation is the concept of quality assurance. Judgements as to whether services are up to the standard expected have traditionally been based on whether the right amount of care was being provided rather than the quality of care. The question ' Are we doing things right?' has been supplemented by the question ' Are we doing the right things?' Below are some of the approaches to determining the quality of care.

Inspection

Since the *NHS and Community Care Act 1990* inspection units were created within social service departments separate from the day to day management function of monitoring residential provision. The latest system of inspection completely separates inspection from those providing residential care. Apart from the physical environment in these homes inspectors should elicit the views of residents and staff. The limitations of this approach are:

- In depth understanding is constrained due to the volume of work to be carried out and the limited contact with everyone concerned.
- It is difficult to be objective when you are working for the same authority responsible for running the home.
- Inspectors will invariably come with their own perceptions and values and may not be able to involve service users or staff as fully as they should.

Reviews

The idea of a review is that an organisation should prepare its plans on a regular basis and that progress towards the achievement of objectives and targets set out in those plans should be subjected to scrutiny. These plans are submitted to central government in accordance with guidelines laid down as part of overall strategic planning. This macro level has its parallel with the micro level of your work with clients. The limitations of reviews are:

- Organisational reviews relate to whether the plan is being conformed with usually in terms

of budget and efficiency. These issues can take precedence over questions of appropriateness and acceptability.
- Service user representatives may be consulted during the process of devising plans but they are primarily the domain of senior management staff.
- The views and expectations of field staff, carers and clients, are not paramount despite rhetoric in mission statements avowing to empower users.

Performance assessment

Central government has begun to issue guidance in the form of national comparative data from many local authorities and social care organisations to judge particular aspects of performance. The white paper *Modernising Social Services* (DoH, 1998??) set out new arrangements to assess the performance of each council within the wider Best Value regime that requires local authorities to achieve improved cost effectiveness. These have been translated into targets for services to attain – for example the number of children on the child protection register, or the number of home care organisers per head of population. Local authorities are awarded star ratings on a range of performance measures. This framework is designed to improve services that people receive by:

- Helping councils develop their own performance management arrangements.
- Ensuring that corporate management and political scrutiny promotes better social services that contribute to community well being.
- Ensuring that councils work effectively with the NHS to address joint health and social care policy and service delivery issues.
- Assessing councils' progress in implementing government policies for social care.
- Identifying and promoting best practice.
- Identifying councils that are performing poorly and ensuring they take action to improve.

They are criticised as crude measures that do not adequately reflect the individual characteristics of different parts of the country, and the levels of need within them. Little account seems to be taken of the differences and distinctions between inner city deprived neighbourhoods, leafy suburbs, or remote rural communities. These misleading measures do not adequately reflect subtle changes and improvements that might disproportionately impact on the quality of service user's lives but do not show up in broad statistical data. The issue of resources is notably absent from the above list. Their limitations are:

- Although they aim to improve standards of care the preparation of performance indicators does not involve the intended beneficiaries.
- Their quantitative nature stresses procedures and outcomes rather than effectiveness and acceptability.
- Their compilation presupposes that local authorities have uniform, accurate, and comprehensive comparable information systems.
- They take little account of variations in the priority given by different authorities to aspects of their care services.

Some of the key indicators used to measure performance include;

- Information on education, employment and training for care leavers.
- Placement stability for looked after children in the short term and longer term.
- The percentage of children looked after in foster placements or placed for adoption.
- The percentage of children on the child protection register.

Satisfaction surveys

The collection of qualitative, highly personal data offers another perspective on the issue of service planning and evaluation of provision. Asking clients what they think of current services seems straightforward, and there are procedures publicised that offer the public an avenue to pursue grievances or register compliments. However satisfaction surveys cannot counterbalance the organisations' attempts to determine performance. The danger is that the act of conducting a survey can be seen as an end in itself. Unless such surveys are backed up with action plans and a set of measurable improvements based on them they can end up being viewed as at best tokenistic and at worse deeply patronising. Further limitations are:

- They often assume that the person asked has knowledge of alternative provision.
- Satisfaction may not tell much about the quality of the service since the client may be starting from a low expectation.

- Data derived from questionnaires is limited when alternatives such as case studies, personal diaries or group interviews could yield richer information.

Process versus outcome

Government will be increasingly concerned with *outcomes* in the future context of public sector budget cuts and value for money arguments. Effectiveness has been interpreted as synonymous with the achievement of predefined goals or outcomes. This approach is limited as it tends to ignore *process* – the means by which outcomes are attained. The concentration on outcome was in reaction to an earlier preoccupation with process – which tended to be equally limited in its focus on the micro aspects of the interactions between workers and clients and neglect their success or otherwise in achieving goals.

The preoccupation with outcomes has concerned many in who feel that it misses important aspects of the values and roles of social work in which – even though hoped for outcomes may not be achieved – the relationship between worker and client has intrinsic value in demonstrating respect and regard for individuals and providing a rewarding relationship for those who might otherwise have none. Thus more recently the concept of evaluation has broadened the approach – going beyond a narrow concern with effectiveness and integrating process and outcome issues. Thus evaluation is concerned not only with the question:

Are we doing things right?

but also:

Are we doing the right things?

Social work requires evaluative skills for several reasons:

- Whilst it is a complex subject dealing with many ill-defined and intangible phenomena if it is to develop and survive as a profession it must employ techniques for studying itself which are more reliable, transferable and credible than the purely intuitive.
- Social work is usually carried on in organisational and policy frameworks to which it is accountable and therefore within which it has to be evaluated.
- The demands of care management require social workers to have a grasp of evaluative concepts in order that they can make decisions

on the purchase and provision of services –
types of decision which were not required of
them before.

- The rights of consumers are increasingly
  recognised and they are entitled to expect that
  social work can account for its success or
  otherwise in serving the public, meeting its
  demands and spending its money.

Therefore it helps to meet these requirements if
social work employs concepts and terms which
are capable of describing in consistent ways some
of the important elements of social work and
social care and which provide a framework for
their evaluation.

Useful terms and concepts

Evaluation is concerned with the relationship
between goals, inputs, outputs and outcomes and
it usually describes this relationship in terms of
effectiveness, efficiency, and equity.

- **Goals** – stated objectives of agencies or
  individuals.
- **Inputs** – human and material resources
  employed.
- **Outputs** – a particular combination of inputs.
- **Outcomes** – effects of outputs (intended or
  not).

It is important to notice here the particular use of
the terms input and output. In this context an
organisation is producing outputs such as social
work or home help by putting money and
personnel into those services – thus from its
perspective money and personnel are inputs,
social workers and home helps are outputs.

- **Effectiveness** – outputs lead to outcomes
  which promote goals.
- **Efficiency** – the maximum outcome for any
  given level of input or output.
- **Marginal productivity** – extra outcome for a
  given additional level of output.
- **Equity** – equal outputs for equal needs.

Case illustration

- **Goal** – to reduce admission of older people to
  residential care.
- **Inputs** – cash grants, wages, worker/hours,
  aids/ adaptations, buildings.
- **Outputs:**
  - grants plus social work.
  - social work plus home care
  - grants plus home care plus adaptations

- **Outcomes:**
  - reduction in admissions
  - delayed admissions
  - increased admissions but less depressed
    carers
- **Effectiveness** – that output is effective which
  leads to reduction in admissions.
- **Efficiency** – the output which requires the least
  inputs to achieve the greatest reduction in
  admissions is the most efficient. Thus, if the
  same outcome is achieved by three hours of
  home help as by three hours of social worker
  time and home help costs less than social work,
  the home help output is the more efficient.
- **Marginal productivity** – the amount outcome
  increases for any given level of output is the
  marginal productivity of that output i.e.
  assume that increasing social worker hours
  from three to five hours per week does not
  keep a person out of care but increasing home
  care hours by the same amount does. If so the
  marginal productivity of home care is greater.
- **Equity** – people of similar dependency receive
  similar levels of home care etc.

This demonstrates the complexity of the issues
because it would be possible to have a situation
where a particular service was effective in
achieving organisational goals but was inefficient
and inequitable. In addition the goals may be
those of the organisation but not of its clients i.e.
older people might not wish to remain at home.

Thus evaluation here would not only be
concerned with the question – was the stated goal
achieved? but with others too such as – was the
goal worthwhile and for whom? Could the goal
be achieved by a more efficient combination of
inputs? Could the level of any output be reduced
without reducing its effect on outcomes (its
productivity)? Did this level and combination of
inputs lead to inequity i.e. were equally
dependent younger people in the area deprived
of home care?

Evaluating social work – the people's perspective

The consumers' perspective has been a feature in
the evaluation of social work for many years –
Mayer and Timms' classic survey of clients in the
1960s showed how the views of social work
clients differed from those of their social workers
about its methods and purpose (Mayer and
Timms, 1970). They referred to this as a clash of

perspective and subsequent research found similar disparities and suggested that social work is more effective in achieving its goals when the views of clients and workers are congruent on what the goals are and how they are to be achieved (Rees and Wallace, 1982; Cheetham et al., 1992; Pawson and Tilley, 1997).

It has often been found that clients judge effectiveness using different criteria than social workers – for example they value practical help more than social workers who value insight and behavioural change more. Evaluation should take such factors into account not only when considering the effectiveness of outputs but in prioritising goals i.e. whose goals and outcomes are more important? However – despite the current high status ostensibly being given to their views – consumers' views are no more 'objective' or 'valid' than those of practitioners' and caution is required in interpreting them for several reasons:

- Previous knowledge of services may colour consumer opinions i.e. unsuccessful encounters with social workers before may lead to less than enthusiastic accounts of current intervention or indeed over enthusiastic accounts of minimal success.
- Levels of expectation will influence consumer feedback – those with very low expectations will be more impressed by any success than those with high expectations.
- Lack of information on alternatives means consumers have no basis on which to judge.
- Anxieties over confidentiality and the results of expressing any negative opinion may lead consumers to give more favourable assessments of services than might otherwise be justified.

Consumers as producers of welfare

Evaluation should take into account not only the welfare produced by the formal organisation but that produced by consumers, carers, and other external providers. Thus in assessing the effectiveness of an output such as intensive home care in avoiding admission to residential care the outcomes for carer well-being should be included. In addition the inputs they make such as the cost of travel, heating, and accommodation should be taken into account. If these costs to carers become too great and they become clients as well, the effectiveness of the intensive home care may be more doubtful because if carers

collapse, the older person will be admitted to residential care. In such circumstances greater efficiency and effectiveness might be achieved by changing the goal to delaying admission rather than avoiding it, putting less home care in and adding social work counselling to prepare the older person and carer for the possibility of admission.

How to evaluate

Many social workers tend to avoid evaluation or to interpret it in such a way that it comes to mean a brief retrospective review of a piece of work or an initiative. You may also hold the view that your agency has to collect so much performance-related information for the government that anything that appears to detract from work with service users and your primary responsibilities has to be avoided. However accountable practice demands that public services need to justify what they do and find useful ways of demonstrating this.

An action evaluation model has been developed in Bradford (Fawcett, 2000) which is based on a partnership between the University, Social Services Department, and the Health Trust aimed at demystifying the evaluation process and providing staff with the tools and support to conduct evaluations. Action evaluations take place in the workplace, and focus on areas viewed as important by those involved with the findings feeding into the services being studied. These are the main characteristics:

- **Outline the current situation** – collect baseline information and establish the service's overall aims and objectives. This can include quantitative data such as the numbers using a service, and qualitative data such as details of service users experiences.
- **Specify available resources**, overall aim and objectives – any project or initiative is likely to have a number of objectives but it is important to be specific about them and what the broad overall purpose of the activity is.
- **Link goals to specific objectives** – identifying the desired outcomes or goals enables you to work backwards through any intermediary stages in the process. This helps to provide progress indicators and how goals can be achieved.
- **Detail why the agreed objectives and goals were decided upon** – no evaluation goes strictly according to plan therefore it is

important to record how the goals were established. A record needs to be kept of the reasoning behind the aims, and any deviation clearly stated and made transparent. This information needs to be easily retrievable so it can be used to explain why goals have changed.

- **Monitor and review the activity** – information from all stakeholders can be collated including recommendations for changing or improving the service. Activity related to goals can be appraised, and evidence of progress summarised. It is important to document how and why progress was made and what obstacles were encountered. This data can be fed back to service purchasers and planners reflecting an inclusive, bottom-up approach to evaluation.

ACTIVITY 11.2

Locate the latest evaluation of your service from your manager or the research and information section of your agency. See whether you can work out the methodology employed and whether the results have or have not influenced working practices.

The social work dilemma

In a climate of public sector financial constraints that impose strict guidelines on the use of resources and requiring demonstrable outcomes for practice, social workers are invariably pulled in different directions. On the one hand there are the familiar overtures to work systematically in a focused manner within budget limits, while on the other hand there are highly vulnerable dependent clients who we are told should have needs led services. This implies that there is no conflict between resource limitations and service user needs, when of course there is. Experienced staff know that in some cases long term support is the only option for some of the most damaged and disadvantaged clients, yet service managers impose artificial limits to the length of time spent on these cases.

We all know that a case closed prematurely will likely reappear in due course and probably be much harder to work. This is particularly the case when clients have experienced losses, neglect and lack of care in their history which are being reproduced in their relationship with their social worker. Finding a way out of this dilemma is one of the modern challenges to professional ethical practice. The task is all the harder because

there is not a reliable robust evidence base to call upon to justify a particular plan of intervention. Social workers seeking evidence-based practice using therapeutic skills and techniques will find the literature on evaluation in this field is rather less than helpful.

There is for example a historical legacy of reluctance among psychotherapists to employ quantitative empirical methods to investigate the effectiveness of their practice. This is partly because therapists have tended to prefer demonstrating results using case study descriptions to support their particular theoretical model. It is also because they have not been trained in these methodologies and are more comfortable with the qualitative research that emphasises the more intangible elements of the subtle processes at work during the therapeutic experience (Target, 1998; Cowie, 1999). If you are trying to implement therapeutic work with a service user this makes it harder to justify your approach. The question of reliability and validity of the research methodology has a bearing on the status of the therapeutic effectiveness.

Reliability chiefly is about whether the same person was assessed on a different day or location, or by another researcher, the result would be similar or different. Validity refers to whether the research is telling you what you think it is – in other words whether what a service users says about how they are, is accurate. These concepts of reliability and validity matter because of the tendency of quantitative research to interpret and generalise from the findings, thereby influencing choice of treatment or intervention. Research is used to justify investment in social work organisation and methods with practitioners left feeling buffeted by changes imposed on their practice and cynical about the underlying rationale.

It is not hard to understand that social work practitioners trained to take account of the social and environmental context of service users lives, also use this to take account of the financial pressures influencing their practice. These pressures are not based on rational evidence-based research methods about effective interventions but on resource constraints. This is the heart of our dilemma in contemporary social work-how to deliver effective services within artificial limits to practice. But rather than descend into brutal cynicism or negative practice we can learn to use the principles of evaluation and effectiveness to our and our clients' advantage. There are ways of using the available research evidence base and combining it with participatory partnership practice to ensure that the arguments for better quality resources and cost effectiveness are articulated.

The old adage about prevention being better than cure has a weight and enduring simplicity that can resonate in the minds of service managers or budget controllers. It is almost impossible to prove that a certain intervention definitely prevented something else from happening, but governments and social policy experts have generated expensive intervention programmes on this basis. For example the multi-million pound Sure Start programme (2002) was based on the untested assumption that such a huge programme would prevent later anti-social, educational, and health problems in the future with a generation of disadvantaged children. It is therefore part of received wisdom that investment of this nature helps.

Reflective and reflexive practice

Contemporary social work literature contains references to reflective practice as well as reflexive practice and it would be unsurprising if practitioners were confused by these terms. They are close in spelling, sound and in meaning but are actually different. They are important because they are linked closely to the concept of evaluation and how to move forward in professional practice from the dilemmas described above. Reflective practice was first considered as early as the 1930s as an active persistent and careful consideration of any belief or supposed form of knowledge in the light of the grounds that support it and the further conclusions to which it tends. This definition was applied to the context of professional practice by later writers who argued that reflective practice consisted of reflection in action or thinking while doing, and reflection on action which occurs after an incident takes place. Reflective practice therefore encompasses the need for a useful outcome to the reflective process that will lead to a change in practice.

Reflection in assessment and intervention practice is crucial because of the need for you to make sense of a lot of information – written, verbal, emotional, including the impact your own working practices on service users and other people connected to them. Reflective practice is the antithesis of standardised routine practice

prescribed by increasingly bureaucratic organisations. It is essential that you maintain a critical, independent stance that enables you to respond pro-actively to diverse situations and meet professional standards of practice because of:

- The often complex conflicts of interest involved in the nature of social problems.
- The unique mix of skills, resources, experience, strengths, weaknesses and gaps involved, particularly where some people's behaviour is defined as 'the problem'.
- The need to understand and unravel the complexities of relationships that perpetuate social problems through self-defeating strategies and mutually defeating interactions: the need for maintenance of the marginal position of the worker.
- The frequent necessity for an exchange model of relationship to achieve effective and lasting change
- The risk that procedures, guidelines, the worker's own behaviour and that of their organisation can contribute to and perpetuate the problems which the worker is intending to resolve.
- The need to identify and respond to unintended and unforeseen consequences of social interventions.

Smale et al., 2000

Reflexive practice is derived from the term reflexivity which gained currency in contemporary debates about the need to conduct research that did not depend on notions of universality and objectivity in social research. Reflexivity is recommended as a critical practice for social research and social work practice that flows from it (Alvesson and Skoldberg, 2000; Pels, 2000). Critical practice is regarded as a challenge to the orthodoxy and contested notions of realism. These debates are connected to broader discussion of the merits of postmodernism, discussed more fully in Chapter 2, which try to consider the best ways of finding out the effects and impact that social work practices have in new ways that challenge the classic models of quantitative research (May, 2002; Walker, 2001). In this context reflexive practice means that you can embrace evaluation from a sceptical position about reality and certainty, whilst working hard to ensure the process of evaluation is culturally competent and conscious of the power relationships between service user and social worker.

Reflexivity suggests that we interrogate previously taken for granted assumptions, it contends that knowledge does not have fixed stable meanings but that it is made rather than revealed thanks to research effort (Taylor and White, 2000). Empowering social work practice can be described and defined as we try to do in this book but actually explaining how it is applied in practice requires reflexivity. Reflective practice assumes that you can become more skilled at applying child developmental theories to your practice for example, whereas reflexivity takes this further and questions whether this is possible.

These debates may seem obscure or irrelevant to your practice, but they find expression in practical ways that have a large impact on the type of social work you can do. The increasing emphasis in strategic planning, government guidance and occupational standards is, as we have noted elsewhere in this book, on risk assessment, risk analysis or risk management. These can be considered as a reaction to the postmodern project of deconstructing orthodox theories and rejecting expert discourses with uncertainty and multiple explanations for social phenomena. It is possible to suggest that the resulting anxiety and lack of guidance naturally produce attempts by organisations and individuals to exert control and authority (Parton, 1994; Dean, 1997). Anxiety can flourish where there is an intellectual vacuum or no eligibility criteria for your service, procedure manuals, mission statements or assessment matrixes to signpost your interventions.

Without these anchors of stability in the turmoil of clients sometimes chaotic, disorganised, and painful lives, you may feel more overwhelmed or driven by the meandering directionless process of a service user's family process. However, if you are sceptical about risk assessment and understand the limitations of contemporary evaluation practice, how can you begin to scrutinise your practice in ways that satisfy intellectual as well as ethical considerations? An empowering and emancipatory social work practice that liberates both client and worker from their mutually helpless positions combined with inner self-knowledge is a powerful prospect. This offers a practical and achievable solution to the dilemmas described above whilst preserving the heart of the value base of social work practice.

ACTIVITY 11.3

Spend a few minutes reflecting on what you have read so far in this chapter. Now begin to jot down some notes to begin to construct an integrated model of evaluation that embraces methodological rigour with the value base of social work.

Commentary

An integrated evaluative model of social work prioritises the task of understanding the experience of the service user whilst preserving the importance of explanatory power in a context of a plurality of social interpretations that embrace a range of explanations. Within this model discriminatory processes can be exposed and resisted while participatory and partnership approaches given legitimacy. It also reminds us of the crucial importance of supervision and the capacity to gain insight into our own feelings and reactions to the distressing circumstances of our clients. Not the supervision of administrative management but the much more valuable supervision based on the psycho-social mandate of social work practitioners that links the inner with the outer worlds. Its characteristics are:

- Offers a both/and rather than either/or position.
- Conserves what is useful and practical.
- Tolerates inconsistency and the messiness of lived experience.
- Bears uncertainty and challenges complacency.
- Accepts that change is continuous while research is static.

The sheer range and quantity of research material available and, thanks to the internet, quickly accessible, is both a blessing and a curse. It is a testimony to the desire of professionals to seek answers to important questions and to find the best way of helping service users. Nobody wants to miss the chance to work more effectively and to the highest possible standard. However the consequence of such a wealth of evidence is that you may find you only have time to concentrate on what is called propositional and process knowledge. The first relates to substantive knowledge related to a discrete area of work, the second relates to material intended to promote skill development (Eraut, 1994). Both can restrict your vision whilst appearing to offer certainty and exactness in specialist areas of work.

One of the dangers in having an uncritical view of evidence based practice is that you are put in the position of a technician whose task is to apply knowledge created elsewhere rather than in assessing its' suitability, relevance and utility in particular practice situations (Taylor and White, 2000). Practitioners often lament the way theory is neatly described and fluently illustrated in social work text books when they contrast this with the imperfection and messiness of daily practice. The gap between theory and practice can feel extremely wide with the consequence that you might be tempted to describe your practice as eclectic, when in fact it is some way from the proper definition of a conscious choice in the selection of methods of work. This can be the case when you feel that your practice is being driven by a reaction to events rather than directed by a planned course of action.

Research methods

The following are a sample of research methods that could be employed in social work contexts. They are not an exhaustive list but they are included to give you an impression of the common formats you might encounter in your work, or in the literature that seeks to inform your practice. It is very important therefore that you understand the way research is organised and the limitations of various designs (Macdonald and Roberts, 1995):

- **Randomised controlled trials** – as mentioned above the randomised controlled trial (RCT), is the method favoured particularly in medical and clinical situations where a high degree of control can be used to try to minimise bias or reliability. By randomly allocating a procedure or intervention the chances of introducing bias into the selection of service users to receive the intervention is reduced. Other external sources of bias such as age, gender, class are discounted by this method because these factors will be equally affecting those clients receiving the intervention and those who are not. However, the RCT cannot help when interpretation of the results occurs because the specific intervention could be affected by other factors such as the characteristics of the practitioner. Or in the case of a group intervention any differences could be due to the specific dynamics of a particular group-however randomly constructed.
- **Quasi-experimental study** – ethical considerations and other factors may mean it is not practical or desirable to evaluate effectiveness by denying one client group a service received by another through a RCT. In order to try to measure the impact of a new or different intervention it is crucial however to try to ensure that alternatives are designed, analysed and interpreted in ways that maximise our knowledge of what works. A common way of doing this is to arrange a study that has the benefit of a control group of service users who continue to receive the standard intervention to a problem, but to compare them with a similar group who receive a new intervention.
- **Non-experimental study** – research designs within this category are evaluated interventions but without a random allocation or any matching of groups for comparative purposes. Results based on studies using these designs are considered to be suggestive rather than conclusive. They can be used as indicators of where further evaluative research might be useful, or when combined with several studies with similar results, their significance can be enhanced.
- **Client opinion study** – these provide valuable information and insights into how service users experience interventions. They offer opportunities to listen to the clients' opinion and perceptions of service provision, what effects and outcomes are produced, and what impact your work has had on service users behaviour or patterns of change. Social workers will feel a natural attraction to this form of evaluation as it fits with client-centred practices and advocacy and empowerment concepts. Recent research into service user opinion consistently demonstrates appreciation of social work support but equally consistently rarely shows clients understand what social workers are attempting to achieve and how they expect to do it.
- **Survey** – this is an important research method that while it may not enable evaluation of practice effectiveness does provide valuable data about the prevalence of particular phenomena. The value of this type of research is that it can mitigate the effects of our assumptions about service user groups we work with constantly. They can be a safeguard against stereotyping and routinised practices derived from failing to notice changes in client populations. In social work, quantitative surveys of large or discrete populations can

remind us of the existence of clients who despite negative indicators of child abuse, risk, or anti-social problems, nevertheless do not become delinquent or damage themselves or their children. They can remind us that it is as important to understand why some people manage to survive personal problems compared to similar people who suffer repetitive crises. Surveys are also useful in attempts to measure the impact of policy initiatives.

- **Cohort study** – this is another sort of survey in which it can be possible to identify factors that have a demonstrable effect. They are especially valuable in determining which kinds of preventive activity are more likely to produce a beneficial effect. Health and social data can be collected from a group or cohort of older people, mentally ill people or children sharing similar characteristics. The research then tracks these people and at regular intervals collects data from them over time. Cohort studies can give some indication of the effects of new social policies introduced by government with the intention of improving service user's lives in some way. They can also permit some predictions about likely problems and challenges to be faced by other service user groups.

What works in practice?

We reviewed some findings related to practice interventions in Chapter 2 to indicate the potential for your selection of practice based on certain theoretical assumptions. Now we can take this further by examining some of the most recent evidence about effectiveness in a selection of practice contexts. It is important to acknowledge that often these individual methods and approaches take place usually in a context of other variables very likely to affect the process and outcome of the work. Most research studies acknowledge these limitations to their findings but this should not detract from examining them and adapting them to your particular practice context. These are intended as an indicative resource to help guide your choice of working practice in child care within your agency resource constraints (Reimers and Treacher, 1995; Macdonald and Roberts, 1995; Alderson et al., 1996; Beresford et al., 1996).

Behavioural and cognitive-behavioural ways of working with clients where child abuse has

occurred or is at risk offer the most convincing evidence of effectiveness. In particular parent training programmes that endeavour to improve parents' capacity to manage and understand their children's behaviour generally show positive results. The following strategies are at the heart of most parent training programmes:

- Emphasising the importance of the maintenance of ground rules and boundaries of acceptable family behaviour, so that children have a growing appreciation of a plan against which to assess their own behaviour.
- Helping parents to gain an understanding of what they can expect from their children in order to acquire a reasonable level of awareness.
- Teaching parents to give clear, rather than mixed messages to their children.
- Training in managing children's behaviour with appropriate rewards for reinforcing desired behaviour and strategies for dealing with unwanted behaviour.

Anger control is a strategy aimed at preventing parents reaching the point where a cycle of poor interaction escalates to a point where anger is expressed violently and physically against a child. It is based on cognitive behavioural work aiming to:

- Teach the parent when to identify the early signs of their levels of anger building, and the typical scenarios where it is more likely to get out of control. The key is to teach recognition and prediction of events before they begin to develop.
- Teach the parent once they have achieved recognition to learn alternative strategies and coping mechanisms such as for example, engaging in an alternative activity, learning to relax by deep breathing, or changing the way they think about the situation.

Multi systemic family therapy based on classic systems thinking combined with cognitive behavioural techniques evidences statistically significant improvement in parent mental health problems, overall stress, and the severity of identified problems in cases of child abuse and neglect. Family therapy in general has its appeal for social workers who are often expected to work with families where children have been identified as in need or on the child protection register. As with much work with children and families in general it is hard to locate methodologically robust meta-analyses that meet the criteria to offer definitive conclusions on effectiveness. In particular studies reflecting service users perceptions are still too rare in the research literature. Nevertheless, given the maxim that any therapy is better than no therapy, and in a climate of resource shortages and waiting lists for specialist therapeutic agencies, social workers can offer something that may well make a difference. Not all social workers are registered family therapists but the skills and techniques are available to be employed as family support as much as psychodynamic or task centred approaches.

The characteristics of family therapy work are:

- Viewing the family as a constantly interacting system.
- Avoiding colluding with individual blaming strategies.
- Reframing problems in ways that offer families positive solutions.
- Using the concept of circular causality to explain the pattern of relationships.
- Actively working to change the way the family system, rather than any individual functions.
- Prescribing tasks and rituals to engage the whole family in problem-solving activity.

An example of a research project in the field of mental health illustrates the importance of seeking service users perceptions of the service they are experiencing. An active outreach team was established with the aim of engaging a group of people who traditionally found it hard to accept help. The researcher spent time with service users using a qualitative methodology that placed them at the centre of the research process.

The innovative outreach project was found to be achieving its aims because:

- Staff were spending more time with clients.
- Service users felt respected and listened to.
- Service users felt their social lives had improved.
- Cash benefits had increased and helped improve mental well-being.

Graley Wetherell and Morgan, 2001

Another example of research addressing the needs of elderly people illustrates how innovative and creative thinking can enable older people to remain in their own homes (McClatchey et al., 2001). Elderly people with dementia are likely to remain in their own homes longer and in much greater numbers than previously (DoH, 2001).

This means social workers in community care contexts will be under pressure to manage the specific needs of this client group. The research team in this study discovered that specialist housing agencies with the capacity to make adaptations and improvements to elderly people's homes can help sustain them for longer. However the home improvement agencies were unable and unwilling to assess the cognitive ability of the elderly people they were assisting. The implications of this research were that social workers working with home improvement agencies could sustain elderly people with dementia in their own homes for longer, rather than precipitate an unwanted admission to residential care. To do this social workers need to think beyond resource-led assessment and intervention and explore other more creative possibilities.

Change and the practice evidence-base

Central to an empowering socially inclusive approach in social work is finding out whether the work has, on the basis of reliable evidence, contributed towards the process of change. Change can be considered as something that is endless, constant and inevitable. How it is perceived and experienced by service users is crucial (Walker, 2003). Various models of intervention permit change stemming from within the psyche of the person to physical changes in their environment and abilities. There are changes imposed on certain clients compulsorily and those that are accepted voluntarily – either of which may lead to long-term benefits for them or their kin. Change is often thought of as something initiated by a social worker in a linear cause and effect process. But it can be useful to think about it in a more circular or reflexive pattern. How much did you change during the course of an intervention? What impact did the client have on you and how did this affect your thinking and behaviour? Indeed most of the change may occur within as you find out more over time about a person and their circumstances compared to the first encounter.

ACTIVITY 11.4

Think about your own personal theory of change. Do you believe that change occurs within a person's psyche and then affects their behaviour? Or do you feel that introducing behavioural changes then affects a person's internal psychology?

Commentary

Change is connected to difference but every stakeholder in the change process has a unique perception of what counts as difference. Pointing out differences to a person might be experienced as empowering but it might equally provoke feelings of fear or anxiety. A minimum amount of help might produce significant changes and equally a substantial amount of intervention results in no change or a worsening of circumstances. Where you choose to look for change may not be where other professionals or the service user is looking. Change can therefore be liberating or constraining, it can generate enlightenment or promote feelings of anger, loss and bereavement. Maintaining a degree of professional optimism with realism and managing uncertainty with a modest and respectful approach offers you the potential for being a useful resource to your clients.

Seven stages of change have been described which serve as a useful tool for social workers trying to evaluate their practice and assess the effectiveness of the chosen intervention with an individual service user (Rogers,1957). The stages can be used with the child, young person or adult, or parent/carer, to include them in the process of insight development and self-reflection:

- Stage 1: Communication is about external events.
- Stage 2: Expression flows more freely.
- Stage 3: Describes personal reactions to external events.
- Stage 4: Descriptions of feelings and personal experiences.
- Stage 5: Present feelings are expressed.
- Stage 6: A flow of feeling which has a life of its own.
- Stage 7: A series of felt senses connecting different aspects of an issue.

The need to expand and refine the evidence base of social work practice in order to demonstrate effectiveness is more important than ever especially in times when the welfare state is contracting and the pressure to find cost-effective solutions is strong. The growing problem requires a concerted effort from all agencies in contact with service users to understand the services they are providing and finding out better ways of measuring success. Three key factors have been identified in defining and explaining why evidence-based practice is not an option, but a necessity (Sheldon and Chilvers, 2000):

- **Conscientiousness** – this means a constant vigilance to monitor and review social work practice and to maintain service user welfare as paramount. It entails keeping up to date with new developments and a commitment to further professional understanding of human growth and development and social problems.
- **Explicitness** – this means working in an open and honest way with clients based on reliable evidence of what works and what is understood to be effective. The principle of explicitness demands a review of the available options with clients based upon thorough assessment of their problems.
- **Judiciousness** – this means the exercise of sound, prudent, sensible, judgement. Potential risks arising from some, or no intervention either in cases or policies, should be thoroughly assessed and evaluated in the knowledge that not all eventualities can be predicted.

The drive to encourage a research-minded profession in order to improve practice standards and accountability is however in danger of producing a confusion of research studies varying in quality and methodological rigour yet producing potentially useful data hidden within the quantity being produced. Practitioner research in social work is being encouraged as a means of influencing policy, management and practice using evaluative concepts moulded by service-user expectations (Fuller, 1996). It is possible to contribute to good quality effectiveness and evaluation studies by working in partnership with your clients to ensure their perspectives are at the heart of this activity. Practice is constantly evolving as society changes and the lives of our clients are influenced by multiple factors beyond their and our control. Maintaining an open mind and a receptive attitude to new learning is important so that we continue to think about (Thompson and Thompson, 2002):

- What we are doing.
- Why we are doing it.
- Whether we are doing it well.
- What we can learn from doing it.

The potential for evidence-based practice to enhance the quality of work and the satisfaction of service users is huge. The history of research and evaluation in social work is patchy and reflects deep ambivalence in practitioners and managers about the nature of the task. However, as the profession develops with the change to a degree level qualification, the establishment of a workforce regulatory council and a national body for collating good practice examples, the importance of good quality, reliable information on which to base practice can not be overstated. The development of evidence-based practice therefore depends on the following (Davies et al., 2000):

- The generation of good quality data concerning effectiveness.
- A workforce able critically to appraise evidence and contribute to the process of systematic reviews of research findings.
- The dissemination of data or research syntheses in a readily accessible form to professionals, managers, policy makers and to service users – a methodological and technical challenge.
- A work and policy environment that facilitates rather than impedes, the development of practices that reflect best evidence.

Your role as a professional social worker includes that of researcher and within that term there are three elements that need to be integrated in order for you to contribute to the knowledge base of social work practice.

1. As a research consumer you need to know how to locate and use research findings, test their reliability and translate them into specific and appropriate interventions.
2. As a knowledge creator and disseminator you will be involved in the production of research findings as part of a proper professional role in participating in systematic efforts to determine effective practice methods. Disseminating the findings can involve a simple written description circulated to team or agency colleagues or submitted to a magazine or journal so that as many social workers as possible can access the results.
3. As a contributing partner in research you can join with others and take responsibility for a specific part of the research process. Collaborative working like this can feel less stressful, be more manageable and ultimately be more powerful.

Chapter summary

We have discussed how in attempting to match resources and services to service users

expectations and perceived needs, social workers are faced with increasing and more complex demands to improve efficiency and effectiveness. Central to all this is the concept of quality assurance which demands a commitment to the pursuit of a high standard of services. Policy statements setting out performance indicators in all areas of social work practice stress the essential role of monitoring and evaluation. You need to know what these terms mean, how they are used, and how you can engage positively with them.

Subjective and objective evaluation are two general ways of thinking about the types of evaluation you might consider. Specific examples include – satisfaction surveys, inspections, joint reviews, performance assessment. They are aimed at measuring quantitative data such as numbers of cases worked or numbers of admissions to residential care. Or they aim to gain qualitative data-the voices and experiences from the service users perspective.

We suggested that a useful framework to consider using in your evaluation practice includes collecting baseline information and establishing the service's overall aims and objectives. Specify available resources, overall aim and objectives. Link goals to specific objectives by identifying the desired outcomes or goals enables you to work backwards through any intermediary stages in the process. Detail why the agreed objectives and goals were decided upon. No evaluation goes strictly according to plan, therefore it is important to record how goals were established. Collate information from all stakeholders including recommendations for changing or improving the service.

Reflective practice as part of evaluation in social work encompasses the need for a useful outcome to the reflective process that will lead to a change in practice. Reflexivity suggests that we interrogate previously taken for granted assumptions, it contends that knowledge does not have fixed stable meanings but that it is made rather than revealed thanks to research effort. Research methods that could be employed in social work contexts include: randomised controlled trials, quasi-experimental study, non-experimental study, client-opinion study, survey, and a cohort study. Probably the most attractive to practising social workers is the service user oriented research that seeks to articulate their experiences and requirements from the personal social services.

References

Adams, R., Dominelli, L. and Payne, M. (1998) *Social Work: Themes, Issues and Critical Debates.* Basingstoke, Macmillan.

Adams, R., Dominelli, L. and Payne, M. (2002) *Critical Practice in Social Work.* Basingstoke, Palgrave Macmillan.

Ahmad, B. (1990) *Black Perspectives in Social Work.* Birmingham, Venture Press.

Alderson, P. et al. (1996) *What Works? Effective Social Interventions in Child Welfare.* Barkingside, Barnardo's.

Alvesson, M. and Skoldberg, K. (2000) *Reflexive Methodology: New Vistas For Qualitative Research.* London, Sage.

Amin, K. et al. (1997) *Black and Ethnic Minority Young People and Educational Disadvantage.* London, Runnymede Trust.

Audit Commission (2000) *Another Country: Implementing Dispersal Under the Immigration and Asylum Act 1999.* London, HMSO.

Babb, P. (2005) *Social Inequalities.* London, Office for National Statistics.

Bagley, C. and Mallick, K. (1995) Negative Self-Perception and Components of Stress in Canadian, British and Hong Kong Adolescents. *Perceptual Motor Skills.* 81: 123–7.

Bagley, C. and Mallick, K. (2000) How Adolescents Perceive Their Emotional Life, Behaviour and Self-Esteem in Relation to Family Stressors: A Six-Culture Study. In: Singh, N., Leung, J. and Singh, A. *International Perspectives on Child and Adolescent Mental Health.* Oxford, Elsevier.

Bailey, R. and Brake, (Eds.) (1980) *Radial Social Work and Practice.* London, Edward Arnold.

Baldwin, M. (2000) *Care Management and Community Care.* Aldershot, Ashgate.

Bamford, T. (1993) Rationing: a Philosophy of Care. In Allen, I. *Rationing of Health and Social Care,* London, Policy Services Institute.

Bandura, A. (1986) *Social Foundations of Thought and Action: A Social Cognitive Perspective.* New Jersey, Prentice Hall.

Banks, S. (2006) *Ethics and Values in Social Work.* 3rd edn, Basingstoke, Palgrave.

Barclay, P. (1982) *Social Workers: Their Role and Tasks.* London, NISW/Bedford Square Press.

Barnes, C. (1991) *Disabled People in Britain and Discrimination.* London, Hurst.

Barnes, C. and Mercer, G. (1997) *Doing Disability Research.* Leeds, The Disability Press.

Barnes, H., Thornton, P. and Maynard, S. (1998) *Disabled People and Employment: A Review of Research and Development Work.* Bristol, Policy Press.

Barry, M. and Hallett, C. (Eds.) (1998) *Social Exclusion and Social Work.* Lyme Regis, Russell House Publishing.

BASW (2002) *Code of Ethics for Social Workers.* Birmingham, BASW.

Bateman N (2000) *Advocacy Skills for Health and Social Care Professionals.* London, Jessica Kingsley.

Beales, D., Denham, M. and Tulloch, A. (Eds.) (1998) *Community Care of Older People.* Oxford, Radcliffe Medical Press.

Beckett, C. (2002) *Human Growth and Development.* London, Sage.

Beckett, C. (2006) *Essential Theory for Social Work Practice.* London, Sage.

Beckett, C. (2007) The Reality Principle: Realism as an Ethical Obligation. *Ethics and Social Welfare*, 1: 3, 269–81.

Beckett, C. and Maynard, A. (2005) *Values and Ethics in Social Work.* London, Sage.

Beckett, C. and Wrighton, E. (2000) What Matters to Me is Not What You're Talking About: Maintaining The Social Model of Disability in Public Private Negotiations. *Disability and Society.* 15: 7, 991–9.

Bennett, G. and Kingston, P. (1993) *Elder Abuse: Concepts, Theories and Interventions.* London Chapman Hall.

Beresford, B. et al. (1996) *What Works in Services For Families With a Disabled Child?* Barkingside, Barnardo's.

Beresford, P. and Croft, S. (1993) *Citizen Involvement: A Practical Guide For Change.* Basingstoke, Macmillan.

Berridge, D. (1997) *Foster Care: A Research Review.* London, HMSO.

Bewley, C. and Glendinning, C. (1994) *Involving Disabled People in Community Care Planning.* York, Joseph Rowntree Foundation.

Bhugra, D. (1999) *Mental Health of Ethnic Minorities.* London, Gaskell.

Bhugra, D. and Bahl, V. (1999) *Ethnicity: An Agenda for Mental Health.* London, Gaskell.

Bichard, M. (2004) *The Bichard Inquiry Report.* London, HMSO.

Bochner, S. (1994) Cross-cultural Differences in The Self-Concept: A Test of Hofstede's Individualism/Collectivism Distinction. *Journal of Cross-Cultural Psychology*, 2: 273–83.

Boyd-Franklin, N., Steiner, G. and Boland, M. (1995) *Children, Families and HIV/AIDS.* New York, Guilford Press.

Bradshaw, J. (1972) The Concept of Human Need. *New Society*, 30: 3, 72.

Braye, S. and Preston-Shoot, M. (1995) *Empowering Practice in Social Care*. Buckingham, Open University press.

Braye, S. and Preston-Shoot, M. (1997) *Practising Social Work Law*. 2nd edn, London, Macmillan Palgrave.

Brearley, J. (1995) *Counselling and Social Work*. Buckingham, Open University Press.

Broadhurst, K. and White, S. (2009) Error Blame and Responsibility in Child Welfare: Problematics of Governance in an Invisible Trade. *British Journal of Social Work*, 39: 1, 15–30.

Butler, I. and Roberts, G. (1997) *Social Work with Children and Families: Getting Into Practice*. London, Jessica Kingsley.

Butrym, Z. (1976) *The Nature of Social Work*. London, Macmillan.

Caplan, G. (1961) *Pinciples of Preventive Psychiatry*. London, Basic Books.

Carpenter, J. and Sbaraini, S. (1997) *Choice, Implementation and Dignity: Involving Users and Carers in Care Management in Mental Health*. Bristol, Policy Press.

Carroll, M. (1998) Social Work's Conceptualization of Spirituality. *Social Thought: Journal of Religion in the Social Sciences*, 18, 2: 1–14.

CCETSW (1989) *Paper 30. Rules and Requirements for the Diploma in Social Work*. London, CCETSW.

Cheetham, J. et al. (1992) *Evaluating Social Work Effectiveness*. Buckingham, Open University Press.

Clarke, N. (2001) The Impact of In-Service Training Within Social Services. *British Journal of Social Work*. 31, 757–74.

Cobb, M. and Robshaw, V. (1998) The Spiritual Challenge of Health Care. Edinburgh, Churchill Livingstone.

Community Care (2010) Getting in the Know: Survey Into Personalisation. *Community Care*, May 8–18.

Compton, B. and Galaway, B. (1999) *Social Work Processes*. 6th edn. Pacific Grove, CA, Brooks/Cole.

Connelly, N. and Stubbs, P. (1997) *Trends in Social Work and Social Work Education Across Europe*. London, NISW.

Connor, A. (1993) *Monitoring and Evaluation Made Easy*. London, HMSO.

Copley, B. and Forryan, B. (1997) *Therapeutic Work with Children and Young People*. London, Cassell.

Corby, B., Millar, M. and Pope, A. (2002) Out of the Frame. *Community Care*, Sept 40–1.

Corker, M. (1999) New Disability Discourse, The Principle of Optimization and Social Change. In Corker, M. and French, S. (Eds.) *Disability Discourse*. Buckingham, Open University Press.

Corrigan, P. and Leonard, P. (1978) *Social Work Practice Under Capitalism: A Marxist Approach*. London, Macmillan.

Coulshed, V. and Orme, J. (2006) *Social Work Practice: An Introduction*. 4th edn. London. Macmillan/BASW.

Cowie, H. (1999) Counselling Psychology in The UK: The Interface Between Practice and Research. *The European Journal of Psychotherapy, Counselling and Health*, 2: 1, 69–80.

CSCI (2005) *Leaving Hospital Revisited: Follow up Study of a Group of Older People Discharged From Hospital in 2004*. London, CSCI.

CWDC (2008) *Building Brighter Futures*. London, Children's Workforce Development Council.

Daines, R., Lyon, K. and Parsloe, P. (1990) *Aiming for Partnership*. London, Barnardo's.

Dallos, R. and Draper, R. (2000) *An Introduction to Family Therapy: Systemic Theory and Practice*. London, Open University Press.

Davies, H., Nutley, S. and Smith, P. (2000) *What Works: Evidence Based Policy and Practice in Public Services*. Bristol, Policy Press.

Davies, M. (Ed.) (1997) *The Blackwell Companion to Social Work*. Oxford, Blackwell.

Davis, A. (1996) Risk Work in Mental Health. In Kemshall, H. and Pritchard, J. (Eds.) *Good Practice in Risk Assessment and Management*. London, Jessica Kingsley.

Davis, A. and Ellis, K. (1995) Enforced Altruism or Community Care. In Hugman, R. and Smith, D. (Eds.) *Ethical Issues in Social Work*. London, Routledge.

Davis, A., Ellis, K. and Rummery, B. (1997) *Access to Assessment: Perspectives of Practitioners, Disabled People, and Carers*. Bristol, Policy Press.

Davis, J., Rendell, P. and Sims, D. (1999) The Joint Practitioner: A New Concept in Professional Training. *Journal of Interprofessional Care*.13: 4, 395–404.

Dean M (1997) *Sociology after Society*. In Owen D (Ed.) *Sociology after Postmodernism*. London, Sage.

Debell, D. and Walker, S. (2002) *Norfolk Family Support Teams Final Evaluation Report*. Chelmsford, APU Centre for Research in Health and Social Care.

Dennis, J. and Smith, T. (2002) Nationality, Immigration and Asylum Bill 2002: Its Impact on Children. *Childright*, 187, 16–7.

DfCSF (2006) *Care Matters: Transforming The Lives of Children and Young People in Care*. London, HMSO.

DfCSF (2008) *Children and Young People in Mind: The Final Report of the National CAMHS Review*. London, HMSO

DfCSF (2009) *Building a Safe, Confident Future: Social Work Taskforce Report*. London, HMSO.

DfES (2003) *Every Child Matters: Change for Children*. Nottingham, DfES.

DfES (2005) *Common Core of Skills and Knowledge for the Children's Workforce*. Nottingham, DfES.

DfES (2006) *Working Together to Safeguard Children: A Guide to Interagency Working to Safeguard and Promote the Welfare of Children*. London, HMSO.

DHSS (1985) *Social Work Decisions in Child Care*. London, HMSO.

Dingwall, R. (1998) Some Problems About Predicting Child Abuse and Neglect. In Stevenson, O. (Ed.) *Child Abuse: Public Policy and Professional Practice.* Hemel Hempstead, Harvester Wheatsheaf.

Doel, M. and Marsh, P. (1992) *Task-centred Social Work.* Aldershot, Ashgate.

DoH (1995) *Child Protection: Messages from Research.* London, HMSO.

DoH (1996) *National Commission of Inquiry Into Child Protection.* London, HMSO.

DoH (1997) *Developing Partnerships in Mental Health.* London, HMSO.

DoH (1998) *Disabled Children: Directions for Their Future Care.* London, HMSO.

DoH (1998) *Modernising Mental Health Services: Safe, Supportive and Sensible.* London, HMSO.

DoH (1998) *Protecting Children: A Guide for Social Workers Undertaking a Comprehensive Assessment.* London, HMSO.

DoH (1999) *Quality Protects Programme: Transforming Children's Services 2000–01.* London, HMSO.

DoH (1999) *Working Together to Safeguard Children.* London, HMSO.

DoH (2000) *Children Act Report (1995–1999).* London, HMSO.

DoH (2000) *Framework for the Assessment of Children in Need and their Families.* London, HMSO.

DoH (2000) *National Service Framework for Mental Health.* London, HMSO.

DoH (2001) *Making it Work: Inspection of Welfare to Work for Disabled People.* London, HMSO.

DoH (2001) *The National Service Framework for Older People.* London, HMSO.

DoH (2006) *Our Health, Our Care, Our Say: A New Direction For Community Services.* London, HMSO.

DoH (2007) *Promoting Mental Health for Children held in Secure Settings.* London, HMSO.

DoH (2008) *Health Profiles, Association of Public Health Observatories.* London, HMSO.

DoH (2008) *Putting People First: Adult Social Care Workforce Strategy.* London, HMSO.

DoH (2009a) *Direct payments.* accessed April 2010 at http://www.dh.gov.uk/en/SocialCare/ Socialcarereform/Personalisa tion/ Directpayments/index.htm

DoH (2009b) *Individual budgets.* accessed April 2010 at http://www.dh.gov.uk/en/SocialCare/ Socialcarereform/Personalisa tion/ Individualbudgets/DH_4125774

DoH (2010) *Prioritising Need in the Context of Putting People First: A Whole System Approach to Eligibility For Social Care.* London: TSO. Accessed May 2010 at http://www.dh.gov.uk/prodconsumdh/ groups/dhdigitalassets/@dh/®@en/@ps/ documents/digitalasset/dh

DoH and DfEE (1996) *Children's Service Planning: Guidance for Inter-Agency Working.* London, HMSO.

DoH/DFES (2002) *The Children Act.* London, HMSO.

DoH/SSI (1991) *Care Management and Assessment. Practitioners Guide to the NHS and Community Care Act 1990.* HMSO.

DoH/SSI (1996) *Caring for People at Home Part 2-Inspection arrangements for Assessment and Delivery of Home Care.* London, HMSO.

DoH/SSI (1997) *At Home with Dementia: Inspection of Services for Older People with Dementia in the Community.* London, HMSO.

DoH/SSI (1997) *Responding to Families in Need.* London, HMSO.

DoH/SSI (1997) *The Cornerstone of Care: Care Planning for Older People.* London, HMSO.

DoH/SSI (2000) *A Quality Strategy For Social Care.* London, HMSO.

Dominelli, L. (1996) De-professionalising Social Work-Equal Opportunities, Competencies, and Postmodernism. *British Journal of Social Work,* 26: 2, 153–75.

Dominelli, L. (1997) *Anti-Racist Social Work.* London, Macmillan/BASW.

Dominelli, L. (1998) Globalisation and Gender Relations in Social Work. In Lesnik, B. (Ed.) *Countering Discrimination in Social Work.* Aldershot, Ashgate.

Dominelli, L. (2002) *Anti-Oppressive Social Work Theory and Practice.* Basingstoke, Palgrave Macmillan.

Dominelli, L. (Ed.) (1999) *Community Approaches to Child Welfare.* Aldershot, Ashgate.

Downrie, R.S. and Telfer, E. (1980) *Caring and Curing: A Philosophy of Medicine and Social Work.* London, Methuen.

du Gay, P. (2001) *In Praise of Bureaucracy.* London, Sage.

Durlak, J. and Wells A (1997) Primary Prevention Mental Health Programs for Children and Adolescents: A Meta-Analytic Review. *American Journal of Community Psychology.* 25: 2, 115–52.

Dwivedi, K.N. (2002) *Meeting the Needs of Ethnic Minority Children.* 2nd edn. London, Jessica Kingsley.

Eastman, M. (Ed.) (1994) *Old Age Abuse: A New Perspective.* London, Chapman and Hall.

Eber L, Osuch R, and Redditt, C. (1996) School-based Applications of The Wraparound Process: Early Results on Service Provision and Student Outcomes. *Journal of Child and Family Studies.* 5: 83–99.

Eraut M (1994) *Developing Professional Knowledge And Competence.* London, Falmer Press.

Farrington, D. (1995) The Development of Offending and Antisocial Behaviour From Childhood: Key Findings From The Cambridgeshire Study in Delinquent Development. *Journal of Child Psychology and Psychiatry.*

Fawcett, B. (2000) Look Listen and Learn. *Community Care.* July 27. 24–5.

Ferguson, I. (2007) Increasing User Choice or Privatising Risk? The Antimonies of

Personalisation. *British Journal of Social Work*, 37: 3, 387–403.

Fernando, S. (2002) *Mental Health Race and Culture*. Basingstoke, Palgrave.

Fletcher-Campbell, F. (2001) Issues of Inclusion. *Emotional and Behavioural Difficulties*, 6: 2, 69–89.

Flynn, N. (2007) *Public Sector Management*. 5th edn, London, Sage.

Fook, J. (2002) *Social Work: Critical Theory and Practice*. London, Sage.

Foucault, M. (1977) *The Archaeology of Knowledge*. London, Tavistock.

Frost, N. (2002) Evaluating Practice. in Adams, R., Dominelli, L. and Payne, M. (Eds.) *Critical Practice in Social Work*. Basingstoke, Palgrave Macmillan.

Fuller, R. (1996) Evaluating Social Work Effectiveness: A Pragmatic Approach. In Alderson, P. et al. (Eds.) *What Works? Effective Social Interventions in Child Welfare*. Barkingside, Barnardo's.

Fuller, R. and Petch, A. (1995) *Practitioner Research: The Reflexive Social Worker*. Buckingham, OUP.

Furedi, F. (2003) *Therapy Culture*. London, Routledge.

Gibson-Cline, J. (Ed.) (1996) *Adolescence: From Crisis to Coping*. London, Butterworth-Heinemann.

Giddings, F.H. (1898) *The Elements of Sociology*. New York, Macmillan.

Girling, J. (1993) Who Gets What and Why? Ethical Frameworks For Managers. In Allen, I. *Rationing of Health and Social Care*. London, Policy Services Institute.

Glisson, C. and Hemmelgarn, A. (1998) The Effects of Organisational Climate and Interorganisational Coordination on The Quality and Outcomes of Children's Service Systems. *Child Abuse and Neglect*, 22: 5, 401–21.

Golightly, M. (2006) *Social Work and Mental Health*. 2nd edn, Exeter, Learning Matters.

Goodman, R. and Scott, S. (1997) *Child Psychiatry*. London, Sage.

Gorell, B.G. (1998) *Family Therapy in Changing Times*, Basingstoke, Macmillan.

Graley-Wetherell, R. and Morgan, S. (2001) *Active Outreach: An Independent Service User Evaluation of a Model of Assertive Outreach Practice*. London, Sainsbury Centre for Mental Health.

GSCC (2009) *Raising Standards, Social Work Education in England*. London, GSCC.

Haralambos, M. (1991) *Sociology: Themes and Perspectives*. 3rd edn. London, Collins Educational.

Hardiker, P. (1995) *The Social Policy Contexts of Services to Prevent Unstable Family Life*. York. Joseph Rowntree Foundation.

Hardin, R. (1990) The Artificial Duties of Contemporary Professionals: The Social Service Review Lecture. *The Social Service Review*, 64: 4, 528–41.

Harding, T. and Beresford, P. (Eds.) (1996) *The Standards We Expect: What Service Users and Carers Want From Social Services Workers*. London, NISW.

Healy, K. (2002) *Social Work Practices: Contemporary Perspectives on Change*. London, Sage.

Healy, K. (2005) *Social Work Theories in Context: Creating Frameworks For Practice*. Basingstoke, Palgrave.

Henderson, P. and Thomas, D. (1987) *Skills in Neighbourhood Work*, London, Allen and Unwin.

Hill, M. (1999) *Effective Ways of Working With Children and Their Families*. London, Jessica Kingsley.

Hills, J. (2010) *An Anatomy of Economic Inequality in the UK: Report of the National Equality Panel*. London, LSE Centre for Analysis of Social Exclusion.

Hills, J., Le Grand, J. and Piachaud, D. (Eds.) (2007) *Making Social Policy Work*. Bristol, The Policy Press.

Hodes, M. (1998) Refugee Children May Need a Lot of Psychiatric Help. *British Medical Journal*, 316, 793–4.

Hogg, M.A. and Abrams, D. (1988) *Social Identification: A Social Psychology of Intergroup Relations and Group Processes*. London, Routledge.

Holman, B. (1983) *Resourceful Friends: Skills in Community Social Work*. London, Children's Society.

Home Office (2008) *Crime in England and Wales*. London, HMSO.

House of Commons (1997) *Child and Adolescent Mental Health Services. Health Committee*. London, HMSO.

Howarth, J. (2002) Maintaining a Focus on the Child? *Child Abuse Review*, 11, 195–213.

Howe, D. (1987) *An Introduction to Social Work Theory*. Aldershot, Gower.

Howe, D. (1994) Modernity, Postmodernity and Social Work. *British Journal of Social Work*, 24, 513–32.

Howe, D. (2009) *A Brief Introduction to Social Work Theory*. Basingstoke, Palgrave.

Howe, D. et al. (1999) *Attachment Theory, Child Maltreatment and Family Support*. Basingstoke, Macmillan.

Howe, G. (1999) *Mental Health Assessments*. London, Jessica Kingsley.

Jack, R. and Walker, S. (2000) *Social Work Assessment and Intervention*. Cambridge, APU.

Jayarajan, U. (2001) *The Demographic Profile of the Children and Young People Referred to Birmingham CAMHS*. Birmingham, Birmingham Children's Hospital Trust.

JCWI (2002) *Joint Council for the Welfare of Immigrants Response to the White Paper Secure Borders, Safe Haven: Integration with Diversity in Modern Britain*. London, JCWI.

Jenkins, R. (2002) *Foundations of Sociology*. Basingstoke, Palgrave Macmillan.

Jones, C. (1997) Poverty. In Davies, M. (Ed.) *The Blackwell Companion to Social Work*. Oxford, Blackwell.

Jung, C.G. (1978) *Psychological Reflections*. Princeton, Bollingen.

Kashani J and Allan W (1998) *The Impact of Family Violence on Children and Adolescents*. London, Sage.

Kelley, D. and Warr, B. (Eds.) (1992) *Quality Counts: Achieving Quality in Social Care Service*. London, Whiting and Birch.

Kemshall, H. (1993) Assessing Competence: Process or Subjective Inference? Do we Really See It? *Social Work Education*, 12: 1, 36–45.

Kim, W.J. (1995) A Training Guideline of Cultural Competence For Child and Adolescent Psychiatric Residencies. *Child Psychiatry and Human Development*, 26: 2, 125–36.

Kinney, M. (2009) Being Assessed Under The 1983 Mental Health Act – Can it Ever Be Ethical? *Ethics and Social Welfare*, 3: 3, 329–36.

Knapp, M. and Scott, S. (1998) *Lifetime Costs of Conduct Disorder*. London, Mind Publications.

Koprowska, J. (2005) *Communication and Interpersonal Skills in Social Work*. Exeter, Learning Matters.

Lader, D., Singleton, N. and Meltzer, H. (1997) *Psychiatric Morbidity Among Young Offenders in England and Wales*, London, HMSO.

Laing, R.D. (1976) *Facts of Life*. London, Allen Lane.

Laming, Lord H. (2003) *The Victoria Climbié Inquiry: Report of an Inquiry*. London, HMSO.

Leonard, P. (1994) Knowledge/Power and Postmodernism: Implications For The Practice of a Critical Social Work Education. *Canadian Social Work Review*, 11: 1, 11–26.

Leonard, P. (1997) *Postmodern Welfare: Reconstructing an Emancipatory Project*. London, Sage.

Lishman, J. (1998) Personal and Professional Development. In Adams et al. (Eds.) *Social Work: Themes, Issues and Critical Debates*. London, Macmillan.

Lishman, J. (Ed.) (2007) *Handbook for Practice Learning in Social Work and Social Care, Knowledge and Theory*. 2nd edn, London, Jessica Kingsley.

Lyon, J., Dennison, C. and Wilson, A. (2000) *Tell Them So They Listen. Messages From Young People in Custody*. Home Office Research Study 201, London, HMSO.

Macdonald, A. (1999) *Understanding Community Care*. Basingstoke, Macmillan.

Macdonald, G. (1999) Social Work and Its Evaluation: A Methodological Dilemma? In Williams, F., Popay, J. and Oakley, A. *Welfare Research: A Critical Review*. London, UCL Press.

Macdonald, G. and Roberts, H. (1995) *What Works in the Early Years?* Barkingside, Barnardo's.

Macdonald, K. and Macdonald, G. (1999) Perceptions of Risk. In Parsloe, P. (Ed.) *Risk Assessment in Social Work and Social Care*. London, Jessica Kingsley.

Madge, N. (2001) *Understanding Difference: The Meaning of Ethnicity For Young Lives*. London, NCB.

Magrab, P., Evans, P. and Hurrell, P. (1997) Integrated Services For Children and Youth at Risk: An International Study of Multidisciplinary Training. *Journal of Interprofessional Care*. 11:1, 99–108.

Martin, G. et al. (1995) Adolescent Suicide, Depression and Family Dysfunction. *Acta Psychiatrica Scandinavica*. 92: 336–44.

Martin, R. (2010) *Social Work Assessment*. Exeter, Learning Matters.

Martslof, D. and Mickley, J.R. (1998) The Concept of Spirituality in Nursing Theories: Differing World-Views and Extent Focus. *Journal of Advanced Nursing*, 27: 294–303.

Massey, A. and Pyper, R. (2005) *Public Management and Public Administration*. Basingstoke, Palgrave.

Masson, J. (1988) *Against Therapy*. London, Collins.

May, T. (Ed.) (2002) *Qualitative Research in Action*. London, Sage.

Mayer, J. and Timms, N. (1970) *The Client Speaks*. London, Routledge and Keegan Paul.

McCaffrey, T. (1998) The Pain of Managing. In Foster, A. and Zagier Roberts, V. (Eds.) (1998) *Managing Mental Health in the Community*. London, Routledge.

McClaren, H. (2007) Exploring the Ethics of Forewarning: Social Workers, Confidentiality and Potential Child Abuse Disclosures. *Ethics and Social Welfare*, 1: 1, 22–40.

McClatchey, T., Means, R. and Morbey, H. (2001) *Housing Adaptations and Improvements For People With Dementia: Developing The Role of Home Improvement Agencies*. Bristol, UWE.

McDonald, A. (2010) *Social Work with Older People*. Cambridge, Polity Press.

McGregor, K. (2010a) Social Workers in Charge: How Are The Social Work Practice Pilots Getting On? *Community Care*, 17th Feb.

McGregor, K. (2010b) Union Members May Boycott Sandwell Looked-After Children Pilot. *Community Care*, 4thMarch.

McIntyre, D. (1982) On The Possibility of 'Radical' Social Work: A 'Radical' Dissent. *Contemporary Social Work Education*, 5: 3, 191–208.

McLaughlin, H. (2009) What's in a Name: 'Client', 'Patient', 'Customer', 'Consumer', 'Expert by Experience', 'Service User' – What's Next? *British Journal of Social Work*, 39: 6, 1101–17.

McLennan, G. (1996) Post-marxism and the Four Sins of Modernist Theorising. *New Left Review*, 218, 53–75.

McReadie, C. (1995) *Elder Abuse: Update on Research*. London, Institute of Gerontology, Kings College.

Mental Health Foundation (1999) *The Big Picture: Promoting Children and Young People's Mental Health*. London. Mental Health Foundation.

Mental Health Foundation (2002) *The Mental Health Needs of Young Offenders*. London, Mental Health Foundation.

Mental Health Foundation (2009) *Mental Health Foundation response to New Horizons Consultation.* London, MHF.

Middleton. L/ (1997) *The Art of Assessment.* Birmingham, Venture Press.

Midgley, J. (2001) Issues in International Social Work-Resolving Critical Debates in the Profession. *Journal of Social Work*, 1: 1, 21–35.

Milne. A. (2002) *Teach Yourself Counselling.* Abingdon, Teach Yourself.

Milner. J. and O'Byrne. P. (2009) Assessment in Social Work. 3rd edn, Basingstoke, Palgrave.

Mishra, R. (1999) *Globalization and the Welfare State.* Northampton MA, Edward Elgar.

Moffic, H. and Kinzie, J. (1996) The History and Future of Cross-Cultural Psychiatric Services, *Community Mental Health Journal*, 32: 6, 581–92.

Morris. J. (1998) *Accessing Human Rights: Disabled Children and the Children Act.* Barkingside, Barnardo's.

Moss, B. (2005) *Religion and Spirituality.* Lyme Regis, Russell House Publishing.

Mullender, A. and Ward, D. (1991) *Self Directed Groupwork: Users Take Action For Empowerment.* London, Whiting and Birch.

Munro, E. (2007) Confidentiality in a Preventative Child Welfare System, *Ethics and Social Welfare*, 1: 1, 41–55.

Murphy, M. (2003) Keeping Going. In Harrison, R. et al. *Partnership Made Painless.* Lyme Regis, Russell House Publishing.

Murphy, M. (Ed) (2001) *Substance Misuse and Childcare.* Lyme Regis, Russell House Publishing.

Nash, M. and Stewart, B. (2002) *Spirituality and Social Care: Contributing to Personal and Community Well-Being.* London, Jessica Kingsley.

NISW (1982) *Social Workers, Their Role and Tasks.* London, NISW.

Nolan, M. and Caldock, K. (1996) Assessment: Identifying The Barriers to Good Practice. *Health and Social Care in the Community.* 4: 2, 77–85.

O'Hagan, K. (1996) *Competence in Social Work Practice.* London, Jessica Kingsley.

O'Hagan, K. (2001) *Cultural Competence in the Caring Professions.* London, Jessica Kingsley.

O'Sullivan, T. (1999) *Decision Making in Social Work.* London, Macmillan.

Oberhuemer, P. (1998) A European Perspective on Early Years Training. In Abbott, L. and Pugh, G. (Eds.) *Training to Work In The Early Years: Developing The Climbing Frame.* Buckingham, OUP.

Office for National Statistics (2008) *Social Tends.* London, HMSO.

OFSTED (1996) *Exclusions from Secondary Schools 1995–96,* London, HMSO.

Oldman, C. Beresford, B. (1998) *Disabled Children and their Families.* York, Joseph Rowntree Foundation.

Oliver, M. (1996) *Understanding Disability; From Theory to Practice.* London, Macmillan.

Oliver, M. and Sapey, B. (1999) *Social Work with Disabled People.* Basingstoke, Macmillan.

Ovretveit, J. (1998) *Evaluating Health Interventions.* Buckingham, Open University Press.

Parsloe, P. (Ed.) (1999) *Risk Assessment in Social Care and Social Work.* London, Jessica Kingsley.

Parton, N. (1991) *Governing the Family.* Basingstoke, Macmillan.

Parton, N. (1994) The Nature of Social Work Under Conditions of (Post) Modernity. *Social Work and Social Science Review*, 5: 2, 93–112.

Parton, N. and O'Byrne, P. (2000) *Constructive Social Work.* London, Macmillan.

Pawson, R. and Tilley, N. (1997) *Realistic Evaluation.* London, Sage.

Payne, M. (2005) *Modern Social Work Theory.* 3rd edn, Basingstoke, Macmillan.

Pearce, J.B. (1999) Collaboration Between The NHS and Social Services in The Provision of Child and Adolescent Mental Health Services: A Personal View. *Child Psychology and Psychiatry Review.* 4: 4, 150–2.

Pearson, G., Teseder, J. and Yelloly, M. (Eds.) (1988) *Social Work and the Legacy of Freud: Psychoanalysis and its Uses.* London, Macmillan.

Pels, D. (2000) Reflexivity One Step Up. *Theory, Culture and Society*, 17: 3, 1–25.

Performance and Innovation Unit (2000) *Prime Minister's Review of Adoption.* London, Cabinet Office.

Phillips, C., Palfrey, C. and Thomas, P. (1994) *Evaluating Health and Social Care.* London, Macmillan.

Pierson, J. (2002) *Tackling Social Exclusion.* London, Routledge.

Pincus, A. and Minahan, A. (1973) *Social Work Practice: Model and Method.* London, Peacock.

Pinkerton, J., Higgins, K. and Devine, P. (2000) *Family Support: Linking Project Evaluation to Policy Analysis.* Aldershot, Ashgate.

Platt, D. and Edwards, A. (1996) Planning a Comprehensive Family Assessment. *Practice*, 9: 2.

Pollock, S. and Boland, M. (1990) Children and HIV infection. *New Jersey Psychologist*, 40: 3, 17–21.

Priestly, M. (1999) *Disability Politics and Community Care.* London, Jessica Kingsley.

Priestly, M. (2001) *Disability and the Life Course: Global Perspectives.* Cambridge University Press.

Pritchard, J. (1995) *The Abuse of Old People.* 2nd edn, London, Jessica Kingsley.

Ramon, S. (1999) Social Work. In Bhui K and Olajide D (Eds.) *Mental Health Service Provision for a Multi-cultural Society.* London, Saunders.

Raval, H. (1996) A Systemic Perspective On Working With Interpreters. *Child Clincal Psychology and Psychiatry*, 1: 29–43.

Reder, P. and Duncan, S. (2003) Understanding Communication in Child Protection Networks. *Child Abuse Review*, 12: 82–100.

Reder, P. and Duncan, S. (2004) Making the Most of the Victoria Inquiry Report. *Child Abuse Review*, 13: 95–114.

Rees, S. and Wallace, A. (1982) *Verdicts on Social Work*. London, Arnold.

Reimers, S. and Treacher, A. (1995) *Introducing User-Friendly Family Therapy*. London, Routledge.

Resnik, M.D., Harris, L.J. and Blum, R.W. (1993) The Impact of Caring and Connectedness on Adolescent Health and Wellbeing. *Journal of Paediatrics and Child Health*.

Richardson, J. and Joughin, C. (2000) *The Mental Health Needs of Looked After Children*. London, Gaskell.

Richmond, M. (1922) *What is Social Casework?* New York, Russell Sage.

Rodgers, A. Pilgrim, D. and Lacey, R. (1993) *Experiencing Psychiatry: Users Views of Services*. London, Macmillan/Mind.

Rogers, R. (1967) *On Becoming a Person: A Therapists View of Psychotherapy*. London, Constable.

Royal College of Psychiatrists (2002) *Parent-training Programmes for the Management of Young Children with Conduct Disorders, Findings from Research*, London, RCP.

Rutter, M. (1999) Resilience Concepts and Findings: Implications For Family Therapy. *Journal of Family Therapy*. 21: 119–44.

Ryan, M. (1999) *The Children Act 1989: Putting it into Practice*. Aldershot, Ashgate.

Samaritans (2010) *Statement to Callers about ...maritans Confidentiality Policy*. London, ...aritans.

...son, H. (1997) *Peoples Plans and Possibilities: ...ring Person Centred Planning*. Edinburgh, ...sh Health Services.

...Children (2001) *Denied a Future? The Right ...tion of Roma/Gypsy Traveller Children in ...*ondon, Save the Children.

... P. (2007) Social Care and The Modern ...Client, Consumer, Service User, Manager ...trepreneur. *British Journal of Social Work*, 37: ...22.

...K. (1992) *The Silent Minority: Children With ...abilities in Asian Families*. London, NCB.

...dlow, S. and Payne, M. (1998) *Contemporary ...sues in Social Work: Western Europe*. Aldershot, ...rena.

..., P. (2000) *The Essentials of Community Care. A ...for Practitioners*. London, Macmillan.

...W. (1997) *Children and Adolescents With ...Health Problems*. London, Bailliere Tindall.

...B. and Chilvers, R. (2000) *Evidence-based ...l Care*. Lyme Regis, Russell House Publishing.

...ir, R., Garnet,t L. and Berridge, D. (1995) *Social ...ork and Assessment with Adolescents*. London, National Children's Bureau.

Smale, G. et al. (1993) *Empowerment Assessment, Care Management and the Skilled Worker*. London, HMSO.

Smale, G., Tuson, G. and Statham, D. (2000) *Social Work and Social Problems*. Basingstoke, Macmillan.

Social Exclusion Unit (2002) *Reducing Re-Offending by ex-Offenders*. London, HMSO.

Social Services Inspectorate (1998) *Partners in Planning: Approaches to Planning Services For Children and Their Families*. London. HMSO.

Solomos, J. (1989) *Race and Racism in Contemporary Britain*. Basingstoke, Macmillan.

SSI (2000) *Excellence Not Excuses. Inspection of Services For Ethnic Minority Children And Families*. London, HMSO.

Stephens, J. (2002) *The Mental Health Needs of Homeless Young People*. London, Mental Health Foundation.

Stepney, P. and Ford, S. (2000) *Social Work Models, Methods, and Theories*. Lyme Regis, Russell House Publishing.

Stevenson, O. (1999) *Elder Protection in Residential Care. What Can We Learn From Child Protection?* London, HMSO.

Stevenson, O. (Ed.) (1998) *Child Abuse: Public Policy and Professional Practice*. Hemel Hempstead, Harvester Wheatsheaf.

Strachan, R. and Tallant, C. (1997) Improving Judgement and Appreciating Biases Within The Risk Assessment Process. In Kemshall, H. and Pritchard, J. (Eds.) *Good Practice in Risk Assessment and Risk Management: Protection Rights and Responsibilities*. London, Jessica Kingsley.

Sue, D., Ivey, A. and Penderson, P. (1996) *A Theory of Multicultural Counselling and Therapy*. New York, Brooks/Cole Publishing.

Suffolk County Council (2010) Fair Access to Care Services, at http://www.suffolk.gov.uk/CareAndHealth/Disabilities/FairAccess.htm (accessed May 2010)

Summit, R. (1983) The Child Sexual Abuse Accommodation Syndrome. *Child Abuse and Neglect*, 7: 2, 177–93.

Sutton, C. (1999) *Helping Families with Troubled Children*. London, Wiley.

Sutton, C. (2000) *Child and Adolescent Behaviour Problems*. Leicester, BPS.

Sveaass, N. and Reichelt, S. (2001) Refugee Families in Therapy: From Referrals to Therapeutic Conversations. *Journal of Family Therapy*. 23: 119–35.

Svensson, K. (2009) Identity Work through Support and Control. *Ethics and Social Welfare*, 3: 3, 234–48.

Swinton, J. (2003) *Spirituality and Mental Health Care*. London, Jessica Kingsley.

Target, M. (1998) Approaches to Evaluation, Counselling and Health, *The European Journal of Psychotherapy*, 1: 1, 79–92.

Taylor, B. and Devine, D. (1993) *Assessing Needs and Planning Care in Social Work*. London, Arena.

Taylor, C. and White, S. (2000) *Practising Reflexivity in Health and Welfare*. Buckingham, OUP.

Taylor, P.J. and Gunn, J. (1999) Homicides by People With Mental Illness: Myth And Reality. *British Journal of Psychiatry*, 174, 9–14.

Thompson, N. (1995) *Theory and Practice in Health and Social Welfare.* Buckingham, OUP.

Thompson, N. (2000) *Theory and Practice in Human Services.* Buckingham, Open University Press.

Thompson, N. and Thompson, S. (2002) *Understanding Social Care.* Lyme Regis, Russell House Publishing.

Tillich, P. (1963) *Christianity and the Encounter of the World Religions.* Washington, Columbia University Press.

Titmuss, R.M. (1958) *Essays on the Welfare State.* London, George Allen and Unwin.

Treacher, A. and Reimers, S. (1995) *Introducing User-Friendly Family Therapy.* London, Routledge.

Trevithick, P. (2000) *Social Work Skills.* Buckingham, Open University Press.

Tucker, N. and Gamble, N. (Eds.) (2001) *Family Fictions.* London, Continuum.

Tucker, S. et al. (1999) Developing an Interdisciplinary Framework For The Education and Training of Those Working With Children and Young People. *Journal of Interprofessional Care*, 13, 261–75.

UNICEF (2000) *Child Poverty in Rich Nations.* New York, Unicef, Innocenti Research Centre.

United Nations (1998) *Human Rights Act.* Geneva, UN.

Valentine, C.A. (1976) Poverty and Culture. In Worsley, P. (Ed.) *Problems of Modern Society.* London, Penguin.

Valentine, L. and Feinauer, L.L. (1993) Resilience Factors Associated With Female Survivors of Childhood Sexual Abuse. *American Journal of Family Therapy*, 21: 3, 216–24.

VanDenBerg, J. and Grealish, M. (1996) Individualized Services and Supports Through The Wraparound Process: Philosophy and Procedures. *Journal of Child and Family Studies.* 5: 7–21.

Vincent, J. and Jouriles, E. (Eds.) (2000) *Domestic Violence: Guidelines for Research Informed Practice.* London, Jessica Kingsley.

Walker, S. (2001) Tracing the Contours of Postmodern Social Work. *British Journal of Social Work*, 31, 29–39.

Walker, S. (2001b) Family Support and Social Work Practice: Opportunities For Child Mental Health Work. *Social Work and Social Sciences Review*, 9: 2, 25–40.

Walker, S. (2002) Family Support and Social Work Practice: Renaissance or Retrenchment? *European Journal of Social Work*, 5: 1, 43–54.

Walker, S. (2003) *Social Work and Child and Adolescent Mental Health.* Lyme Regis, Russell House Publishing.

Walker, S. (2004b) Çommunity Work and Psychosocial Practice: Chalk and Cheese or Birds of a Feather? *Journal of Social Work Practice*, 18: 2, 161–75.

Walker, S. (2005) *Culturally Competent Therapy: Working With Children and Young People.* Basingstoke, Palgrave.

Walker, S. (2007) Family Therapy and Systemic Practice. In: Lishman J (Ed.) *Handbook for Practice Learning in Social Work and Social Care.* London, Jessica Kingsley.

Walker, S. and Akister, J. (2004) *Applying Family Therapy: A Guide For Professionals in The Community.* Lyme Regis, Russell House Publishing.

Walker, S. and Thurston, C. (2006) *Safeguarding Children and Young People: A Guide to Integrated Practice.* Lyme Regis, Russell House Publishing.

Watkins, D. and Gerong, A. (1997) Culture and Spontaneous Self-Concepts Among Filipino College Students. *Journal of Social Psychology.* 137: 480–8.

Weersing, V. and Weisz, J. (2002) Mechanisms of Action in Youth Psychotherapy. *Journal of Child Psychology and Psychiatry*, 43: 1, 3–29.

Weisz, J., Weiss, B. and Donenberg, G. (1992) he Lab Versus The Clinic: Effects of Child an Adolescent Psychotherapy. *American Psyc* 47,1578–85.

White, M. and Epston, D. (1990) *Narrative N Therapeutic Ends.* New York, W.W Nort

White, S., Hall, C. and Peckover, S. (2009 Descriptive Tyranny of the Common Framework: Technologies of Categoris Professional Practice in Child Welfare. *Journal of Social Work*, 39: 1197–217.

Wolbring, G. (2001) Surviving Eugenics. I M. (Ed.) *Disability and the Life Course.* Can University Press.

Yeo, S. (2003) Bonding and Attachment of Austi Aboriginal Children. *Child Abuse Review*, 12: 292–304.

Zavirsek, D. (1995) Social Innovations: A N Paradigm in Central European Social W *International Perspectives in Social Work,* University of Ljubljana.